A FALCON GUIDE®

Hiking Ohio

A Guide to Ohio's Greatest Hiking Adventures

Mary Reed

FALCON®

GUILFORD, CONNECTICUT
HELENA, MONTANA

AN IMPRINT OF THE GLOBE PEQUOT PRESS

Photo on page 279 by Attila Horvath. All other photos by
Mary Reed.
Maps created by XNR Productions © The Globe Pequot
Press.

Library of Congress Cataloging-in-Publication Data
Reed, Mary T., 1968-
    Hiking Ohio: a guide to the Buckeye State's greatest
    hiking adventures / by Mary Reed. p. cm.
    "A FalconGuide"
    ISBN 0-7627-2476-5
    1. Hiking–Ohio–Guidebooks. 2. Trails–Ohio–Guide-
books. 3. Ohio–Guidebooks. I.Title.
    GV199.42.03R44 2003
    796.51'09771–dc21

                                    2003049101

Manufactured in the United States of America
First Edition/First Printing

*To all the Ohio conservationists,
past and present, who have had
the foresight to protect our wild
places. Without them this book
would not be possible.*

Contents

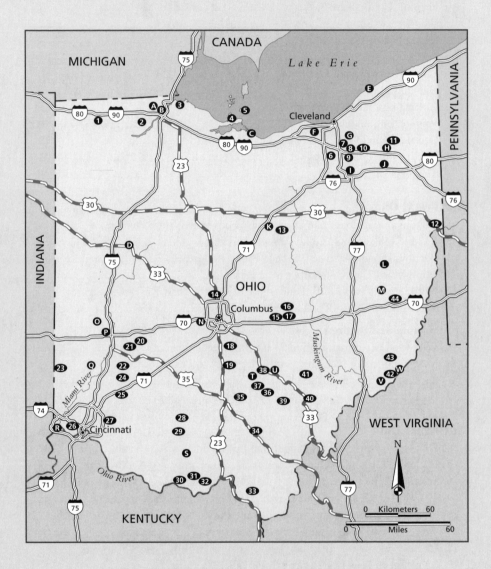

Central Ohio

Southwest Ohio

Southeast Ohio 193

Acknowledgments

I'd like to begin by thanking all the folks I met on the trail who provided me with knowledgeable feedback and tips. Thanks to Buckeye Trail Association members Jim Sprague, Dana Zintek, and Lisa Daibel, who helped out off the trail with feedback and even with a bed and hot shower when I needed it. Thanks also to all the folks who picked me and my hiking partners up when we were hitchhiking from one trailhead to another. We couldn't have done it without you.

There are too many public and private land managers and naturalists to acknowledge by name. Thanks for giving me information and tips on your area and again for reviewing my finished manuscripts.

Thanks to my editor at The Globe Pequot Press, Scott Adams, for asking all the right questions and taking me to task to write an informative and (hopefully) entertaining guidebook for everyone who wants to hit Ohio's trails.

One of the most enjoyable aspects of writing this book was time spent with family and friends on the trail. Thanks to those who hiked with me, including Robert Reed, Kathleen Reed-Brown, Josephine Brown, Mark Steinmetz, Colin Donohue, Kathryn Clayton, Paul Tescher, Marisa Alcorta, Cindy Braly, Susan Heitker, Padam Khatri, Bob Harrington, Matt Peters, Ron Kittle, the Greenfields—Michelle, Geoff, Aidan, and Robin—Mary Stallings, Jeremy Ernst, Cheryl and Lauren Sara, Larry Saylor, Susan Burgess and Kate Leeman, Heather Cautino, and James Cochran.

Thanks to all the women from the annual Women's Backpacking Trip for agreeing to stay in Ohio this year: Lisa King, Cat Cutcher, Timi Singley, Michelle Sampson, Jody Schaub, and Jessica Maguire.

Finally, a special thanks to Attila Horvath, who served as chauffeur, photography assistant, editor, number-one supporter, and model. His handsome face is the one that graces so many of the photographs in this book. It would have been very difficult to do it without you.

Introduction: The Buckeye State

"Ohio" comes from the Iroquoian word meaning "beautiful waters." Indeed, the state is largely defined by water. The Wisconsinan Glacier, which retreated from Ohio twelve to fifteen thousand years ago, gouged out Lake Erie to the north and forced the rivers in the central and southern part of the state to flow south, where they now drain into the Ohio River, the country's ninth longest. Rock deposits and the impressive glacial grooves on Kelley's Island are visible results of the glacier's advance and retreat. Along the former ice sheet's terminal edge, which cuts through the state, now lies one of the most biodiverse areas on the continent, where more than 1,500 plant species grow. In the unglaciated southeastern part of Ohio, forested ridges dominate the landscape.

The Ohio buckeye is the state tree.

Evidence of Ohio's human prehistory still exists in the earthworks built by the Adena, Hopewell, and Fort Ancient cultures at the famous Serpent Mound and elsewhere. The state was later home to the Wyandot and Ottawa in the north and the Shawnee, Miami, Mingo, and Delaware in the central and south. The first Europeans were French trappers and British settlers. They all came for the wealth of natural resources in the Ohio territory. The Native American tribes, the French, and the British fought fiercely over Ohio lands at the end of the eighteenth century.

At the time of European settlement, the state was more than 95 percent covered in forests, mostly beech-maple but also oak-hickory and mixed mesophytic forests in the unglaciated southeast portion of the state, with the Ohio buckeye, the state's namesake tree, found throughout. The forests were almost completely felled to fuel iron and charcoal furnaces, access coal seams, and make way for settlement and agriculture. However, a few remnants of virgin forest still remain, and footpaths exist to help you explore them. The largest tracts of second- and third-growth forest are in southeast Ohio, and the state's longest and most secluded trails are here.

Ohio was once home to such animals as the gray wolf, cougar, black bear, wood bison, Carolina parakeet, and passenger pigeon. These species are now either extinct or extirpated (driven out). But if you hike quietly on most Ohio trails today, you're sure to see white-tailed deer, wild turkey, ruffed grouse, beaver, and fox. In the eastern part of the state, the black bear is also making a comeback. There are innumerable bird species, from the ubiquitous state bird, the cardinal, to the less common but growing bald eagle population.

The late nineteenth and twentieth centuries brought a wave of agricultural and urban development to Ohio, seriously diminishing the state's wild areas. To those who haven't spent the time to explore it, Ohio may seem to contain only these urban areas and farmlands. Taking to the trails—whether a short day hike or an extended backpacking trip—is an excellent way to see all the state has to offer. A sampling of hikes presented in these pages will take you along beaches, over boardwalks, through gorges, past waterfalls, into caves, near wildlife, under forest canopies, and through carpets of wildflowers.

Weather and Seasons

Ohio generally offers four-season hiking, especially in recent years with increasingly mild winters and daily winter temperatures that often rise above freezing. The general exception is the snowbelt, east of Cleveland, where cross-country skiing usually replaces hiking in winter. Winter is the time to bundle up and survey the lay of the land. After a winter storm, head to your favorite spot to look at newly formed icicles and a quieting blanket of snow.

Spring is the best time of year in most of Ohio to view wildflowers. Do not be discouraged by the rain! Put on your rain gear and get out in the springtime, because the wildflower show is unparalleled between mid-April and early June. This is

Dogwood in spring.

also the time when many birds are migrating and nesting. Just be sure to plan ahead and consider what kinds of stream crossings your hike will require, since springtime is also flooding time. Also keep an extra set of dry clothes in the car or back at camp.

Summer is the best time to tackle the longer hikes and backpacking trips; the days are long and warm. Actually, summer would more accurately be described as incredibly hot and humid, with daytime temperatures often in the sticky 80s and 90s Fahrenheit. And the bugs do swarm, especially mosquitoes! Go to your local outdoors retailer and try out an effective, nontoxic bug repellent. Summer is also the best time to plan hikes that are farther afield, since campgrounds tend to be open seasonally.

Late summer and early fall feature the year's second wildflower season, mostly in open fields. Then the birds begin their southward migration. Fall is a good time to search out hikes with vistas so that you can enjoy the colorful foliage. It's also the driest time of the year, with comfortable temperatures.

Find your favorite spots and visit them in every season to witness the annual cycle of life that continues, whether you are there to witness it or not.

Ohio's Natural Regions

Some 300 to 500 million years ago, Ohio was periodically covered by seas. The sediment that piled up in layers on the sea bottom makes up Ohio's sedimentary bedrock. Three or four ice ages have occurred in Ohio more recently—geologically speaking—over the past two million years. The glaciers that advanced and retreated over the land probably have been the primary force shaping the landscape and its variations. As anyone who observes nature can tell you, it's the "edge" areas—where different conditions (forest, water, fields) or entire ecosystems meet—that harbor the most life. Depending on whom you ask, Ohio has four to six distinctive ecoregions, each with its own distinct geology, climate, and species.

Lake Erie Plains

To the north are the Lake Erie Plains, home to a flat landscape and more than 200 miles of shoreline. Temperatures here are moderated by the lake, and you'll find species that dominate here and not inland. This region was formerly home to the Great Black Swamp, and remnants of the swamp-oak forests hang on in preserves. Look for an abundance of cattails and grasses such as little bluestem, bluejoint, slough grass, and the nonnative, invasive phragmite grass. Showy flowers include wild sunflower, goldenrod, aster, lupine, and wild coreopsis. Common tree species include ash, walnut, maple, basswood, and sycamore. Shorebirds include an abundance of eagles, terns, gulls, herons, cranes, ducks, and geese.

Western Allegheny/Appalachian Plateau

The Western Allegheny Plateau is Ohio's hill country, located along the east and southeast portions of the state. The glaciated northern Allegheny, or Appalachian, Plateau was covered by the Wisconsinan Glacier. The resulting landscape is characterized by rounded hills, broad valleys, and many wetlands. The unglaciated Western Allegheny Plateau, in southeast Ohio, is home of sharp ridges 300 to 600 feet above the valleys. The forests along the Western Allegheny Plateau are often dominated by oak and hickory on the ridges and maple and beech in the lowlands. Many of the east- and north-facing slopes are home to mixed mesophytic forests. Twenty to twenty-five tree species are common, including the aforementioned oak, hickory, beech, and maple, as well as tulip poplar, ash, elm, hemlock, walnut, and locust; but no single species dominates the canopy. More then 1,500 species of flowering plants can be found throughout the region.

The Teays River was the major watershed draining the eastern portion of what's now the United States until the Kansan Glacier (700,000 years ago) dammed the river and reversed drainage patterns. In the unglaciated southeast portion of Ohio, evidence remains in the landscape of the former Teays River valley.

Ohio's Natural Regions

MICHIGAN

Lake Erie

PENNSYLVANIA

Lake Erie Plains

Glaciated Western
Allegheny Plateau

INDIANA

O H I O

Till Plains

Unglaciated Western
Allegheny Plateau

WEST
VIRGINIA

N

KENTUCKY
Bluegrass Region or
Low Interior Plateau

0   Kilometers   60

0   Miles   60

Lexington Plain/Bluegrass

Jutting up from Kentucky into portions of three Ohio counties is the Interior Low Plateau, also known as the Lexington Plain or Bluegrass ecoregion of Ohio. This region shares some features with the Western Allegheny Plateau, since it was also once part of the ancient Teays River watershed and was also unglaciated. The bluegrass is home not only to sandstone and shale bedrock but also to the more resistant dolomite. The resulting landscape has higher ridges—as high as 750 feet above the creek valleys—than the rest of southern Ohio. Also characteristic of this ecoregion is the presence of barrens and glades, which are small prairie communities. These were once common but are now rare. Shallow soils support grasses and sedges as well as some oaks and cedars. The Edge of Appalachia preserve, owned by The Nature Conservancy, is an excellent place to explore this ecoregion.

Till Plains

Most of the western half of Ohio is known as the Till Plains, so named for the rich layer of glacial debris, or till, that makes up its fertile soil. The landscape here is flat, and river drainages are shallow. Many of these rivers and creeks have high sustained water flows and support a wide variety of species. The Big Darby Creek, west of Columbus, is home to 100 of the 166 fish species found in Ohio. When European settlers arrived this land was mostly covered in beech-maple forests and dotted with prairie openings. John Deere's invention of the steel plow helped transform this landscape drastically. Today, 95 percent of the land in this region is either urbanized or cultivated into large fields of corn and soybeans. A remnant Till Plain forest exists in Hueston Woods, and several city and state parks have worked to restore or maintain remnant prairie lands, which include such species as echinacea (cone flower), prairie dock, and big bluestem grass.

Precautions

Hunting is allowed in most areas covered in this guide. Be sure to contact the land administrators to find out the dates of hunting seasons, specifically firearm seasons. It's probably best simply to avoid areas where hunting is allowed during the season. However, if you do decide to hike then, be sure to wear hunter-orange clothing.

Poison ivy is everywhere! Wearing long pants is usually enough protection against this irritant. When you finish a hike, wash with cool water and soap and launder your clothing. Your pet can pick up poison ivy oil and pass it on to you, so be sure to wash your dog if it has come into contact with the plant. If you don't already know how to identify poison ivy, it comes in two basic forms: In summer you will see it along edge areas and in full sun as a creeping vine with leaflets of three. The leaves tend to have one noticeable notch, and the stems are reddish; the fall berries are white. The second form of poison ivy grows into huge, hairy vines up the sides of trees. If you are a tree hugger, watch out for the PI!

Land Ownership and Oversight

Wayne National Forest

The Wayne, covering a patchwork of 232,900 acres in southeast Ohio, is a multiple-use area. Environmental groups have been successful in halting mining and timbering operations in the past several years, but the USDA Forest Service plans to continue with extraction. Many trails in the Wayne are open to off-road vehicles, horses, and mountain bikes. Hikers are allowed on these multi-use trails, but it's safest and most pleasant to stick to the hiking and backpacking trails. Leashed dogs are permitted, and hunting is allowed.

State Forests

Ohio state forests are largely managed for logging but are also open to recreational opportunities. Most trails, in terms of sheer mileage, are for off-road vehicles and horses, but some parks also have many miles of hiking trails. Some state forest lands are pretty beat up, and some hiking trails skirt clearcuts. The Shawnee State Forest is home not only to some of the largest public land logging operations but also to Ohio's only wilderness area; a backpacking trail allows you to explore it. Leashed dogs are allowed on hiking trails, and hunting is allowed in the forests.

State Parks

Ohio's state parks are managed for recreation. No resource extraction occurs on state park land, and trails are generally well developed and marked. Most state parks have campgrounds and other resources, such as concessions, beaches, pools, amphitheaters, miniature golf, and so on. Several state parks have lodges. These are good destinations for seeing some of Ohio's scenic treasures without "roughing it." State parks are generally not the best place to find solitude, especially during summer weekends, when campgrounds and trails are usually overrun with people. Naturalist programs are often offered between Memorial Day and Labor Day. Leashed dogs are allowed on state park trails, and hunting is allowed in some state parks.

Metroparks

Many Ohio cities have well-developed metroparks. These parks tend to be well managed, with nature centers, naturalist programs, guided hikes, and environmental restoration projects. Most metroparks do not offer camping options. Because of their proximity to large population centers, metroparks often have heavily used trails, but they are generally well maintained in response to this high demand. These are great options for nearby day hikes but not for finding solitude. Leashed dogs are usually allowed in metroparks, but hunting is generally not allowed.

Natural Areas and Preserves

The Ohio Department of Natural Resources maintains a Department of Natural Areas and Preserves (DNAP). These preserves are managed for the land itself, not for you! DNAP preserves exist to protect biologically significant lands. These parcels are generally pretty small but quite beautiful. Camping, pets, and picnicking are not permitted on DNAP lands, but there's an upside to all of this: Trails on state nature preserve lands are among the nicest in the entire state. A number of preserves are accessible by permit only. Contact DNAP for more information (see Appendix B: Resources).

Private Preserves

A few private preserve hiking trails are covered in this guide. These preserves, although open to the public, tend to have strict rules to protect the ecological integrity

Mushrooms in the understory.

of the land. These, too, are some of the most attractive and biologically significant areas in the state. Dogs are not permitted on most private preserves, and hunting is generally prohibited. Be considerate of preserve rules, and encourage others to do so, too, since these lands are only open to the public at the goodwill of preserve owners. Also consider helping maintain these preserves with a monetary donation.

Difficulty Ratings

Ultimately, you have to know your own strengths and limits when hitting the trail. The following descriptions should serve as guidelines as to what to expect from the ratings used in this book.

Easy hikes are less than 5 miles in length and are on mostly flat, well-worn trails.

Moderate hikes can be from 1 to 5 miles in length with steep ascents and descents or from 5 to 10 miles long but generally flat or with moderate ascents.

Difficult hikes are approaching 10 miles in length or longer and are on hilly terrain.

Contacting Your Representatives

Most of the hikes covered in this book are on publicly owned lands. That public is you and me. Contact your state representative and senator and let them know about your support for public lands. Encourage funding levels that allow these lands to be managed and staffed at full capacity. Also watch closely at how funds are allocated, and follow up on your support for recreational opportunities.

Legislative Public Information Office: (800) 282–0253

State of Ohio home page legislature link: www.legislature.state.oh.us

Volunteering

The most important resource when it comes it Ohio's trails is you. Many of the hikes described in this book were built by volunteers. If you live near a park or preserve, contact the manager and find out if a volunteer trail organization already exists. If it doesn't, start one. Contact the Buckeye Trail Association (800–881–3062) for information on trail building.

Getting around Ohio

Area Codes

Ohio, a very population-dense state, has twelve area codes:

Toledo/northwest Ohio—**419** and **567**

Cleveland—**216**

Cleveland east/west suburbs—**440**

Akron, Canton, and Youngstown—**330** and **234**

Southeast Ohio—**740**

Columbus—**614** and **380**

Cincinnati—**513** and **283**

Dayton/Springfield and southwest Ohio—**937**

By Road

They say that there are two seasons in Ohio: winter and road repair. For links to up-to-date information on weather, road conditions, and road closings—or if you have a breakdown or other problem—contact the **Ohio State Highway Patrol** at (877) 7–PATROL or www.state.oh.us/ohiostatepatrol/. For more esoteric information on Ohio's transportation system (that is, roads) contact the **Ohio Department of Transportation (ODOT)** at www.dot.state.oh.us/. You can reach the **Ohio Turnpike Commission** at (440) 234–2081 or www.ohioturnpike.org/.

By Air

Ohio is serviced by numerous regional airports. Most flights, however, are concentrated at three major airports: Cleveland, Columbus, and Cincinnati.

Cleveland Hopkins International Airport, (216) 265–6000; www.cleve-landairport.com/. The airport is accessible by train from downtown. For more information contact the Greater Cleveland Rapid Transit Authority (RTA) at (216) 566–5227 or www.gcrta.org/.

Port Columbus International Airport, (614) 239–4000; www.port-colum bus.com/. The airport is accessible by public bus. Contact the Central Ohio Transit Authority at www.cota.com.

Cincinnati/Northern Kentucky International Airport, (859) 767–3151; www.cvgairport.com/. The airport is accessible by public bus. Visit www.tankbus.org for information.

Akron/Canton Regional Airport, www.akroncantonairport.com/.

Dayton International Airport, www.flydayton.com/.

Toledo Express Airport, (419) 865–2351; www.toledoexpress.com/.

Warren-Youngstown Regional Airport, (330) 539–4233; www.yngwrn air.com/.

The airports also host car rental companies and taxi services to help you get to your ground destination. (Most hikes in Ohio are not accessible by public transportation.) To book your reservations, contact an airline directly by phone or Web, or work through your local travel agent. To book reservations online, go to an airline's Web site or a general travel Web site. Some popular ones are www.travelocity.com, www.expedia.com, www.cheaptickets.com, and www.priceline.com.

By Train

Amtrak serves Youngstown, Akron, Alliance, Bryan, Cleveland, Elyria, Sandusky, Fostoria, and Toledo across the northern part of the state. Trains stop in Columbus in central Ohio; in southern Ohio, Amtrak serves Cincinnati and Hamilton. For information and reservations, call (800) USA–RAIL, or log on to www.amtrak.com/.

By Bus

Greyhound serves most medium-sized and large cities in Ohio. For fare and schedule information, call (800) 229–9424 or log on to www.greyhound.com. All of Ohio's major cities have local bus services.

Visitor Information

For statewide travel and tourism information, call (800) BUCKEYE or visit www.ohiotourism.com. Almost every county in Ohio has a local convention and visitor bureau. To find a local bureau, log on to www.ohiotourism.com/visitor/local_tour_org.asp.

How to Use This Book

Hiking Ohio is designed to be highly visual and quickly referenceable. We've split up Ohio into five regions: Northwest Ohio, Northeast Ohio, Central Ohio, Southwest Ohio, and Southeast Ohio. Each region begins with a **Section Intro,** where you're given a sweeping look at the lay of the land. Following each Section Intro are the hikes within that region.

Each hike within a region begins with a short summary. You'll learn about the trail terrain and what surprises each route has to offer. If your interest is piqued, read on. If not, skip to the next hike.

The **Hike Specifications** are fairly self-explanatory. Here you'll find the quick, nitty-gritty details of the hike, including where the trailhead is located, hike distance, approximate hiking time, difficulty, type of trail surface, best hiking season, what other trail users you may encounter, nearest town, any fees and permits required, and other key information. **Finding the trailhead** section provides dependable directions from a major intersection or a nearby town or city right down to where you'll want to park. **The Hike** is the meat of the chapter. Detailed and honest, it's the author's carefully researched impression of the trail. While it's impossible to cover everything, you can rest assured that we won't miss what's important. **Miles and directions** provides mileage cues to identify all turns and trail name changes, as well as points of interest. At the end of each hike, you'll find sources of additional local information. We'll also tell you where to stay, where—and sometimes what—to eat, and what else to do and see while you're hiking in the area.

Honorable Mentions details hikes that didn't make the cut. In many cases it's not because they aren't great hikes, but rather that they're overcrowded or environmentally sensitive to heavy traffic. Be sure to read through these. A jewel might be lurking among them.

Don't feel restricted to just the routes and trails described here. Show your adventurous spirit and use this guide as a platform to dive into Ohio's backcountry and discover new routes for yourself. (One of the simplest ways to begin this is to hike the trail in reverse. The change in perspective is often fantastic, and the hike should feel quite different. It'll be like getting two distinctly different hikes on each map.)

Slip this guide into your backpack and begin your adventure. Enjoy your time in the outdoors—and remember to pack out what you pack in.

Map Legend

70	Limited access highway
23	U.S. highway
20	State highway
26	County Road
——	Paved road
═══	Gravel road
= = = = =	Unimproved road
- - - - - - -	Trail
▬▬▬▬	Featured route
⊓	Bench
⇒	Boat launch
⋈	Bridge
▲	Camping
†	Cemetery
⸸	Church
•—•	Gate
⌇	Golf course
▬	Lodge
◙	Overlook/viewpoint
P	Parking
⊼	Picnic area
▪	Point of interest
▶	Ranger station
♿	Rest room
‖‖	Stairs
START ⛱	Swimming
🚶	Trailhead
⊌	Water for drinking
∥	Waterfall

Northwest Ohio

Northwest Ohio's Great Black Swamp, once more than 100 miles long and 30 miles wide, was one of the last places to be settled east of the Mississippi because of its inhospitable swampy soil, weather, and bug conditions. But settlement did occur, and most of the swamp has since been drained. The soil proved very fertile, and today northwest Ohio largely comprises farmland. Most hikes located here are short, but some of the state's best hiking and bird-watching destinations lie in remnants of the Great Black Swamp. Several Lake Erie islands are nearby, with Kelleys Island providing the most hiking opportunities, as well as views of stunning glacial grooves.

The southern shore of Lake Erie is a bird-watcher's paradise. In springtime, birds migrating to the north must stop before making the long trip over the lake, often taking a day to rest and prepare. Single-day bird counts have numbered in the tens of thousands—for each species! Shorebirds include bald eagles, gulls, terns, herons, swans, egrets, and red-winged blackbirds, just to name a few.

Swamp oak forests stand in small parcels and are home to such animals as fox, muskrat, mink, and weasel. Spring wildflowers are abundant in the wooded portions of this ecoregion; marsh and meadow flowers are most conspicuous in late summer and early fall. Although less than 10 percent of Ohio's original wetlands remain, these lands produce the most diverse wildlife of any habitat in the state. The Toledo Metropark's Oak Openings Preserve, home to sandy soils left behind by glacial lakes, is a great place to see yet more diversity of life in a slightly upland region bordering the Great Black Swamp.

The Ottawa and Wyandot Indians were living in this region when European settlers arrived. In the War of 1812 the American forces under Commodore Oliver Hazard Perry defeated the British in the Battle of Lake Erie. (Perry's Victory and International Peace Memorial stands at Put-in-Bay.) The Erie Canal and later the St. Lawrence Seaway opened the Great Lakes for development, and large cities grew along their shores. Vacation destinations in northwest Ohio are within a half day's drive of tens of millions of people. Historic, amusement, and nature parks draw tourists, yet seclusion can be found just a few miles into a trail.

Look forward to hiking inland among remnant swamp forests, along the sandy shores of Lake Erie, on wetland boardwalks, and among sand dune communities. Most lakeside hikes in northwest Ohio are best tackled in summer. Volatile weather conditions and heavy winds can make cold-weather hiking uncomfortable.

1 Cottonwood to Toadshade Loop

Goll Woods State Nature Preserve

The 170-acre "near-virgin" forest is a remnant of the Great Black Swamp, character-ized by towering trees 200 to 400 years old, with a few specimens as old as 500 years. Hike around the preserve on a 3.0-mile outer loop; it won't take long to see that you're in a special place. Unusually tall and broad tree specimens include cottonwood, oak, tulip tree, ash, maple, beech, hickory, and linden (basswood). The dark and clear understory is quite swampy in areas and gives you a taste of what the Great Black Swamp was once like, all the way down to the mosquitoes. Take a respite from every-day living to view the process of life, death, and rebirth in a natural ecosystem.

Start: From the trailhead next to the parking lot and rest rooms
Distance: 3.0-mile loop
Approximate hiking time: 1 to 1^1/$_2$ hours
Difficulty: Easy; flat and clear
Trail surface: Dirt trail
Blaze: None, all junctions are marked.
Seasons: Best in spring and fall, when there's a night frost to keep the mosquitoes down
Other trail users: Hikers only
Canine compatibility: Dogs not permitted
Water: The spigot at the trailhead is dry, bring your own water.

Land status: State nature preserve
Nearest town: Archbold
Fees and permits: No fees or permits re-quired
Schedule: Open daily from dawn to dusk
Maps: Usually available at the trailhead kiosk. USGS quad: Archbold; Maptech Terrain Navi-gator: Ohio Lima/Toledo/Northwest.
Trail contacts: Goll Woods Nature Preserve, Archbold, OH; (419) 445-1775; www.ohiodnr.com/dnap/location/goll_woods. html

Finding the trailhead: From the junction of State Routes 2 and 66 north of Archbold, con-tinue north on SR 66 for 1 mile to County Road F. Turn west (left) and drive 2.8 miles to County Road 26. Turn south (left) and drive 0.2 mile to the parking lot on the left. *DeLorme: Ohio Atlas and Gazetteer:* Page 25 D5.

The Hike

When the Goll family purchased land for a homestead in northwest Ohio in 1837 (for $1.25 per acre), they probably couldn't have imagined that in less than 150 years their land would be designated a natural treasure—simply because the trees hadn't been cut. In fact, the only reason this small tract of magnificent forest exists is because the Goll family preserved the woods through four generations before selling it to the state in 1966.

The forest at Goll Woods is characterized by towering trees 200 to 400 years old, thick clouds of mosquitoes, and everything in between. This area was the last to be settled east of the Mississippi. It was eventually drained with the help of an exten-

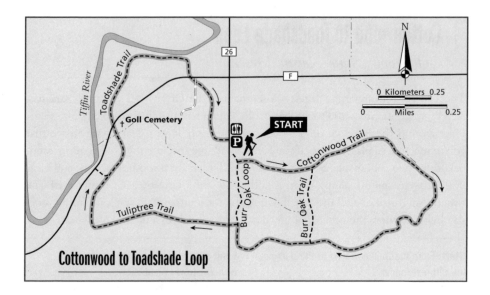

Cottonwood to Toadshade Loop

sive ditching project and now is home to almost a million acres of productive farm-land. Getting to Goll Woods requires a long drive through what seems to be cease-less cornfields, making it hard to imagine the vast expanse of forest that once existed here. Goll Woods was left untouched until World War I, and even then only a few trees were cut. The entire preserve encompasses 321 acres, and the 170 acres of near-virgin timber within the preserve are listed as a National Natural Landmark.

► **Check out the Homestead Ice Cream shop on County Road F just east of State Route 66 (419-446-2663). Try their Black Swamp flavor, made with homemade French silk ice cream, chocolate-covered peanuts, and crushed Al-Meda toffee. There's a nice patio where you can sit, relax, and eat your well-deserved treat after your hike.**

Start the hike just past the trailhead kiosk, which may have self-guided nature trail brochures stocked. Begin by taking a left onto the Cottonwood Trail to make a clock-wise loop around the preserve. It won't take long to see that you're in a special place. Un-usually tall and broad trees, including the namesake cottonwood as well as oak, tulip tree, ash, maple, beech, hickory, and linden (basswood) tower above, creating a dark and clear understory that's quite swampy in areas.

The dark forest and dark swampy bottomlands are what gave the Great Black Swamp its name. This wide variety of evenly distributed tree species is known as a mixed mesophytic forest. Although this land is quite flat, look for very subtle changes in elevation. The wetter soil supports elm and ash, while the drier soil is home to beech and maple. As the swamp was drained over the years, beech and maple trees began to take hold. As the soil continues to become drier, the beech-maple com-munity will eventually dominate this forest.

Continuing to the Burr Oak Trail, take note of the most impressive big trees, a few of which are estimated to be almost 500 years old. (See the "elder of the woods" at Post 8, which was growing here in the sixteenth century!) Also note the process of life, death, and rebirth in a natural ecosystem. Snags stand here and there, providing habitat and food for birds and other animals. Other trees have been blown down during storms and left to rot, helping to create the rich soil that supports this forest. Look and listen for the red-headed woodpecker, common to Goll Woods but not so common elsewhere. In the understory look for the native pawpaw tree and the strong-smelling spicebush, both of which can grow in low light conditions.

The next portion of the route is the Tuliptree Trail, named for the tree that produces yellow-and-orange tuliplike flowers in the spring. Look on the trail for fallen

A magnificent oak tree towers in the canopy at Goll Woods.

flowers, because you won't be able to see them in the trees themselves—the tall, straight tulip tree prunes itself, and the first branches are 40 to 50 feet above the ground. The tulip tree is one of the oldest tree species on the planet. Fossil records show evidence of tulip trees growing one hundred million years ago. Tulips are excellent lumber trees, but they were often just burned as settlers cleared the Great Black Swamp.

▶ **Goll Woods is home to two state champion trees (the largest trees in the state of their species): black ash and rock elm.**

These remnant tracts of virgin forest are important to scientists and the rest of us because they provide a living record of history, including natural history of fires, droughts, wet years, and so on. These forests also provide a benchmark for what a natural, healthy forest should look like, which is critical when land managers undertake restoration projects. And, of course, these forests are simply remarkable, beautiful places in and of themselves, whether or not we visit them for a respite from everyday life.

The final leg of the loop is on the Toadshade Trail, which parallels the Tiffin River for a stretch. Toadshade is a common name for a maroon or green trillium with mottled leaves. Other spring wildflowers found here include bloodroot, columbine, cut-leaved toothwort, phlox, Dutchman's breeches, wood anemone, and mitrewort. In fall look for the uncommon dwarf ginseng in addition to the common black-eyed Susan, thistle, jewelweed (spotted touch-me-not), and tick trefoil. As the trail turns away from the river, it enters a pine plantation. This is a fragrant portion of the trail and offers a much-needed respite from the mosquitoes. It's nonnative, however, and will someday be naturally displaced by the native deciduous trees.

Miles and Directions

0.0 Start at the trailhead located beyond the rest rooms and the trailhead kiosk. The trail begins at a fork. Take the left fork to begin a clockwise loop around the entire preserve, starting with the Cottonwood Trail.

0.2 Pass a junction with the Burr Oak Trail on the right. Continue straight. **Option:** Take a right to do only the Burr Oak Trail, a 1.5-mile loop.

1.1 At the end of the Cottonwood Trail, come to another fork for the Burr Oak Trail. Take a left.

1.3 Come to another fork. Take a left to begin the Tuliptree Trail. **Option:** Take the right fork to return directly on the Burr Oak Trail for a 2.2-mile loop.

1.4 Cross CR 26 and pick up the trail on the other side, a little bit to the right.

1.9 Arrive at the junction with the Toadshade Trail. Continue straight. (The Tuliptree Trail continues to the right.)

2.0 Pass a junction with an access trail from the left.

2.2 Come to CR F. Turn right and walk about 100 yards along the road and then pick up the marked trailhead on the other side.

2.6 Pass a seasonal river-overlook deck on the left.

2.7 Cross CR F again.

3.0 Arrive at CR 26. Cross the road and return to the parking lot where you began.

Hike Information

Local information

Wauseon Chamber of Commerce, Wauseon, OH; (419) 335–9966; www.wauseonchamber.com/.

Local events and attractions

Sauder Village historical farm and crafts, Archbold, OH; (800) 590–9775; www.sauder village.com.

Accommodations

Sauder Village has an inn and a campground; (800) 590–9775.

Restaurants

The Barn at Sauder Village; (800) 590–9775.

Organizations

Toledo Naturalists Association, Bowling Green, OH; www.wcnet.org/~tna/.

2 17 Mile Trail

Oak Openings Preserve Metropark

The 17 Mile Trail is simply one of the best long hikes in the state. It takes you along inland sand dunes, characteristic of the oak openings region, home to beaches thousands of years ago when Lake Erie was much higher than it is today and its shores extended this far. Walk through oak forests, through canopy openings and prairies, through pine forests, along creekbeds, and on sandy trails. Tackle it in a day, or take two days to explore this long and winding path, which is easy to do with plenty of nearby amenities. Other shorter trails in the park also allow you to explore this ecosystem, which exists only in this part of the state.

Start: At the Springbrook picnic area
Distance: 17.6-mile loop
Approximate hiking time: 6 to 9 hours
Difficulty: Difficult due to length
Trail surface: A flat, well-maintained dirt trail that often crosses other trails
Blaze: Yellow
Seasons: Best April through October
Other trail users: Hikers only
Canine compatibility: Leashed dogs permitted
Water: Available at both the Springbrook and White Oak picnic areas along the trail

Land status: Toledo Metropark
Nearest towns: Whitehouse, Swanton
Fees and permits: No fees or permits required
Schedule: Open daily from 7:00 A.M. to dark
Maps: The Metropark map shows all trails in the park. USGS quads: Swanton, Whitehouse; Maptech Terrain Navigator: Ohio Lima/Toledo/Northwest.
Trail contacts: Oak Openings Preserve Metropark, Swanton, OH; (419) 826-6463; www.metroparkstoledo.com

Finding the trailhead: From I-475 southwest of Toledo, exit on U.S. 24 west (exit 4) and drive 4.4 miles to State Route 64 in Waterville. Turn north (right) and drive 10.1 miles to the Springbrook picnic area parking on the left (watch for turns on SR 64). *DeLorme: Ohio Atlas and Gazetteer:* Page 26 D2.

The Hike

If you're an über-hiker, tackle it in a day, but if you're a mere mortal, take two days to explore this long and winding path. Walk along inland sand dunes (a signature characteristic of the oak openings), in oak woodlands, through canopy openings and prairies, through pine forests, along creekbeds, past attractive ponds, and on sandy trails.

Oak openings refers to the region that reaches from the Maumee River to Detroit, west of Toledo. The region extends about 25 miles in length and is only a few miles wide. It's characterized by a ridge of sand that sits atop clay soil. The sand was deposited by a series of three glacial lakes that were higher than present-day Lake Erie. Originally this region was a sandy beach. Over the years, as the water

At some spots in Oak Openings Preserve, fern carpet the forest floor.

receded plant communities moved in. Today there are some spots where the inland sand dunes still shift and move and pile as high as 35 feet above the clay subsoil. In other places the water table rises to just 3 feet below the surface. Native Americans once regularly set fire to the woodlands understory to keep it clear for game hunting. European settlers found that they could drive their Conestoga wagons through the clear understory beneath widely spaced oak trees. Thus, the name "oak openings."

The preserve, at under 4,000 acres, is home to more than 1,000 plant species, a number of which are rare or endangered. These include flowering plants such as Skinner's foxglove and the carnivorous sundew. Rare butterflies found here include the Frosted elfin and Persius dusky-wing. Expect to see some of the park's resident deer, which number in the hundreds. Nesting birds include larks, sparrows, indigo buntings, whippoorwills, and bluebirds.

The hike begins and ends at the Springbrook picnic area, where the Wabash Cannonball (Rails-to-Trails) Trail bisects the park. Start by walking through the first of many plantations of white, red, and Scotch pines, as well as some spruce and fir stands that were planted by the Metroparks system when it first acquired the land around 1940. Notice how these nonnative species are all in various stages of being replaced with native deciduous forests. The Metroparks is allowing this natural progression to happen and does not intend to plant more evergreens.

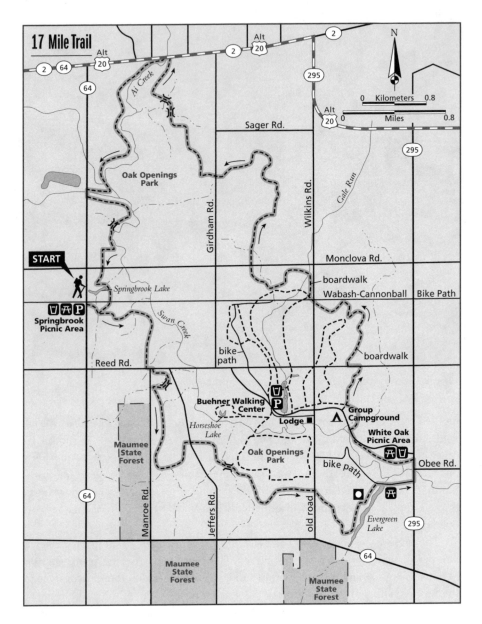

The 17 Mile Trail is thoughtfully designed, rarely joining the bridle trails or following a road. It's mostly flat and on hard-packed dirt. But, as you will see, a main characteristic of the oak openings is the sandy soil. It's an interesting experience to walk along the sand in an oak forest. The trail most often winds through native black and white oak with a varying understory. In some places look for a vast, open forest floor covered in cinnamon or bracken fern. In other spots look for the characteristic oak savannas, or oak openings, with widely spaced oak trees and tallgrass

prairie species growing underneath, including blazing star, lupine, bird's-foot violet, puccoon, and little bluestem grass. Enter a full-on prairie with no trees and then look in spots for yucca, which is well adapted to the sandy soil. The trail passes three attractive bodies of water: Evergreen Lake, Swan Creek, and Springbrook Lake.

You'll have time to reflect on the many who have walked here before you. Archaeologists believe that humans inhabited the region 12,000 years ago. Recorded history of the oak openings begins with European explorers, who used the slightly upland oak openings as part of a transportation route. The region's population was booming around the time the Miami and Erie Canal opened in 1842, but today the main use of the canal towpath is as a right-of-way for hiking trails.

If you're looking for a hike considerably shorter than 17 miles, Oak Openings Preserve can provide that, too. Try the 1.7-mile Sand Dunes Trail to best experience the park's inland dunes. Most of the preserve's other trails are accessible from the Buehner Center for the Oak Openings. Oak Openings Preserve also has an all-purpose trail and a handicap-accessible trail. Pick up the park map for more details.

Miles and Directions

Note: The trail has undergone some changes, so mileage signposts may not be exact. As the trail continues to be maintained, some of the mileages listed here may not be exact.

0.0 Start at the Springbrook picnic area. Walk to the junction of Route 64 and the Wabash Cannonball bike path. Cross over the junction and walk on a short mowed path to the trailhead, marked with a wooden sign. Walk past a brush pile and into a pine plantation.

0.3 Walk straight past a side trail; in about 100 feet hit a four-way intersection. Continue straight.

0.5 Come to a fork; take the right fork.

0.9 Walk straight through a four-way intersection.

1.0 Walk straight past a side trail and come to a fork. Take the right fork.

1.2 Reach a five-way intersection. Walk straight past the gate, and then hit a four-way intersection. Take a left and walk about 200 feet out to Oak Openings Parkway and Manroe Road. Take a left and walk along the road.

1.4 Cross the road to the south side and reenter deciduous woods.

1.5 Hit a fork and take a left out to the intersection of Oak Openings Parkway and Jeffers Road. Turn right onto Jeffers Road. In about 100 feet take a right back into the woods.

1.8 Come to a four-way intersection. Walk straight through the intersection, and then take an immediate right at a fork.

2.4 Walk straight past a side trail and join a doubletrack.

2.6 Come to a fork and take the left fork off the doubletrack.

2.9 Cross Jeffers Road and enter a white pine plantation.

3.2 Reach a four-way intersection with the horse trail. Continue straight. The trail crosses the horse trail four times in the next half mile or so. Stay on the narrow yellow-blazed trail.

3.9 Cross the horse trail at a four-way intersection and enter a section of forest where the floor is covered in bracken fern.

4.0 Enter a dying spruce plantation and hit a junction. Take a left; in about 200 feet walk straight through a four-way intersection.

4.1 Cross over a fire road.

4.2 Come to a junction marked with an OAK SAVANNA 2000 sign. Cross straight over the horse trail; cross it again a couple more times in the next several hundred yards.

4.5 Cross South Wilkins Road and enter the Lou Campbell tallgrass prairie. Then reenter the woods.

4.9 Cross an access/fire road; cross it again in about 100 feet. Then hit another access road road/bridle trail. Take a left and follow the road briefly before taking a right off the road into the pines, near the edge of Evergreen Lake.

5.0 Come to a T-intersection with a horse trail/road. Take a right and walk through a picnic area. (**FYI:** This would make a good rest/lunch stop. There's a shelter and rest rooms but no water.)

5.7 Cross the horse trail.

5.9 Come to a T intersection with a gravel road/dam. Take a right and walk to the other side of the dam and a junction. Continue straight, toward the picnic area access road. Take a left back onto the footpath just before the road.

6.1 Come out at State Route 295 and take a left. Follow the road and cross Swan Creek. The trail reenters the woods on the other side of the road bridge.

6.5 Come out to a field and walk straight through it. (To the right is the White Oak Picnic area with water, rest rooms, and a shelter.)

6.8 Cross the horse trail.

7.1 Hit Oak Openings Parkway and take a left. Follow the road over the creek and then turn left, off the road again. In about 150 feet hit a junction with an access road on the right. Take a right onto the access road/horse trail. (There's a rest room on the left.)

7.4 Come to a fork. Take the right fork to leave the horse trail.

7.9 Come to a junction. Take a right and cross Reed Road in about 30 feet.

8.6 Arrive at a junction with the horse trail and take a right.

8.8 Pass a side trail on the right and hit a fork, just before the road. Take the right fork.

8.9 Walk diagonally across the intersection of Wilkins Road and the Wabash Cannonball bike path. On the other side of the road, the trail forks immediately. Take the right fork.

9.1 Cross the horse trail.

9.4 Cross an old road; in a couple hundred feet cross a faint trail.

9.9 Cross the horse trail and then cross Monclova Road.

10.3 Cross an access road/horse trail.

10.8 Come to a junction with the horse trail. Take a right and follow the horse trail.

11.2 At a post for the horse trail, hit a four-way intersection. Take a left, following the yellow blaze. Cross another old road and enter a white pine plantation.

11.6 Still in the pines, cross Girdham Road.

12.1 Come to a T-intersection with a gravel road; turn left onto the road.

12.3 Reach a junction and take a right, leaving the gravel road.

12.5 Hit a junction and take a left.

13.0 Come to a T intersection with an abandoned asphalt road; take a right.

13.1 Take a left, off the road and back onto the trail.

13.2 Just before Airport Highway, take a left and parallel the road. After crossing the creek on the roadway, take a left back into the woods. Then walk, essentially, though some backyards. Begin closely paralleling Swan Creek.

13.6 Come to a fork. Take the left fork and join a doubletrack road for about 100 feet. Take another left, off the road and back onto a singletrack trail.

13.9 At another junction, the trail rejoins the doubletrack for about 50 feet. Then take another left to leave the doubletrack.

16.1 At a junction, go straight and cross two footbridges.

16.3 Come to a fork take the right fork. (The left fork leads to a group camp and is also blazed yellow.)

16.5 In the pines, reach a four-way intersection and take a left.

16.6 Come to Monclova Road. Pass the brown gate and cross the road. Pick up the trail again on the other side of the road, about 20 feet to the left (east).

16.9 Just past Springbrook Lake on the right, hit a four-way intersection. Take a right (to the left is the camp; the trail is also blazed yellow). In a couple hundred feet, cross a doubletrack road.

17.1 Cross directly over the Wabash Cannonball bike trail and then hit a T intersection.

17.2 Come to a four-way intersection near the trailhead. A sign directs you to the right for the Springbrook picnic area.

17.6 Return to the trailhead.

Hike Information

Local information
Toledo Convention and Visitors Bureau; (800) 243-4667; www.toledocvb.com.

Local events and attractions
The Wabash Cannonball Trail is a 63.0-mile multiple-use trail from Maumee to Montpelier. Contact the Northwest Ohio Rails-to-Trails Association, Inc., at (800) 951-4788.

Accommodations
Betty's Country Campground, Whitehouse; (419) 875-6696.

Twin Acres Campground, Whitehouse; (419) 877-2684.

The Mill Bed and Breakfast, Grand Rapids; (419) 832-6455; www.themillhouse.com.

Restaurants
Loma Linda's, Swanton; (419) 865-5455.

Organizations
Maumee Valley Volkssporters walking club; (734) 847-0641; www.geocities.com/Yosemite/Gorge/4120.

Volunteers in Parks (VIPs); (419) 535-3057, ext. 143.

Hike tours
Naturalist-led hikes are offered regularly. Call the preserve for up-to-date information at (419) 826-6463, or visit www.metroparks toledo.com.

Other resources
Metroparks Magazine is a quarterly publication for Metroparks members; call (419) 535-3050.

3 Boardwalk Trail

Maumee Bay State Park

Maumee Bay State Park is home to a 2.4-mile boardwalk that takes you through the heart of a marsh ecosystem. Enjoy this fun little loop that weaves through a swamp forest of swamp white oak, ash, willow, hackberry, and red maple. Look for large birds, including great blue herons, as well as amphibians and reptiles. The swamp forest gradually gives way to an open marsh. The invasive purple loosestrife and phragmite grass join thick expanses of cattail, with showy swamp rose mallow providing color in summer and early fall. Take the spur trail to the overlook. It's only about 10 feet high, but that's all you need here. From atop the overlook deck, gaze out over a sea of cattails, with Lake Erie to the north, swamp forests to the south, and development in the distance.

Start: From the Trautman Nature Center
Distance: 2.4-mile loop
Difficulty: Easy; short and flat and even hand-icap-accessible
Trail surface: Boardwalk
Blaze: None; junctions are marked.
Seasons: Best in the summer
Other trail users: Hikers only
Canine compatibility: Dogs not permitted on the boardwalk trail
Water: Available at the nature center

Land status: State park
Nearest town: Oregon
Fees and permits: No fees or permits required
Schedule: Open daily until 11:00 P.M. year-round
Maps: USGS quad Reno Beach; Maptech Terrain Navigator Ohio Lima/Toledo/Northwest
Trail contacts: Maumee Bay State Park, Oregon; office (419) 836-7758; nature center (419) 836-9117; www.ohiodnr.com/parks/parks/maumebay.htm

Finding the trailhead: From State Route 2 east of Toledo, turn north onto North Curtice Road and drive 3.1 miles to the nature center entrance on the right. *DeLorme: Ohio Atlas and Gazetteer:* Page 27 C5.

The Hike

If you're a bird-watcher, this is the place for you. The western basin of Lake Erie is situated along both the Mississippi and Atlantic flyways; northward migrating birds gather here in vast numbers in spring. They often stop along the southern shore of the lake to wait for good crossing conditions. The marshes that line Lake Erie are home to about 300 bird species for at least part of the year, and during spring migration tens of thousands of birds gather along the shoreline here. These wetlands teem with animal life among the thick cattail and reed stands. Water levels vary, and trying to walk here can be quite a challenge. The solution: Build a boardwalk.

Swamp rose mallow stands out among the cattail in Maumee Bay State Park.

Maumee Bay State Park is a special place, in part, because Ohio has lost 90 percent of its wetlands since European settlers arrived. Begin the walk from the Trautman Nature Center, which features exhibits on the flora and fauna you will encounter along the boardwalk. Interactive exhibits make this a kid-friendly place, and a giant window in the back of the center allows for comfortable bird-watching.

Begin the walk in a swamp forest of swamp white oak, ash, willow, hackberry, and red maple. Look for turtles (often seen sunning on a log in the pond nearest the nature center) and amphibians. Soon you will notice the abundant presence of two invasive exotic species, the attractive purple loosestrife and phragmite grass.

The swamp forest gradually gives way to an open marsh. The phragmite grass joins thick expanses of cattail, with showy swamp rose mallow providing color in summer and early fall. Take the spur trail to the overlook. It's only about 10 feet high, but that's all you need here. From atop the overlook deck, gaze out over a sea of cattails, with Lake Erie to the north, swamp forests to the south, and development in the distance. The largest birds here are white egrets and great blue herons, which stand 4 feet tall and have 6-foot wingspans. Other common marsh birds include red-winged blackbirds, kingfishers, mallards, and Canada geese. From the overlook, return to the main boardwalk trail and complete a loop back to the nature center.

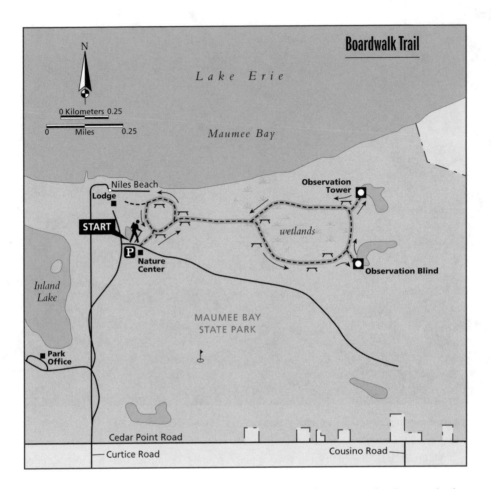

Maumee Bay has become one of Ohio's most popular state parks, due no doubt to its many amenities: a new lodge overlooking the lake, cabins, an eighteen-hole golf course, a campground, and two beaches (one along Lake Erie, the other an inland lake). Nearby natural areas that are more conducive to bird-watching than hiking include Crane Creek State Park, Magee Marsh Wildlife Area, and Ottawa National Wildlife Refuge.

Miles and Directions

0.0 Start from the side or back door of the nature center and begin walking east on the boardwalk.

0.1 Come to a junction at Post 2. Take a right and walk part of the Short Loop.

0.2 Arrive at a second junction at Post 3. Take another right and walk on the connector section of the boardwalk.

0.3 Hit a T intersection. Take a right and begin circling the One Mile Loop.

0.6 Pass a side trail on the right that leads to cabins.

0.8 Come to a junction with a side trail to the right to a bird blind. Take the spur to the bird blind, return to this spot, and then continue in a counterclockwise direction.

1.1 Arrive at the junction with the spur trail to the observation tower. Take a right and check out the observation tower. (**FYI:** Don't forget to bring a quarter for the binoculars.)

1.4 Return to the main loop and take a right.

1.9 Finish the One Mile Loop at a junction with the connector trail. Take a right.

2.1 Come to a T intersection with the Short Loop. Take a right.

2.2 Arrive at a triangular intersection. To the right is the lodge; take a left to return to the nature center.

2.3 Pass the Short Loop trail on the left and continue straight.

2.4 Arrive back at the nature center.

Hike Information

Local information

Toledo Convention and Visitors Bureau; (800) 243-4667; www.toledocvb.com

Local events and attractions

Kite Weekend is the third weekend in July; contact the park for up-to-date information. Crane Creek State Park, Oak Harbor; (419) 836-7758; www.ohiodnr.com/parks/parks/cranecrk.htm.

Magee Marsh Wildlife Area and Ottawa National Wildlife Refuge; contact the ODNR Division of Wildlife District 2 offices at (419) 424-5000 or (800) WILDLIFE; www.ohiodnr.com/wildlife/default.htm.

Accommodations

Maumee Bay Resort/Quilter Lodge; (419) 836-1466 or (800) 282-7275.

Maumee Bay State Park campground; (419) 836-8828.

Restaurants

Quilter Lodge dining room; (419) 836-1466.

Organizations

Black Swamp Bird Observatory, Oak Harbor; (419) 898-4070; www.bsbobird.org/.

Hike tours

Naturalist-led hikes are offered in season. Contact the nature center for up-to-date information at (419) 836-9117.

INVASIVE EXOTICS

According to the ODNR Division of Natural Areas and Preserves, about 3,000 species of plants grow in Ohio. Of these, about 75 percent are native to the state. The other 25 percent are exotic plants, meaning that they were introduced from elsewhere, mostly by early European settlers. Some of these exotics are invasive, which means they displace other, native plant species. Among those on DNAP's "hit list" of invasive exotics are Japanese honeysuckle, garlic mustard, multiflora rose (brought here for use as a natural fence—oops!), and, in northern Ohio's wetlands, common reed/phragmite grass and purple loosestrife. You can help avoid further spread of these species by not planting them in your yard and by pulling them out whenever you have the opportunity. Also try to avoid picking up "hitchhikers," carrying seeds from one place to the next.

4 South Beach Trail

East Harbor State Park

No matter where you stand in East Harbor State Park, you are no more than 200 yards from the water. East Harbor's 7 miles of trails are mostly located on a peninsula, surrounded by the main body of Lake Erie to the east and natural harbors to the west. Walk along the Wetlands Trail, where boardwalks help when conditions get too muddy. Then hit the South Beach Trail and walk along inland sand dunes under towering cottonwood trees. Watch boats navigating in and out of the channel that links East Harbor and Lake Erie. You have the option to return along the beach. Check out the West Harbor Trail, which narrows to a spit of land less than 20 feet across with West and Middle Harbors on either side.

Start: From the south beach parking lot trailhead

Distance: 3.0-mile loop, with spur loop

Approximate hiking time: 1 to 1^1/$_2$ hours

Difficulty: Easy; short and flat

Trail surface: A wide, flat trail on grass, boardwalks, and sand

Blaze: None, marked at junctions

Seasons: Best late-April through late-September

Other trail users: In winter, trails are open to snowmobiles.

Canine compatibility: Leashed dogs permitted

Water: Available at the North Beach rest rooms/concession area

Land status: State park

Nearest town: Lakeside-Marblehead

Fees and permits: No fees or permits required

Schedule: The park is open daily until 11:00 P.M.

Maps: USGS quad: Gypsum; Maptech Terrain Navigator: Ohio Northeast/Cleveland/Canton

Trail contacts: East Harbor State Park, Lakeside-Marblehead; (419) 734-4424; www.ohiodnr.com/parks/parks/eharbor.htm

Finding the trailhead: From Sandusky, follow State Routes 2 and 269 over Sandusky Bay. When the highways split, take SR 269 north 3.6 miles to the park entrance. Turn right into the park and drive 1.1 miles to the beach area. The road forks here; take a right into the south beach parking lot. *DeLorme: Ohio Atlas and Gazetteer:* Page 28 D3.

The Hike

East Harbor State Park is located on the Marblehead Peninsula, which juts more than 5 miles into Lake Erie. This area contains remnants of the Great Black Swamp that once dominated the landscape of northwest Ohio. By the middle of the nineteenth century, timbering and swamp draining had led to the extirpation of such species as ruffed grouse, wild turkey, river otter, bison, wolverine, mountain lion, gray wolf, and even deer. The remaining marshes that surround East Harbor State Park are still home to a relatively high diversity of species, including mammals such as red fox, woodchuck, and muskrat. A lot of reptiles and amphibians also call this place home,

The invasive phragmite grass crowds around the boardwalk at East Harbor State Park.

including the green frog, American toad, water snake, fox snake, and painted turtle. The park's main attraction for many hikers, though, is the birding. Look for such species as great blue heron, white egret, mute swan, and black-crowned night heron.

Walk along the Wetlands Trail in, well, a wetland. Boardwalks help when conditions get too muddy. Growing around you is common reed or phragmite grass, a highly invasive nonnative plant. Some small cedar trees dot the landscape. Walk quietly and bring binoculars in hopes of seeing a lot of bird activity. East Harbor is visible to your right. As you near the end of the peninsula, jump onto the South Beach Trail. This short loop takes you through inland sand dunes beneath towering cottonwood trees. As you circle the edge of the peninsula, you will see boats coming in and out of the narrow harbor channel and trophy homes on the other side of the channel. On your return trip you have the option to walk along the beach.

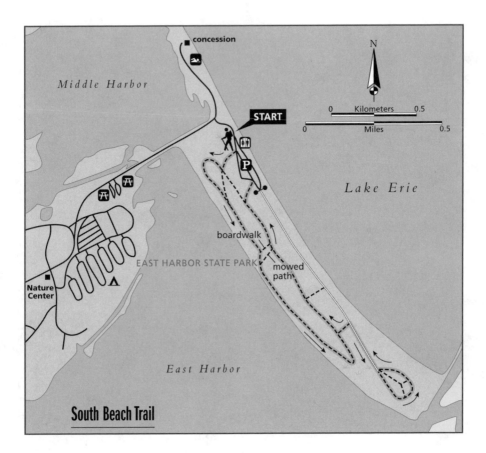

South Beach Trail

While you're here, try out the West Harbor Trail. This 1.1-mile out-and-back trip starts along the North Swimming Beach and then curves around to the west, along a spit that's less than 20 feet wide. From this trail West Harbor is to the north and Middle Harbor game sanctuary is to the south.

The entire Marblehead Peninsula is a popular tourist attraction. Several wineries operate in this grape-growing region. From East Harbor State Park, stop at roadside stands or pick-your-own places for fresh fruit. Then make your way to the east end of the peninsula and the famous Marblehead Lighthouse. Johnson's Island, on Sandusky Bay, is the site of a Confederate cemetery. It's a short jaunt to Cedar Point Amusement Park and a short ferry ride to Kelleys Island. The Ottawa National Wildlife Refuge is several miles west along the lakeshore.

▶ East Harbor is Ohio's second most visited state park (Cleveland Lakefront is number one), with more than three million visitors annually. It also has the largest campground in the state park system, with 585 sites.

Miles and Directions

0.0 Start from the trailhead sign near the South Beach parking lot, next to the rest rooms. In about 100 feet there's a side trail, which rejoins the main trail a few hundred feet farther on.

0.5 Approach a boardwalk on the left; continue straight.

1.0 Come to a fork at a red post; take a right and walk to a gravel road. Take a right and walk south down the gravel road to the end. **Option:** Continue straight to return directly for a 1.3-mile loop.

1.4 Leave the road and hit a fork. Take the South Beach Loop Trail in either direction, and return to this point.

2.7 Return the way you came on the gravel road to the junction on the Wetlands Trail. Take a right and head north.

3.0 Return to terminal trailhead at the parking lot, just south of where you started.

Hike Information

Local information

Marblehead Peninsula Chamber of Commerce; (419) 798-9777; www.marbleheadpeninsula. com/.
Ottawa County Visitors Bureau; (800) 441-1271; www.lake-erie.com.

Local events and attractions

Other activities in the park include camping, swimming, fishing, and boating from a fully equipped marina.

Accommodations

East Harbor State Park campground; (419) 734-4424.

Restaurants

The Crow's Nest restaurant overlooks West Harbor; (419) 734-1742.
Frontwater's Restaurant and Brewing Co., Marblehead; (419) 798-8058.

5 North Shore Loop, North Pond, and East Quarry Trails

Kelleys Island State Park and North Pond State Nature Preserve

Explore Kelleys Island by a combination of bicycle and foot to enjoy the unique natural features this charming tourist trap has to offer. Take a ferry to this Lake Erie island and head to the famous Glacial Grooves State Memorial. From there hike on the self-guided North Shore Trail to the water's edge, where you have views of other Lake Erie islands nearby and the horizon beyond. Also check out the North Pond State Nature Preserve on a boardwalk through a wetland. Hit the East Quarry Trail and walk around Horseshoe Lake, which was created when rainwater filled this former limestone quarry. The surroundings are dotted with cedar trees, and the trail is reminiscent of a hike out west more than Ohio.

To reach Kelleys Island from State Routes 2 and 269 west of Sandusky, cross Sandusky Bay to Marblehead Peninsula. When SR 2 and SR 269 split, continue on SR 269 for 2.2 miles to a T intersection with State Route 163. Turn east (right) and drive 5.4 miles to the Kelleys Island Ferry Boat Line parking on the left. Take the ferry to the island (888–225–4325; www.kelleysislandferry.com). **Option:** Approach Kelleys Island from Sandusky or Port Clinton via the Island Rocket Express Ferry (800–854–8121; www.islandrocket.com). *DeLorme: Ohio Atlas and Gazetteer:* Page 28 D4.

Fees and permits: Ferry rides to Kelleys Island start at $9.00 per person round trip and $16.00 per car. No fees or permits are required for hiking.

Schedule: Open daily from dawn to dusk. Check seasonal ferry service hours.

Maps: USGS quad: Kelleys Island; Maptech Terrain Navigator: Ohio/Toledo/Northwest

Trail contacts: Kelleys Island State Park, Kelleys Island; (419) 746-2546; www.ohiodnr.com/parks/parks/lakeerie.htm

The Hikes

Kelleys Island is a bona fide tourist trap, but it has managed to retain its charm and has set aside several natural areas for exploration. The only public transportation to the Lake Erie Islands is ferryboat, so just *getting* to Kelleys Island is fun. Begin with a twenty-minute ferry ride to Kelleys and then explore the 2-by-3-mile island by a combination of bicycle and foot.

From the ferry dock, stop by Inscription Rock, a large limestone boulder where Native Americans carved now-faint pictographs 300 to 500 years ago. Then head north out of downtown on Division Street to Glacial Grooves State Memorial. This excavated spot is known as the world's largest and clearest example of striations caused by glaciers scouring out bedrock. Glaciers produced Lake Erie and the islands in this area.

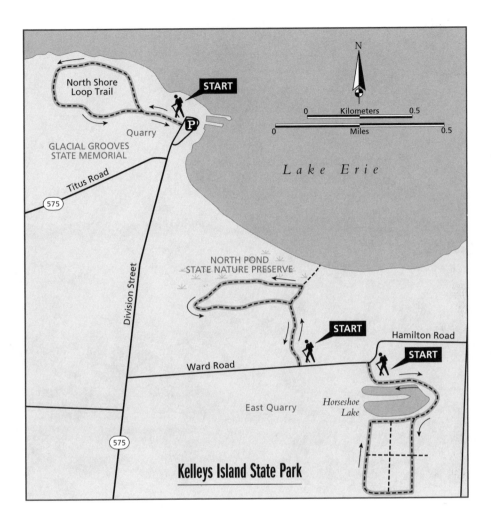

Kelleys Island State Park

From the glacial grooves to the trailhead for the North Loop Trail, pass an old limestone quarry. The history of Kelleys Island is tied to its natural resource base. Quarrying was once a dominant industry here, and the old quarries remain, some now filled with water. Eastern red cedar trees grow out of this calcium-rich rock and dot the landscape. The land is also suitable for fruit orchards and vineyards, and several wineries exist on Kelleys and other Lake Erie islands. Many people have also made their living fishing the abundant waters of Lake Erie, dominated by walleye, perch, bass, and catfish.

The North Loop Trail is a self-guided nature trail (ask for a map and guide at the campground). Begin by walking alongside the North Quarry, opened in 1830 and operated for more than seventy years. The trail winds by an old loader, used to load crushed limestone onto rail cars, and then past an old spoil bank composed of by-products from the limestone crushing process. Walk through second- and third-

The North Shore Trail on Kelleys Island takes a hiker to the water's edge.

growth deciduous forests of water-loving cottonwood, ash, and hackberry, identified by its "treads" of corky bark. The evergreens are red cedar. Underfoot, watch out for poison ivy and Virginia creeper. The trail loops around but has plenty of access trails to the north shore of Kelleys Island.

From the north shore, watch waves crash up against the rocks. If you look closely you'll see where glacial grooves are evident here as well. To the west you can identify Put-in-Bay by the tall monolith that marks Perry's Victory and International Peace Memorial. Oliver "Hazard" Perry led U.S. troops in Lake Erie to a victory over the British in the War of 1812, helping turn the tide to an American victory. Return on the loop trail to where you started along Division Street.

▶ Campsites 85, 87, 89, 91–93, 95, 97, 101, 103, and 104 at Kelley's Island State Park are situated along the water.

Round out a day of hiking by heading down to Ward Road and two more worthwhile hikes. The North Pond State Nature Preserve features a 1.0-mile boardwalk through a lovely forest and wetland. Birding is excellent here; a bird observation tower overlooks the wetland. A spur trail leads to a rare barrier-beach ecosystem. Since this is a nature preserve, you can't bring your dog along on this one.

Just down the road is the East Quarry Trail, which winds around Horseshoe Lake, created when water filled the old quarry. This is an excellent trail for views of the lake and a wetland. You'll be walking mostly on limestone, dotted with red cedars. Due to all the rock and the evergreens, the trail is more reminiscent of western states than Ohio. This is also a self-guided nature trail, so request a map from the state park campground office.

North Shore Loop Trail

Start: At the boat parking lot north of the glacial grooves
Distance: 1.7-mile lollipop
Approximate hiking time: 45 minutes to 1 hour
Difficulty: Easy; short and flat

Trail surface: Flat dirt trail
Other trail users: Bicyclists
Canine compatibility: Leashed dogs permitted
Water: Available at the campground
Land status: State park

Finding the trailhead: From the ferry dock—by foot, car, golf cart, or bicycle—turn left and continue to the stop sign. Go straight and travel westward on East Lakeshore Drive 0.5 mile to downtown. Turn right (north) onto Division Street and travel 1.7 miles to its end, where there is a parking lot. The trailhead is on the west side of the parking area.

Miles and Directions

0.0 Start at the trailhead sign off the parking lot return road. Walk straight past the trailhead sign; in about 25 feet pass a side trail on the left.

0.1 The trail joins a doubletrack road and then forks. Take a right to begin the loop.

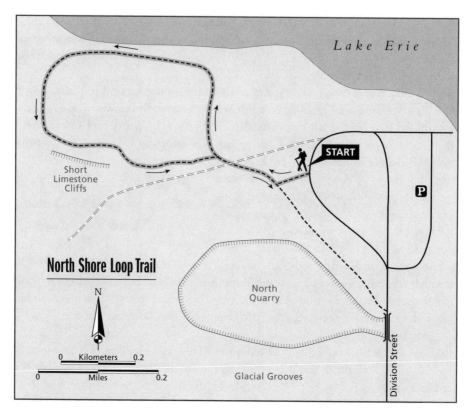

North Shore Loop Trail

0.2 A side trail leads to an old quarry spoil bank (Post 3). Continue straight.

0.6 The trail forks. Take the left fork to continue on the trail, but first take the right spur to the lakeshore. (Several spur trails off of the main trail lead to the lake and good lunch spots.)

1.1 After passing a half dozen side trails to the right, the trail curves sharply left (south) and arrives at a T intersection. Take a left (east).

1.3 Post 9 describes old foundations and quarry roads. Side trails explore these features. Continue straight.

1.5 The trail rejoins the doubletrack road and continues straight.

1.7 Return to the trailhead.

North Pond State Nature Preserve Trail

Start: At the trailhead kiosk off of Ward Road
Distance: 1.1-mile loop
Approximate hiking time: 30 to 45 minutes
Difficulty: Easy; short and flat
Trail surface: Recycled plastic boardwalk

Other trail users: Hikers only
Canine compatibility: Dogs not permitted
Water: Available at the campground and at Memorial Park downtown
Land status: State Nature Preserve

Finding the trailhead: From the junction of East Lakeshore and Division, travel north 0.9 mile to Ward Road. Take a right and go 0.4 mile to North Pond State Nature Preserve on the left.

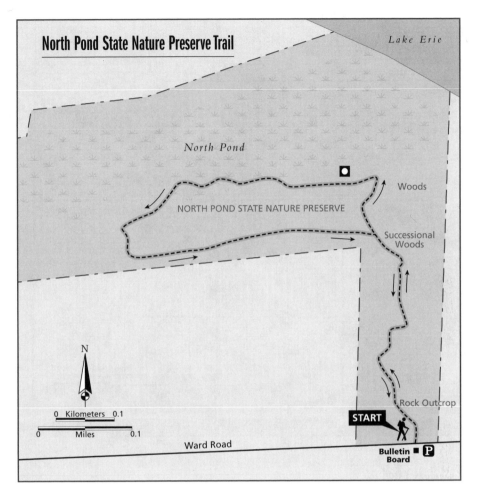

Miles and Directions

0.0 Start at the trailhead kiosk off Ward Road.

0.2 Come to a fork. Take the right fork and begin a counterclockwise loop.

0.3 Come to a junction with the spur trail to the beach on the right. Continue straight.

0.4 Arrive at the wetland overlook deck. Return from the deck and continue in a counterclockwise direction.

0.9 Return to the first junction. Take a right.

1.1 Return to the trailhead.

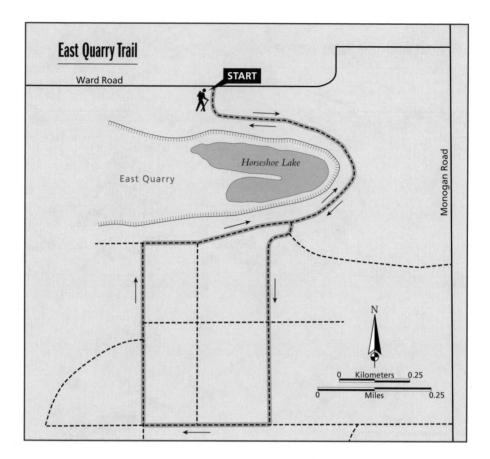

East Quarry Trail

Start: At the trailhead off of Ward Road, marked with a map and a SWIMMING/DIVING PRO-HIBITED sign

Distance: 2.5-mile loop

Approximate hiking time: 1 hour

Difficulty: Easy; short and flat

Trail surface: A broad, flat trail on rock and dirt

Other trail users: Bicyclists

Canine compatibility: Leashed dogs permitted

Water: Available at the campground and Memorial Park downtown

Land status: State park

Finding the trailhead: From the junction of East Lakeshore and Division, travel north 0.9 mile to Ward Road. Take a right and go 0.8 mile to the trailhead on the right. (If you reach a sharp left in the road, you've gone too far.)

Miles and Directions

0.0 Start at the trailhead, located on the south side of Ward Road. Walk past the sign.

0.1 Come to a four-way intersection just before the quarry. Take a left and begin walking around the quarry.

0.6 Reach another four-way intersection. Take a left, turning away from the quarry. In about 20 feet, reach a fork (Post 4). Take the right fork.

0.7 Pass Post 6 on the left and come to a four-way intersection. Continue straight.

1.0 Pass Post 7 on the right and come to a T intersection. Take a right.

1.2 Pass Post 9 and hit a junction. Continue straight.

1.3 Come to a four-way intersection. Take a right.

1.4 Pass a side trail on the left.

1.5 Now on a dirt road, pass another side trail on the right.

1.6 Hit a T intersection, now back at the quarry. Take a right. (**FYI:** Check out the wetland and views of the lake from here.)

1.9 Return to the four-way intersection at Post 4. Continue straight, returning the way you came.

2.5 Return to the trailhead.

Hike Information

Local information
Kelleys Island Chamber of Commerce; (419) 746-2360; www.kelleysislandchamber.com.

Local attractions
Birding, cycling, fishing, boating, and jet-skiing are all popular activities at Kelleys Island. Check out the **Kelleys Island Wine Company;** (419) 746-2678; www.kelleysislandwine.com/.

Islandfest is an annual event, usually held the last weekend in July.

Accommodations
Kelleys Island State Park campground; (419) 746-2546.
Contact the Kelleys Island Chamber of Commerce for a full listing of bed-and-breakfasts on the island; (419) 746-2360.

Restaurants
Island Cafe and Brewpub; (419) 746-2314. **Water Street Cafe;** (419) 746-2468; www.waterstcafe.com.

Hike tours
The Kelleys Island Audubon Society offers monthly bird walks; (419) 746-2258. Contact Kelleys Island State Park for information on summer programs; (419) 746-2546.

Organizations
Kelleys Island Audubon Society, Kelleys Island; (419) 746-2546.

Transportation
Caddy Shack Rentals for bicycles; (419) 746-2664.
Kelleys Cove for golf carts; (419) 746-2622.
Unc'l Dik's; (419) 746-2462.

Northwest Ohio Honorable Mentions

A Wildwood Metropark Upland Woods Trail

Toledo's Wildwood Preserve Metropark could be named Wildly Popular Metropark, and its popularity is consistent with the spirit of its origins. In 1973 a developer's plans were thwarted by the Citizens' Campaign to Save the Stranahan Estate. Two years later the former estate of the Champion Spark Plug Company cofounder Robert A. Stranahan became Wildwood Metropark. Try the 2.3-mile Upland Woods Trail and hike in a forest of maple, oak, sassafras, and witch hazel. Enjoy outstanding wildflower displays from spring through fall as well as wildlife and a floodplain ecosystem. Don't be afraid to take the narrower, less-traveled side trails and explore the many verdant streambeds that drain into the Ottawa River.

Trail contacts: Wildwood Metropark Metz Visitor Center; (419) 535–3058; www.metroparkstoledo.com.

Finding the trailhead: From I–475 northwest of Toledo, exit east on U.S. Highway 20 (exit 13) and drive 1.6 miles to the park entrance on the left. Follow signs to the visitor center, where all trails originate. *DeLorme: Ohio Atlas and Gazetteer:* Page 26 C3.

B Miami and Erie Canal: Farnsworth Metropark to Providence Metropark

Nature and history meet along an 8.0-mile ramble on the Miami and Erie Canal towpath, which parallels the Maumee River near Toledo. Begin walking upstream from the popular Farnsworth Metropark. Just a couple of miles in, arrive at Bend View Metropark, accessible only by the self-powered. Enjoy views of the towering cottonwoods, sycamores, and maples. Keep an eye out for ospreys and bald eagles. Continue all the way to Providence Metropark for the "canal experience," complete with a mule-drawn canal boat replica, a restored lock and mill, and interpretive guides dressed in period clothing. Shuttle or return the way you came for a 16.0-mile out-and-back hike.

Trail contacts: Providence Metropark; (419) 832–6004. Farnsworth/Bend View Metroparks; (419) 878–7641; www.metroparkstoledo.com.

Finding the trailhead: From I–475 southwest of Toledo, exit west on State Route 24 (exit 4) and drive 5.5 miles to the Roche de Bout Shelterhouse parking on the left. To shuttle, continue west 8.0 miles to the entrance to Providence Metropark, also on the left. *DeLorme: Ohio Atlas and Gazetteer:* Page 36 A2.

C Sheldon Marsh State Nature Preserve Trails

The 2.0-mile out-and-back trail at Sheldon Marsh is mostly along an asphalt path that was once part of the original automobile road to Cedar Point amusement park. This short jaunt allows you to explore a swamp forest, a cattail marsh, and a barrier beach—a remnant of this once-common ecosystem in the Sandusky Bay region. Springtime brings such showy wildflowers as Dutchman's breeches, trout lilies, and trilliums, as well as migrating birds, including colorful warblers. Throughout the year this small preserve sees as many as 300 bird species. Look for large conspicuous birds such as great blue herons and bald eagles. From May 1 to September 30, the beach is off-limits to hiking in order to protect the nesting grounds of the federally endangered piping plover and the state endangered common tern. The beach provides ideal nesting habitat for these two birds. Across the water Cedar Point's roller coasters rise from the horizon.

Trail contacts: Sheldon Marsh State Nature Preserve, Huron; (419) 433–4919; www.ohiodnr.com/dnap/location/sheldon.html.

Finding the trailhead: From State Route 2 in Huron, exit north onto State Route 6 (Rye Beach Road). At the stoplight, take a left (west); drive 0.6 mile to the preserve entrance on the right.

D Buckeye Trail: Minster to 40 Acre Lake

This is not a wilderness trail; rather it's a 13.0-mile slice of rural and small-town America. Start just north of the town of Minster and walk through farmland, New Bremen, more farmland, and then through the attractive little burg of St. Marys. Continue to a finish at 40 Acre Lake. This portion of the Buckeye Trail follows the Miami–Erie Canal Towpath Trail; amenities (water, food, rest rooms) are available along the way. Be sure to check out the Bicycle Museum in Bremen. Avoid this hike during full summer sun, since it's quite exposed. The St. Marys section of the Buckeye Trail map has detailed directions.

Trail contacts: Buckeye Trail Association, Worthington; (800) 881–3062; www.buckeyetrail.org.

Finding the trailhead (north trailhead): From I–75 near Wapakoneta, drive west 10.5 miles on U.S. Highway 33 to State Route 66. Turn north onto SR 66 and drive 2.1 miles to Glynwood Road (Township Road 160). Turn west (left) and drive 1.6 miles to a pullout near the bridge that crosses over the north end of 40 Acre Lake. *DeLorme: Ohio Atlas and Gazetteer:* Page 45 D4.

Finding the trailhead (south trailhead): From I–75 between Wapakoneta and Sidney, turn west onto State Route 119 and drive 12.5 miles through Minster (watch for the turns—if you hit the railroad tracks, you've just passed the trailhead). Pull off onto the right side of the road and hop on the towpath. *DeLorme: Ohio Atlas and Gazetteer:* Page 55 A5.

Northeast Ohio

When the Connecticut Western Reserve was admitted into the U.S. Confederation in 1786, this land was already known as "Ohio," a word borrowed from the Iroquois language meaning "beautiful waters." In northeast Ohio today, little more than names are left to remind us of who inhabited or frequented these lands before Europeans: Erie, Wyandot/Huron, Delaware, Ottawa. When U.S. forces and Native American nations signed the Treaty of Greenville in 1795, much of Ohio was opened for settlement. The following year, surveyor Moses Cleaveland landed on the shores of Lake Erie (and, as the joke goes, said "We'll just stay until the weather clears").

The completion of the Erie Canal in 1825, connecting the Atlantic Ocean with the Great Lakes, and then the Ohio and Erie Canal in 1832, connecting Lake Erie with the Ohio River, fueled the population growth of northeast Ohio. The steel industry employed a large segment of the workforce, and by the beginning of the twentieth century, Cleveland (the named was shortened to fit a newspaper headline) was the nation's sixth largest city. The Cleveland Metroparks system was established in 1917, and today it provides an "emerald necklace" of greenspace around the sprawling metropolitan area. Excellent multiuse and hiking trails ring the city in this well-run park system.

Yet another strip of greenspace connects Cleveland and Akron, surrounding the Cuyahoga River and the old Ohio and Erie Canal. The Cuyahoga Valley National Recreation Area was established in 1970, and it was upgraded in 2000 to become Ohio's only national park. Cuyahoga Valley National Park is home to more than 125 miles of trails, including the 20-mile Ohio and Erie Canal Towpath Trail. Northeast Ohioans love their trails, and several hiking organizations get together to hike and help with trail maintenance around Cuyahoga Valley National Park and several cities' metroparks.

The statewide Buckeye Trail begins its route from the north at Headlands Dunes State Nature Preserve and Mentor Headlands State Park. A spur from here leads to a 1,300-mile loop around the entire state. A number of other state parks and preserves are concentrated in the Western Allegheny or Appalachian Plateau, which extends from Pennsylvania into Ohio. Because the last glacier advanced this far, the hills are more rounded here than in the southeastern portion of the state. Natural ponds, bogs, and wetlands are more prevalent, especially closer to the shore of Lake

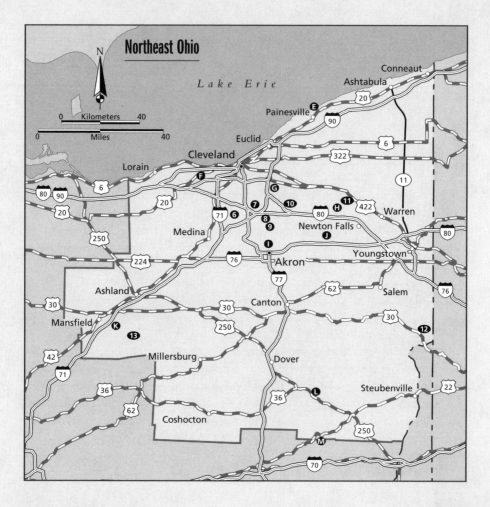

Erie. Wildlife species that once struggled in Ohio are coming back nicely, such as beaver, white-tailed deer, bald eagle, and now black bear.

In far northern Ohio, rivers flow north into Lake Erie; rivers in the rest of the state flow south to the Ohio River. The Muskingum River watershed, south of the state's watershed divide, encompasses much of the landmass in northeast Ohio. The Muskingum Watershed Conservancy District manages 54,000 acres of land in the watershed for flood control, conservation, and recreation. A number of reservoirs, including Tappan and Piedmont Lakes, are home to plenty of lakeside hiking opportunities.

6 Hinckley Lake to Whipps Ledges Trail Loop

Hinckley Reservation

Hinckley Reservation is one of the best known in the Cleveland Metropark system. The reservation gets its fifteen minutes of fame every year with the return of the buzzards. For locals its 25 miles of trails are just as popular. Try a 6.7-mile loop around Hinckley Lake (a reservoir created by damming the East Branch Rocky River) and continue on the Buckeye Trail to Whipps Ledges, an area of 40-foot-high Sharon conglomerate rock ledges. In the meantime enjoy views of the lake, lakeside birds, wildflowers, and forest.

Start: At the Spillway Pool Picnic Area
Distance: 6.7-mile loop with spur loop
Approximate hiking time: 2.5 to 3.5 hours
Difficulty: Moderate due to length
Trail surface: Crushed gravel and dirt trail
Blaze: Hinckley Lake Trail, blue heron silhouette; Buckeye Trail, blue paint; Whipps Ledges Trail, oak leaf silhouette
Seasons: Best mid-April through mid-October and after a winter snowfall
Other trail users: Hikers only
Canine compatibility: Leashed dogs permitted
Water: Available at the rest rooms/changing rooms.

Land status: Cleveland Metropark
Nearest town: Brunswick
Fees and permits: No fees or permits required
Schedule: Open daily year-round from dawn to dusk
Maps: USGS quad: West Richfield; Buckeye Trail Section Map: Medina; MapTech Terrain Navigator: Ohio Northeast/Cleveland/Canton
Trail contacts: Hinckley Reservation, Cleveland Metroparks, Hinckley; (216) 351-6300; www.clemetparks.com/

Finding the trailhead: From State Route 303 east of Brunswick, turn south on State Route 606 and drive 0.8 mile to Bellus Road. Turn left (east) and drive 0.2 mile to the parking lot on the left, next to the ranger station. *DeLorme: Ohio Atlas and Gazetteer:* Page 41 C5.

The Hike

Bird-watchers and other curious folks gather every March to celebrate the harbinger-of-spring return of the buzzards, large bald-headed scavengers, also known as turkey vultures. The Annual Return of the Buzzards is a park event every March 15, when the buzzards supposedly return like clockwork. The celebration motto is "No one spots a buzzard until the Official Buzzard Spotter spots one first!"

The central feature of Hinckley Reservation is Hinckley Lake, a dammed reservoir on the East Branch Rocky River. This body of water provides good birding year-round, where great blue herons, kingfishers, ducks, and Canada geese are as common as the buzzards. The Hinckley Lake Loop Trail encircles the entire lake, providing good views of the lake, its human and avian visitors, deciduous and ever-

Whipps Ledges are a popular destination at Hinckley Reservation.

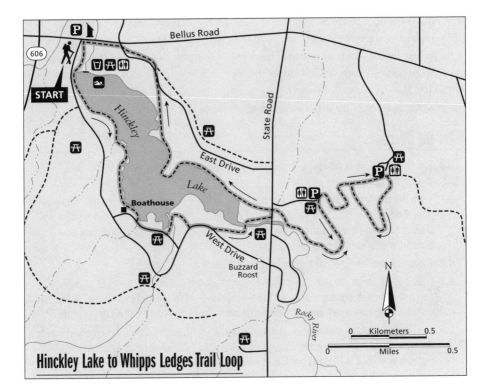

Hinckley Lake to Whipps Ledges Trail Loop

green forests, and plentiful wildflowers. This well-used lake and its surrounding trails are enjoyed by hikers, joggers, cyclists, anglers, canoeists, and kayakers (you can rent canoes and kayaks from the boathouse).

The trail begins near the swimming area below the dam spillway and generally hugs the lakeside all the way to the river. You will pass wetlands, home to more birds as well as willows, cattails, and grasses. As you hike, disregard the various side access trails to the main (crushed gravel) trail and to fishing spots. Look for water lily in the lake and forget-me-not, St. John's wort, and Canada lily along the trail.

At the source of the lake, cross the road and jump on the Buckeye Trail (BT), which serves as a connector path to the Whipps Ledges Trail. This short section of the statewide BT is an attractive narrow footpath that parallels the edge of the East Fork Rocky River for a stretch. In this sunny, wet area look for horsetail (scouring rush), wild rose, and willow.

The trail then joins Whipps Ledges, another highlight of Hinckley Reservation. The trail starts at the bottom of these 50-foot Sharon conglomerate outcroppings, which are made up of rounded quartz pebbles cemented into sedimentary sandstone. The quartz pebbles come from ancient streams that rounded their shape and deposited them in layers. Beech and maple trees grow up between the many rock ledges and passageways, where you can expect to see rock climbers on nice days. The trail continues up a stone stairway to the top of the ledges. Oaks and hickories grow up here, and you can peer down to where you climbed from.

The last leg of the trail rejoins Hinckley Lake's east side, where stands of spruce join the deciduous forest. Walk along the asphalt all-purpose trail to finish the loop. Hinckley Reservation is home to more than 25 miles of hiking, bridle, and all-purpose trails to explore on another day.

Miles and Directions

0.0 Start on the asphalt all-purpose trail where it begins along Bellus Road. Walk south, toward the spillway.

0.1 From the bottom of the spillway, take the stairs to the top and reach a four-way intersection. You'll see the first blue heron blaze ahead. Walk straight through the intersection and begin paralleling the lakeshore. Stay on the broad crushed-gravel path and walk past numerous side access and fishing trails.

0.4 The trail forks. Take the left fork, staying near the lake.

1.2 Pass a junction on the left and continue straight toward the boathouse. Walk straight along the asphalt access road, past the boathouse, and to the all-purpose trail. At the all-purpose trail, take a left and pick up the crushed-gravel path again. Pass the rest rooms.

1.3 As you walk into the picnic area, look for a junction to the right. Take this unmarked trail to the right through a small wetland. Walk straight to the all-purpose trail again. At the all-purpose trail, take a left and parallel the trail to the end of the reservoir.

1.5 Pass a picnic area on the left and cross over a footbridge on the all-purpose trail. Just past the footbridge, reach a junction. Take a left and pick up the crushed-gravel path, blazed now with both the heron and the blue Buckeye Trail blaze.

2.3 Come to a T intersection with the all-purpose trail. Take a left and follow the all-purpose trail over the bridge.

2.5 At a four-way intersection, take a right and cross State Road at the WHIPPS LEDGES PICNIC AREA sign. Walk past the sign to a split-rail fence. At the fence pick up the Buckeye Trail to the right, marked with a blue blaze.

2.8 At the river's edge reach a fork. Take the left fork and ascend the slope.

3.1 Come out at a picnic area, behind the rest rooms. Turn right; in about 50 feet the trail forks. There are no visible blazes here; take the right fork, where the trail is more level.

3.3 The trail approaches the ledges. Take a left here and walk along the bottom of the rocks.

3.4 Between two rock faces, follow stone steps to the top of the rocks. At the top of the steps, take a right, turning away from the blue blaze. In about 50 feet, come to a post with blazes for both the BT and Whipps Ledges. Disregard the arrows on the post and continue straight ahead.

3.5 The trail forks. Stay right and continue to the picnic area. (Water is available here.) Come to a T intersection with a dirt path and a post. Take a right and follow the trail into the woods.

3.8 The trail forks. Either fork descends to the top of the ledges. At the top of the ledges, turn right and return to the intersection for the BT and Whipps Ledges. Take a left and return to the top of the stairs. Return the way you came to reach State Road.

4.9 Cross State Road and pick up the crushed-gravel path again, marked with the blue heron blaze.

5.9 Pass a side trail on the right and continue straight into a patch of spruce trees.

6.0 Cross East Drive and join the all-purpose trail. Follow it to the end of the road.

6.5 Come to a T intersection with Bellus Road. Turn left and cross East Drive, staying on the all-purpose trail, paralleling Bellus Road.

6.7 Return to the trailhead.

Hike Information

Local information

Medina County Convention and Visitors Bureau; (800) 860-2943; junior.apk.net/~mccvb/.

Local events and attractions

The annual **Return of the Buzzards** is celebrated every March 15 and again the following Sunday (unless, of course, the fifteenth is a Sunday). Cuyahoga Valley National Park is less than 10 miles east of Hinckley Reservation; (216) 524-1497; www.nps.gov/cuva.

Organizations

Buckeye Trail Association, Worthington; (800) 881-3062; www.buckeyetrail.org.

Hike tours

Ranger-led walks are available; contact the park for up-to-date information.

Other resources

Cleveland Metroparks produces a newsletter, *The Emerald Necklace,* available free at visitor centers and by subscription; (216) 351-6300.

7 Buckeye Trail: Red Lock to Boston Store

Cuyahoga Valley National Park

This is your best bet for a longer, more secluded quality hike in the Cuyahoga Valley. Begin and end this 8.7-mile loop at the Cuyahoga River, and in between climb to the top of the ridge and walk in a deciduous forest with a few nice spots where water, rocks, and hemlocks meet. A short spur takes you to Blue Hen and Buttermilk Falls. Walk by the historic Boston Store and return on the Ohio and Erie Canal Towpath.

Start: From the Red Lock parking area
Distance: 8.7-mile loop
Difficulty: Moderate due to length and one steep ascent and a steep descent
Approximate hiking time: 3 to 5 hours
Seasons: Best mid-April through mid-October
Trail surface: Dirt trail ascends to ridgetop then back down to the crushed-gravel canal towpath
Blaze: Blue
Other trail users: Hikers only
Canine compatibility: Leashed dogs permitted
Water: Don't rely on seasonal hours of operation at Jaite park headquarters or Boston Store; bring your own.
Land status: National park
Nearest town: Peninsula
Fees and permits: No fees or permits required
Schedule: Open daily dawn to dusk; visitor centers are closed on Thanksgiving, Christmas, and New Year's Day.
Maps: USGS quad: Northfield; Buckeye Trail Section Map: Bedford; Maptech Terrain Navigator: Ohio Northeast/Cleveland/Canton
Trail contacts: Cuyahoga Valley National Park, Brecksville; (216) 524-1497; www.nps.gov/cuva, www.dayinthevalley.com.

Finding the trailhead: From I-77 in Brecksville, exit east on State Route 82 (Chippewa Road). Pass State Route 21 and drive 0.2 mile to Chippewa Creek Drive. Turn right (south) and drive 1.8 miles to Riverview Road. Turn right (south) onto Riverview and drive 2.4 miles to Vaughn Road. Turn left (east) and drive 0.5 mile, crossing the railroad tracks and the river. Just past the river and on the left is the parking lot for Red Lock. *DeLorme: Ohio Atlas and Gazetteer:* Page 41 B6.

The Hike

With more than 125 miles of trails, this is one of Ohio's premier hiking areas. Add a well-developed outdoor adventure infrastructure, and you can easily spend several days or longer discovering all the nooks and crannies of this lush greenway. The two best ways to do this are by cycling the Ohio and Erie Canal Towpath and by hiking some (or all) of the park's footpaths.

Upgraded from national recreation area to national park in 2000, Cuyahoga Valley National Park straddles a 22-mile north-south section of the Cuyahoga River between Cleveland and Akron. Tracing a line right down the center of it all is a section of the statewide Buckeye Trail (BT). For a relatively long and secluded hike in

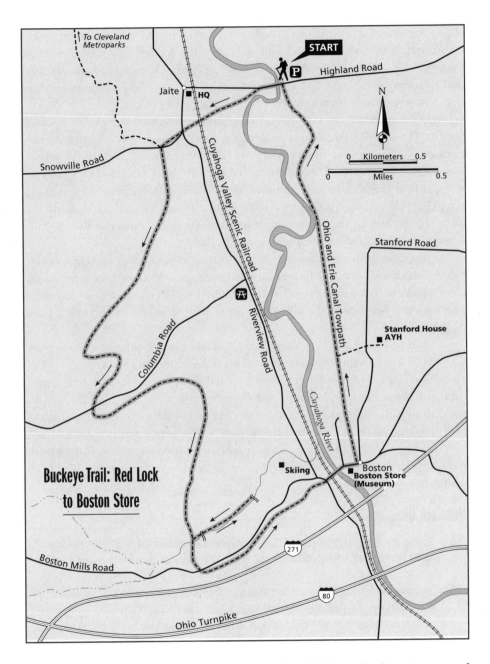

To Cleveland Metroparks

START

Highland Road

Jaite ▪ HQ

N

Kilometers 0 0.5

Miles 0 0.5

Snowville Road

Cuyahoga Valley Scenic Railroad

Stanford Road

Ohio and Erie Canal Towpath

Columbia Road

Riverview Road

Stanford House ▪ AYH

Cuyahoga River

Buckeye Trail: Red Lock to Boston Store

▪ Skiing

Boston
Boston Store (Museum) ▪

271

Boston Mills Road

80

Ohio Turnpike

this popular park, tackle the BT from Red Lock and hike to the historic town of Boston, then return on the canal towpath.

Starting from Red Lock, cross the Cuyahoga River. The beauty of this winding river does not belie the struggles it still has with pollution. (Park literature euphemistically says that water quality "varies.") In late summer you'll be walking in sun-loving grasses and wildflowers such as wingstem, bottlebrush, bergamot, gold-enrod, and ironwood. Soon you will walk past the former mill company town known as Jaite. Today this collection of buildings serves as park headquarters. The trail then crosses the road and steeply ascends to the top of the ridge. Power line rights-of-way provide occasional views of the river valley below.

Atop the ridge, hike in a nicely maturing hardwood forest dominated by oak and hickory. Occasionally you'll cross cool ravines that are lined by hemlock and mus-clewood. Spring greens and wildflowers include coltsfoot, jack-in-the-pulpit, mayapple, and ramps (wild leek). Toward the end of this stretch along the ridgetop, arrive at Blue Hen Falls, pouring into a shale creekbed. Take the spur trail that passes Blue Hen Falls and continue to Buttermilk Falls, a beautiful cascade that's worth the short trip. Return to the BT and cross the road again, then descend steeply back down to the river across from Brandywine Ski Resort.

As you cross the bridge back over the Cuyahoga, look to the north side. You may see the wooden remains of a former dam that long ago impounded water for a mill. Take a break and stop at the restored Boston Store, which is now a canal and canal boat museum. Across from the old Boston Store, pick up an ice-cream cone at Lock 32 general store.

Return to Red Lock by walking north on the crushed-gravel canal towpath. Completed in 1827, the Ohio and Erie Canal linked Cleveland and Lake Erie with Portsmouth and the Ohio River. Towns boomed along the canal, including Cleve-land and Akron but also Peninsula and Boston. Look across the river for railroad tracks. Railroads displaced canal transport by the end of the nineteenth century, and now the automobile has rendered this railway a sentimental scenic byway. As you walk north, pass Stanford House Hostel on the right. If you're staying at the hostel, this would be the obvious start and end point. Otherwise, continue to the Red Lock trailhead.

Miles and Directions

0.0 Start at the Red Lock trailhead, off Vaughn/Highland Road. Take the spur to the towpath. At the towpath turn left (south) and cross Highland Road. Turn right and cross the river on the road.

0.1 Just past the ENTERING CUYAHOGA COUNTY road sign, take a left and pick up the trail, blazed with a signpost that might be obscured.

0.6 Walk under power lines and cross the railroad tracks. Another trailhead comes in from the right here.

0.7 Come to a junction with Riverview and Snowville Roads. Cross Riverview Road and walk along the edge of Snowville Road. In a few hundred feet, a blue-blazed post points you across the road to the left and into the woods. Ascend to the top of the ridge.

3.1 Cross Columbia Road.

4.9 Come to a junction with the spur trail to Blue Hen and Buttermilk Falls. Taking a left onto the spur trail; Blue Hen Falls is almost immediately on the right. Continue downstream.

5.4 Approach an old cement foundation. Walk around to the far side of the foundation, and then cross the stream again. Follow the sound to the top of Buttermilk Falls.

5.9 Return the way you came to the BT, and take a left.

6.0 Walk through a parking area and come to Boston Mills Road. Cross the road and walk along a doubletrack road for about 40 feet. Take a left into the young woods. A large silver maple is blazed blue.

6.2 Come out of the woods and see a building ahead. Walk along the road, but don't cross it. Instead, pick up the gravel road.

6.3 Take a right off the gravel road at a trailhead sign, next to two abandoned buildings.

6.7 Come out at Boston Mills Road and take a right. Cross Riverview Road, and then cross the bridge over the Cuyahoga.

6.9 Walking on the sidewalk now, pass the Boston Store on the right and reach the canal towpath trail. Take a left and walk north.

7.1 Pass a spur trail on the right that leads to Stanford House Hostel.

8.7 Return to the Red Lock trailhead.

THE CUYAHOGA RIVER

The Cuyahoga River was formed with the retreat of the last Ice Age glaciers about 12,000 years ago. The resulting changes in landscape rerouted the drainage of this river from a south-flowing body of water to its current U-shape. The 100-mile Cuyahoga begins flowing south but abruptly turns north where it drains into Lake Erie at Cleveland, just 30 miles west of its mouth. The shape lends to the name Cuyahoga, which means "crooked river."

By the mid-nineteenth century, pollution pressures on the Cuyahoga included raw sewage and industrial waste, including oil. The first fire on the Cuyahoga actually occurred in 1936, but the huge blaze in 1969 catapulted Cleveland to national attention as the "mistake on the lake." Even today, the Great Lakes Brewing Company features the Burning River Pale Ale.

With the 1972 Clean Water Act and ensuing EPA guidelines on pollution emissions, the Cuyahoga is no longer a "dead" river. Its headwaters are protected by natural bogs, fens, and other wetlands. It even supports a warm-water fishery. But the navigable portion of the Cuyahoga near its mouth, still lined with industry, continues to suffer serious water quality problems. Cuyahoga Valley National Park is upstream from this section and is one of the state's most underrated outdoor recreation areas. Still—don't drink the water.

Hike Information

Local information

Convention and Visitors Bureau of Greater Cleveland, Cleveland; (216) 621-4110 or (800) 321-1001; www.travelcleveland.com/.
Akron/Summit Convention and Visitors Bureau, Akron; (330) 374-7560 or (800) 245-4254.

Local events and attractions

Other attractions in the park include the Cuyahoga Valley Scenic Railroad, the 20-mile Ohio & Erie Canal Towpath, Blossom Music Center, Porthouse Theater, several visitor centers, Hale Farm and Village, Brandywine and Boston Mills ski resorts, the Cuyahoga Valley Environmental Education Center, and a slew of park-sponsored events. Most services are cut back during winter months.

Accommodations

Stanford House—Hosteling International; (330) 467-8711.
The Inn at Brandywine Falls; (330) 467-1812. No camping is available in the park.

Restaurants

Fisher's Cafe & Pub in Peninsula; (330) 657-2770
Winking Lizard in Peninsula; (330) 657-2770

Organizations

Cuyahoga Valley Trails Council; www.nps.gov/cuva/friends/cvtc.htm.
Cleveland Hiking Club; www.clevelandhikingclub.com.
Cuyahoga Valley Hiking Association; pw1.net com.com/~toph/cvha.html.

8 Stanford House to Brandywine Falls Loop

Cuyahoga Valley National Park

Approaching Brandywine Falls from Stanford House on foot is one of the nicest experiences you can have in the Cuyahoga Valley. Take this 4.0-mile loop to the 67-foot cascade, a signature attraction of this national park. Return by paralleling a beautiful valley cut by Brandywine Creek. Stanford House makes a good base for exploring the park's 125 miles of trails, including the 20.0-mile Ohio and Erie Canal Towpath.

Start: From Stanford Hostel

Distance: 4.0-mile loop, including observation deck spur

Approximate hiking time: 2 hours

Difficulty: Moderate due to some hilly sections, stairs, and a stream crossing

Trail Surface: Dirt

Blaze: Junctions are marked with signs.

Seasons: Best April through October and after a snowfall in winter

Other trail users: Hikers only

Canine compatibility: Leashed dogs permitted; owners are expected to clean up after pets.

Water: No potable water is available along the trail; bring your own.

Land status: National park

Nearest town: Peninsula

Fees and permits: No fees or permits required

Schedule: Open daily dawn to dusk; visitor centers are closed on Thanksgiving, Christmas, and New Year's Day.

Maps: USGS quad: Northfield; Maptech Terrain Navigator: Ohio/Cleveland/Northeast

Trail contacts: Cuyahoga Valley National Park, Brecksville; (216) 524-1497; www.nps.gov/cuva, www.dayinthevalley.com

Finding the trailhead: From I-77 in Richfield, exit onto I-271 East and travel 6.2 miles to State Route 303 East. Drive 3.7 miles to Riverview Road. Turn left (north) and drive 1.7 miles to Boston Mills Road. Turn right (east) and cross the Cuyahoga River. Take the second left onto Stanford Road. Stanford House is 0.5 mile on the right. Pull into the driveway and park behind the barn. There is a trailhead kiosk.

From I-80 in Boston Heights, exit south onto State Route 8. In 0.25 mile turn right (west) onto Boston Mills Road. Travel 4.0 miles to Stanford Road and turn right (north). Stanford House is 0.5 mile on the right. Pull into the driveway and park behind the barn. There is a trailhead kiosk. **DeLorme: Ohio Atlas and Gazetteer: Page 41 B6.**

(**Note:** The Cuyahoga Valley is not accessible by public transportation.)

The Hike

Brandywine Falls is one of the most scenic spots in Cuyahoga Valley National Park. The trail begins and ends at Stanford House Hostel, an 1843 Greek Revival farmhouse, which is listed on the National Register of Historic Places. This is a great home base for exploring the entire park, especially due to its proximity to the 20.0-mile multiple-use Ohio & Erie Canal Towpath. Parking, information, and a picnic area are all available here. Bring your own water.

Brandywine Falls is a signature attraction in the Cuyahoga Valley National Park.

Begin the Stanford Trail by walking through an open field and then into an oak-hickory forest. Expect to see a variety of birds, wildflowers, and perhaps a large herd of white-tailed deer. The trail can be muddy in wet weather, but its overall quality is quite good, thanks to local hiking groups who donate their time to trail maintenance. Walk across boardwalks and down wooden steps into a nice valley. Look here for such wildflowers as coltsfoot, trillium, bloodroot, mayapple, corn salad, angelica, and bluets.

Ascend out of the valley to Stanford Road, where you will hear Brandywine Falls before they come into view. A wooden boardwalk and observation deck take you close to the 67-foot cascade, a signature attraction of the Cuyahoga Valley. You may even encounter a wedding party here on summer weekends. The trail then takes you to the lip of the falls, where you can peer closely at the water tumbling over a relatively hard layer of Berea sandstone. The softer layers below, worn over millions of years, are composed of Bedford and Cleveland shales.

This spot is also the former site of a sawmill, built by George Wallace in 1814. For decades the town of Brandywine thrived. Now little evidence of the mill or the town remains. The Inn at Brandywine Falls is the restored James Wallace House, another option for accommodations.

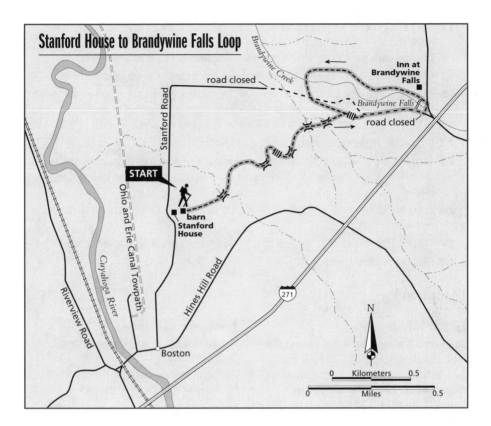

Stanford House to Brandywine Falls Loop

As you cross the top of the falls, you will walk toward the inn. Don't forget to pet the goats and horses out back. Here you will pick up the Brandywine Gorge Trail. The path descends into a fairly narrow gorge, cut by Brandywine Creek. Enjoy the shimmering water, hemlocks, rocks, and forests in this very attractive valley. To cross the stream, walk across a line of quarried stones. (**Note:** The crossing is impossible in high water, so plan accordingly.) The trail soon connects with the Stanford Trail, where you will return the way you came.

Miles and Directions

0.0 Start at the trailhead kiosk behind the barn at Stanford House.

0.2 Cross a footbridge over the creek and enter the woods.

0.7 Arrive at the halfway point to Brandywine Falls, marked with a wooden sign.

0.8 Come to a junction with a spur trail to Averill Pond. Turn right to continue toward Brandywine Falls.

1.2 Come to the junction for the Brandywine Gorge Loop. Turn right and ascend the stairs out of the valley.

1.4 The trail dead ends into Stanford Road. Take a right and pass the gate. Walk along the road for a few hundred feet and take a left at the boardwalk. Follow the boardwalk and then the steps down to the lower observation deck overlooking Brandywine Falls.

1.7 Return to the main boardwalk. Take a left and walk past the lip of the falls.

1.9 Come to a parking area. Take a left and walk the roadway over the creek, toward the Inn at Brandywine Falls. Pick up the trail again along the wooden fence. Walk downstream and keep an eye out across the grass for the trailhead sign for the Brandywine Gorge Trail.

2.2 A spur trail on the left leads to a bench overlooking the creek.

2.4 Approach a sign warning (a bit late) that crossing the creek in high water is impossible. The trail forks just after the sign. Take the left fork and cross the creek on quarried stepping-stones.

2.6 Come to Stanford Road again. Cross the road to the left of the gate, and pick up the trail on the other side.

2.7 Return to the junction with Stanford Trail. Take a right and return the way you came.

4.0 Finish at Stanford House.

Hike Information

Local information

Convention & Visitors Bureau of Greater Cleveland, Cleveland; (216) 621–4110 or (800) 321–1001; www. travelcleveland.com/.
Akron/Summit Convention and Visitors Bureau, Akron; (330) 374–7560 or (800) 245–4254.

Local events and attractions

Other attractions in the park include the Cuyahoga Valley Scenic Railroad, the 20.0-mile Ohio & Erie Canal Towpath, Blossom Music Center, Porthouse Theater, several visitor centers, Hale Farm and Village, Brandywine and Boston Mills ski resorts, the Cuyahoga Valley Environmental Education Center, and a slew of park-sponsored events. Most services are cut back during winter months.

Accommodations

Stanford House—Hosteling International; (330) 467–8711.
The Inn at Brandywine Falls; (330) 467–1812. No camping is available in the park.

Restaurants

Fisher's Cafe & Pub in Peninsula; (330) 657–2770
Winking Lizard in Peninsula; (330) 657–2770

Organizations

Cuyahoga Valley Trails Council; www.nps.gov/cuva/friends/cvtc.htm.
Cleveland Hiking Club; www.clevelandhikingclub.com.
Cuyahoga Valley Hiking Association; pw1.net com.com/~toph/cvha.html.

9 Haskell Run to Ledges Trail

Cuyahoga Valley National Park

This easy 2.0-mile loop is a fun trail that takes you along the base of striking Sharon conglomerate rock ledges and then out to an overlook that provides an expansive view of the Cuyahoga Valley. The vista is especially nice in the fall, but the trail is good year-round, with spring wildflowers, cool hemlock coves in summer, and attractive ice formations in the winter.

Start: From Happy Days Visitor Center; water is available here when visitor center is open.
Distance: 2.3-mile loop
Approximate hiking time: 1 hour
Difficulty: Easy due to length and little elevation gain
Trail surface: Dirt and stone
Blaze: Junctions are marked with signs
Seasons: Best April through October; attractive but icy after a winter storm
Other trail users: Cross-country skiers
Canine compatibility: Leashed dogs permitted; owners are expected to clean up after pets.

Water: Available year-round in the rest rooms at the Ledges Shelter
Land status: National park
Nearest town: Hudson
Fees and permits: No fees or permits required
Schedule: Open daily dawn to dusk; visitor centers are closed on Thanksgiving, Christmas, and New Year's Day.
Maps: USGS quad: Northfield; Maptech Terrain Navigator: Ohio Northeast/Cleveland/Canton
Trail contacts: Cuyahoga Valley National Park, Brecksville; (216) 524-1497; www.nps.gov/cuva, www.dayinthevalley.com

Finding the trailhead: From I-77 in Richfield, turn east onto I-271. Travel 6.2 miles to State Route 303 and turn right (east); drive 4.0 miles to the Happy Days Visitor Center. Take a left into the parking lot, and then follow a pedestrian underpass to the visitor center. From the visitor center, walk to the south side of the parking lot to the trailhead kiosk. *DeLorme: Ohio Atlas and Gazetteer:* Page 41 C6.

(**Note:** The Cuyahoga Valley is not accessible by public transportation.)

The Hike

If you've never hiked the Ledges Trail in Cuyahoga Valley National Park, you're in for a treat. Just a few miles south of downtown Cleveland, you can hop on this short trail and walk along the base of tall Sharon conglomerate ledges before climbing to the top for a sweeping vista of the Cuyahoga River Valley. Begin and end at one of the several excellent visitor centers located in Ohio's only national park.

Beginning with Yellowstone National Park in 1872 and continuing for the next century, the U.S. National Park Service concentrated its lands in beautiful but remote settings, often inaccessible to the vast majority of the nation's population. But the 1970s saw a trend toward establishing parks close to urban areas. In 1970 Cuya-

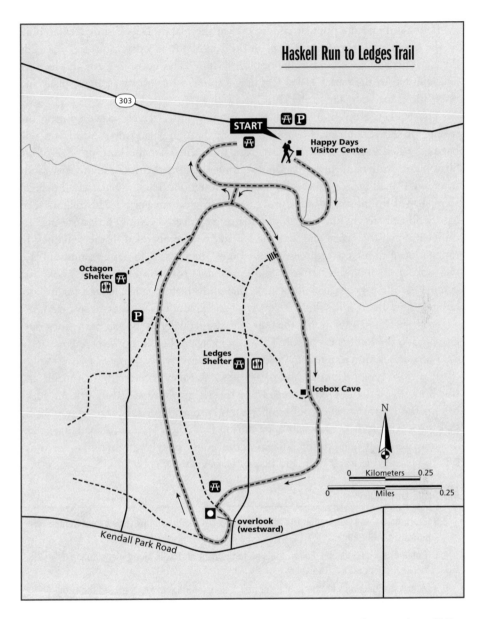

START

⛺ P

Happy Days
Visitor Center

Octagon
Shelter ⛺

P

Ledges
Shelter ⛺

Icebox Cave

N

overlook
(westward)

Kendall Park Road

| 0 | Kilometers | 0.25 |

| 0 | Miles | 0.25 |

303

hoga Valley National Recreation Area was established. In 2000 the Cuyahoga Valley was upgraded to a national park. Around 1978 Cuyahoga Valley National Park took over administration of what had long been known as Virginia Kendall Park, named after the mother of Haywood Kendall, a wealthy Clevelander who owned the property in the early 1900s.

◀ *Stone steps lead hikers through narrow passageways along the Ledges Trail in Cuyahoga Valley National Park.*

Begin and end the popular Ledges hike at the Happy Days Visitor Center, built by the Civilian Conservation Corps in the late 1930s as a day camp for area children. In addition to informational displays, Happy Days hosts concerts and lectures and is home to the park's Travel Planning Center, where you can make plans and reservations for your stay in the Cuyahoga Valley.

The Haskell Run Trail begins by descending into a creek valley. Look in the spring for skunk cabbage, sometimes poking through a late snow. Soon you will begin the Ledges Trail. For the most part, this trail skirts the bottom edge of tall Sharon conglomerate ledges. Sharon conglomerate is made up of sedimentary sandstone with small quartz pebbles embedded throughout. These white, round pebbles were shaped by moving water during the Pennsylvanian Period 320 million years ago. Sediment slowly piled up in seas that once covered Ohio. The quartz pebbles tumbled down the rivers and into the sea and were embedded in the sediment. In time (a lot of time), the sediment formed into Sharon conglomerate sandstone. You will want to include time in your hiking schedule to explore the many nooks and crannies of these geological attractions, including Icebox Cave, named for its cool temperatures. Bring a flashlight if you want to explore the 50-foot-deep cavern.

At about the halfway point, the trail ascends gradually to the top of the rock outcropping to the Ledges Overlook. This is an excellent lunch spot, where you can sit on a broad rock outcropping and take in an expansive view of the Cuyahoga Valley. (Keep a close eye on children and pets here.) The valley is forested, with maple and beech mostly in the low-lying areas. These species give way to mostly oak and hickory on the ridgetops. The cool temperatures around the ledges also support hemlock trees. This spot is especially nice during fall, when leaves are changing color. The trail descends again to the bottom of the ledges, which you follow on the other side to return to Haskell Run and Happy Days Visitor Center.

Miles and Directions

0.0 Start the Haskell Run Trail at the trailhead kiosk behind the Happy Days Visitor Center. Follow the gravel path.

0.1 Come to a T intersection. Follow the sign to the right and walk along the wide, hard-packed trail down into the valley.

0.3 Reach the junction with the connector trail. Take a left here to head toward the Ledges Trail. Ascend the stairs.

0.4 Come to the junction with the Ledges Trail. You can walk this loop in either direction; taking a left, walk toward the Ledges Shelter. In a few hundred feet, approach steps to the right that take you to the Ledges picnic shelter. Take a few minutes to explore the rock outcroppings here. Then continue straight, walking along the ledges.

0.5 Come to Icebox Cave on the right.

0.6 Pass another junction for the Ledges picnic shelter.

1.0 Cross an access road to the shelter. Stay on the gravel path, passing rest rooms on the left and an open field on the right.

1.1 Come to a T intersection and follow the signs to the left for the Ledges Overlook. Continue in the same direction past the overlook.

1.2 Reach another T intersection. Take a right and continue your descent to the junction with the Pine Grove Trail connector. Stay to the right, following signs for the Octagon Shelter.

1.7 Pass a spur trail on the left for the Octagon Shelter. Walk upslope a little to join the rocks again, and continue in the same direction (north).

1.8 Another spur from the Octagon Shelter comes in from the left. Continue straight about 100 feet to steps taking you down and a little to the left, passing another spur trail on the left.

1.9 Take some steps down to a footbridge and then approach a signpost leading you straight. (Informal trails to the right explore the ledges some more.)

2.0 Come to a T intersection and take a left to take the connector trail back to the Haskell Run Trail. When you reach the Haskell Run Trail, take a left to complete the loop.

2.2 The trail emerges from the woods. From here walk across the grassy field back to the visitor center.

2.3 Return to the Happy Days Visitor Center.

Hike Information

Local information

Convention & Visitors Bureau of Greater Cleveland, Cleveland; (216) 621–4110 or (800) 321–1001; www.travelcleveland.com/.
Akron/Summit Convention and Visitors Bureau, Akron; (330) 374–7560 or (800) 245–4254.

Local events and attractions

Other attractions in the park include the Cuyahoga Valley Scenic Railroad, the 20.0-mile Ohio & Erie Canal Towpath, Blossom Music Center, Porthouse Theater, several visitor centers, Hale Farm and Village, Brandywine and Boston Mills ski resorts, the Cuyahoga Valley Environmental Education Center, and a slew of park-sponsored events. Most services are cut back during winter months.

Accommodations

Stanford House—Hosteling International; (330) 467–8711.
The Inn at Brandywine Falls; (330) 467–1812. No camping is available in the park.

Restaurants

Fisher's Cafe & Pub in Peninsula; (330) 657-2651
Winking Lizard in Peninsula; (330) 657-2770

Organizations

Cuyahoga Valley Trails Council; www.nps.gov/cuva/friends/cvtc.htm.
Cleveland Hiking Club; www.clevelandhiking club.com.
Cuyahoga Valley Hiking Association; pw1.net com.com/~toph/cvha.html.

10 Seven Ponds, South Point, and Lonesome Pond

Loop Trails *Tinkers Creek State Nature Preserve*

Prepare for the bugs and head out to link all three short trails in this preserve for a 2.4-mile hike. When the last glacier came and retreated, it left piles of boulders and smaller debris (moraines), circular hills (kames), and long serpentine embankments (eskers). Today you'll see peat bogs, swamps, and marshlands from your slightly upland spot in a forest of swamp white oak, beech, and maple, with some sections of pine plantations. Purple pickerel weed and buttonbush grow along the pond edges. Look for dragonflies, birds large and small, and beavers and deer—and listen for bullfrogs.

Start: From the trailhead parking lot on Old Mill Road

Distance: 2.4-mile trail system

Approximate hiking time: 1 to 1$\frac{1}{2}$ hours

Trail surface: Flat dirt path

Blaze: None, junctions are marked

Seasons: Because of mosquitoes, the preserve is best during dry spells or when nights freeze.

Other trail users: Hikers only

Canine compatibility: Dogs not permitted

Water: No potable water available at the preserve; bring your own.

Land status: State nature preserve

Nearest town: Aurora

Fees and permits: No fees or permits required

Schedule: Open daily year-round from dawn to dusk

Maps: USGS quad: Twinsburg; Maptech Terrain Navigator: Ohio Northeast/Cleveland/Canton

Trail contacts: Tinkers Creek State Nature Preserve, Aurora; (330) 527-5118; www.ohiodnr.com/location/tinkers.html

Finding the trailhead: From I-480 and State Route 14 in Streetsboro, exit east on Frost Road and take an immediate left onto Aurora-Hudson Road. Travel north 0.4 mile to a T intersection. Turn right and continue on Aurora-Hudson Road 1.8 miles to Old Mill Road. Turn west (left) and travel 0.6 mile to the Tinkers Creek State Nature Preserve parking lot on the right. *DeLorme: Ohio Atlas and Gazetteer:* Page 41 B7.

The Hike

Next time you're at a dinner party and the subject of kettle lakes, kames, and eskers comes up, you'll be ready. You'll have hiked the trails at Tinkers Creek State Nature Preserve and seen the results of retreating glaciers in this upland spot in northeastern Ohio. You might even have a story or two—historical or your own—to tell. Tell your friends of the birds and wildflowers you saw or, better yet, of the swamps and marshlands full of sinkholes and quicksand.

Buttonbush swamp (in the foreground) meets ponds at Tinkers Creek State Nature Preserve.

Geologically, the features at Tinkers Creek Preserve are direct results of the Wisconsinan Glacier that came through 12,000 to 15,000 years ago. Where glaciers stopped, they left piles of boulders and smaller debris, called moraines. Huge blocks of ice broke free from the glaciers and created large indentations in the land. When the ice melted, it created kettle lakes. Deposits of sand and gravel made their way through openings, tunnels, or waterways in the glacier and created kames (circular hills) and eskers (long serpentine embankments).

Geography is the key to why Native Americans populated this area. Located along Ohio's watershed divide, the Cuyahoga River flows north into Lake Erie, while the Tuscarawas makes its way south, eventually draining into the Ohio River. By canoe, it is possible to travel from Lake Erie to the Ohio with only an 8-mile portage. When Europeans arrived, they reportedly feared these marshlands with their "sinkholes"

▶ Forty-three of Ohio's 124 state nature preserves are accessible by permit only. These preserves are limited access to protect their sensitive natural features. They often have no formal hiking trails. For more information contact the ODNR Department of Natural Areas and Preserves in Columbus; (614) 265-6453; www.ohiodnr.com/dnap.

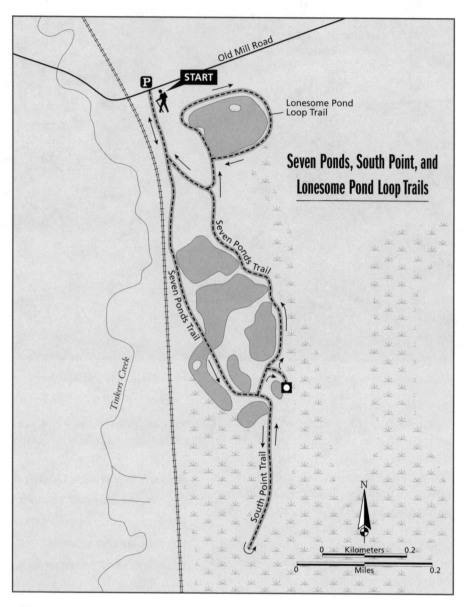

Seven Ponds, South Point, and Lonesome Pond Loop Trails

Old Mill Road

START

Lonesome Pond Loop Trail

Seven Ponds Trail

Seven Ponds Trail

Tinkers Creek

South Point Trail

N

0   Kilometers   0.2

0   Miles   0.2

and "quicksand." But development did occur, and many wetlands were drained. Ironically, when the New York, Chicago, and St. Louis (Nickel Plate) Railroad was built at the end of the nineteenth century, it helped back up some of the water and preserve some swampland. The railroad tracks still border the west edge of the preserve.

Prepare for the bugs and head out to link all three short trails in the preserve. You're sure to see some of the prominent features—peat bogs, swamps, and marsh-lands. Swamp white oak, beech, and maple grow in the canopy, with some sections of pine plantations. The purple pickerel weed grows along the pond edges, as does buttonbush, aptly named for its round flower heads. Look for dragonflies and listen for bullfrogs. Keep an eye out for beaver and deer, or at least their signs—dens and tracks. More elusive but still here are mink, weasel, and muskrat. Birds are quite con-spicuous, especially larger species like great blue herons, Canada geese, and several duck species. In spring many colorful warblers migrate through these parts.

Don't confuse Tinkers Creek State Nature Preserve with Tinkers Creek State Park, its neighbor with 3.5 miles of trails. Also well known is Tinkers Creek Gorge, which cuts a scenic path on its way to the confluence with the Cuyahoga River in Cuyahoga Valley National Park.

Miles and Directions

0.0 Start from the parking lot on Old Mill Road. Cross the road and pick up the trailhead. In 0.1 mile reach the trailhead kiosk.

0.2 Hit a junction where the Seven Ponds Trail diverges. Continue straight.

0.6 Come to a fork. Take a right to walk the out-and-back South Point Trail.

1.0 Return to the junction with the Seven Ponds Trail. Turn right.

1.1 Come to a junction with a side trail to an overlook platform. Take a right to the platform, return to this point, and continue north.

1.5 Arrive at the junction with the Lonesome Pond Loop Trail. Take a right.

1.6 Hit a junction and go straight to begin a clockwise loop around the pond.

1.9 After circling the pond, return to junction and take a left.

2.1 Return to the junction with the Seven Ponds Trail. Continue straight.

2.2 Return to the first junction where the Seven Ponds Trail began its loop. Take a right.

2.4 Return to the trailhead and parking lot.

Hike Information

Local information

Portage County Convention and Visitors Bureau, Aurora; (800) 648-6342; www.portagecountycvb.com.

Local events and attractions

Tinkers Creek State Park, Streetsboro; (330) 562-5515; www.ohiodnr.com/parks/parks.

Six Flags Worlds of Adventure, Aurora; (330) 562-7131; www.sixflags.com.

Accommodations

Ravenna Country Acres, Ravenna; (330) 358-2774; www.gocampingamerica.com/countryacres.

Woodside Lake Park, Streetsboro; (866) 241-0492; www.woodsidelake.com.

Hike tours

Naturalist-led hikes are offered in season; contact the preserve manager for more information; (330) 527-5118.

11 Cascade Falls to Devil's Icebox Loop

Nelson-Kennedy Ledges State Park

Once you've dropped down to your ideal weight from your summer hiking regimen, head over to Nelson-Kennedy Ledges State Park and hike through trail sections with such names as Fat Man's Peril, The Squeeze, and The Narrows. These ledges and mini-canyons are not for the claustrophobic or acrophobic, but they are ideal for a day of summer fun. Explore the Sharon conglomerate outcroppings and slump blocks in a beech-maple-hemlock forest. Walk by waterfalls and through caves; climb to the top of the rocks and then back down. All told, you can cover 2 miles worth of trails, but the scenery is so good, you should plan extra time for exploring.

Start: From the northern trailhead, across from the picnic area
Distance: 1.8-mile loop
Approximate hiking time: 1 hour
Difficulty: Moderate due to some steep or slick terrain and tight squeezes
Trail surface: Dirt and rock
Blaze: White, red, yellow, and blue
Seasons: This is a nice summer hike when the trails are dry yet cool.
Other trail users: Hikers only
Canine compatibility: Leashed dogs permitted
Water: Available in the picnic area

Land status: State park
Nearest Towns: Garretsville, Parkman
Fees and permits: No fees or permits required
Schedule: Open dawn to dusk year-round.
Maps: USGS quad: Garrettsville; Maptech Terrain Navigator: Ohio Northeast/Cleveland/Canton
Trail contacts: Nelson-Kennedy Ledges State Park, c/o Punderson State Park, Newbury; (440) 564-2279; www.ohiodnr.com/parks/parks/punderson.htm

Finding the trailhead: From I-271 in North Randall, turn east on U.S. Highway 422 and drive 26 miles to State Route 282. Turn south (right) and drive 1.7 miles to the Nelson-Kennedy Ledges parking lot on the left. *DeLorme: Ohio Atlas and Gazetteer:* Page 42 B3.

The Hike

The formation of Nelson-Kennedy Ledges began when ancient streams smoothed out, tumbled quartzite pebbles downstream, and deposited them into a sea that once covered most of what is now Ohio. These pebbles became embedded in sediment, and today's resulting rock is Sharon conglomerate sandstone. When the Wisconsinan Glacier retreated from Ohio some 12,000 years ago, it left a thick layer of debris that covered most rock outcrops. The outcrops at Nelson-Kennedy Ledges, however, remained exposed. The process of weathering through freeze and thaw cycles has created slump blocks, where parts of the cliff have slumped off and are now lying on the ground nearby.

Striking rock formations at Nelson-Kennedy State Park.

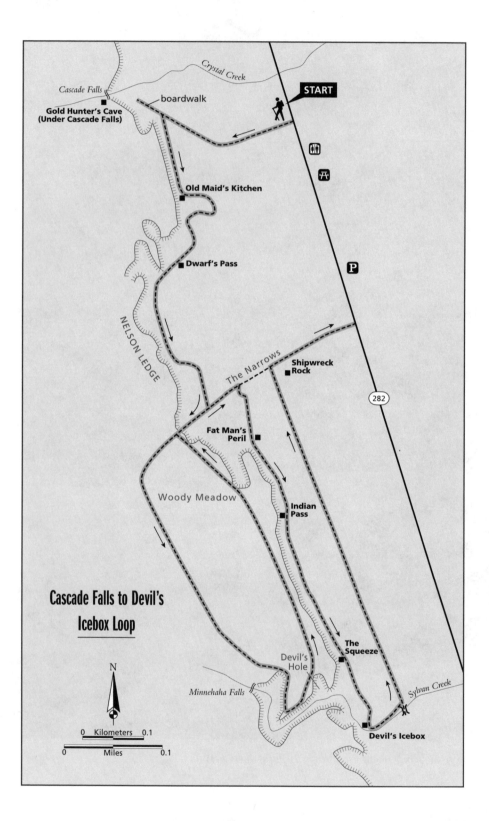

Crystal Creek

Cascade Falls

START

boardwalk

**Gold Hunter's Cave
(Under Cascade Falls)**

Old Maid's Kitchen

Dwarf's Pass

NELSON LEDGE

The Narrows

**Shipwreck
Rock**

282

**Fat Man's
Peril**

Woody Meadow

**Indian
Pass**

**Cascade Falls to Devil's
Icebox Loop**

N

0   Kilometers   0.1

0   Miles   0.1

Devil's
Hole

**The
Squeeze**

Minnehaha Falls

Sylvan Creek

Devil's Icebox

The hike begins immediately among the slump blocks and ledges. Walk through a forest of hemlock, beech, and maple while winding around the many rock faces. Make your way to Cascade Falls, which tumble 35 feet down the rock face. Under Cascade Falls is Gold Hunter's Cave, which got its name during a gold rush of sorts around 1870. But as it turns out, the gold diggers who came here found only fool's gold.

Reverse direction and walk through a dark cave named Old Maid's Kitchen. Work your way out of the cave, and then shortly down the trail do a limbo move to walk under the aptly-named Dwarf's Pass. In springtime these cool recesses are home to abundant wildflowers, including the rare red trillium, spring beauty, solomon's seal, and hepatica. A multitude of ferns grow out of the rocky soil and directly out of the rocks themselves. Look for the common wood, Christmas, and maidenhair fern, as well as the less common polypody, grape, and marginal shield fern.

The trail soon reaches the top of the ledges and continues through a mature maple-beech forest. From this vantage you can look down on the two-part Minnehaha Falls and into the slot canyon the falls create. The upper falls are 20 feet high; the lower falls are 35 feet high. Cliffs are as high as 60 feet, so exercise caution, especially if you're hiking with children. This portion of the trail loops back and returns to the bottom of the ledges, where the passageways narrow considerably. The next part of the path has a couple of very small squeezes that aren't even big enough for both you and your day pack. After wiggling through these tight spots, enjoy the cool damp and the acoustics of Devil's Icebox. From here return farther downslope into a cool-weather-loving forest that includes hemlock, Canada yew, and yellow birch. End the hike at the southern trailhead next to the parking lot.

Miles and Directions

0.0 Start from the north trailhead, across the road from the picnic area. Facing the trailhead signs, take off to the right and follow the yellow-blazed trail around the ledges to Cascade Falls.

0.1 A boardwalk leads to Cascade Falls. After viewing the falls, retrace your steps for about 100 feet to a fork. Take a right, staying near the rocks and ascending slightly. Then walk into the Old Maid's Kitchen cave.

0.2 Exit the cave to the left, just past the boardwalk. Outside the cave, take a right. At the end of the rock face to your right, turn right again into the rocks and then follow another boardwalk through Dwarf's Pass. After crossing a second boardwalk, continue straight and ascend out of the cool rock shelters.

0.4 Walk atop the rocks to a four-way intersection, marked with white blazes. Take a right.

0.7 Before reaching the chain-link fence, the trail curves to the left, overlooking some nice views from the top of the rocks, including Minnehaha Falls.

0.8 A wooden footbridge to the right allows you to peer into the mini-slot canyons below. Walk to the footbridge then turn back, looking for the white blazes.

1.0 Return to the four-way intersection. Take a right and walk about 100 feet. To the left is a metal yellow hiker blaze. Across from this blaze, look for a narrow squeeze between two rocks, marked with a faint red blaze. Walk through this opening.

1.2 About 50 feet past another narrow squeeze, come to a fork. Turn right and head upward. At the top of the rocks, there's a red-blazed beech tree. Just past the beech tree, descend into the gorge again. (**FYI:** Be careful here; it's a slick spot.)

1.3 Come out of the last squeeze and look left for a blaze. Beyond that, a double blaze indicates a turn to the right.

1.4 Arrive at Devil's Icebox. After exploring, walk downstream toward a footbridge. Instead of crossing the footbridge, turn left and walk north for the return trip, following the blue blazes.

1.8 Return to the southern trailhead, across from the parking lot.

Hike Information

Local information

Portage County Convention and Visitors Bureau; (800) 648-6342; www.portagecounty cvb.com.

Local events and attractions

Eagle Creek State Nature Preserve, Garretsville; (330) 527-5118; www.ohiodnr. com/dnap/location/eaglecreek.html.

Century Village living historical museum, Burton; contact the Geauga County Historical Society at (440) 834-1492; www.geauga historical.org/html/century_village.html.

Accommodations

Punderson State Park campground, Newbury; (440) 564-2279; www.ohiodnr.com/parks/ parks/punderson.htm.

West Branch State Park campground, Ravenna; (330) 296-3239; www.ohiodnr.com/parks/parks/westbrnc.htm.

Restaurant

Welshfield Inn, Welshfield; (800) 882-1144.

12 Vondergreen Trail

Beaver Creek State Park

Little Beaver Creek was the first designated Wild River in Ohio. It's also a National Scenic River, and it does not disappoint. The 10.0-mile out-and-back Vondergreen Trail follows the edge of Little Beaver Creek, providing views of whitewater, steep forested slopes, and plentiful wildlife. The hike begins and ends near Gaston's Mill and Pioneer Village. It also follows the route of the former Sandy & Beaver Canal, so you will walk by old canal locks as well. The park is excellent for wildlife viewing; if you're quiet and lucky you might see a bald eagle or a black bear.

Start: From the red steel bridge near the pioneer village

Distance: 10.0-mile out-and-back or 5.0-mile point-to-point shuttle

Approximate hiking time: 3.5 to 5 hours

Difficulty: Moderate due to some poor trail conditions

Trail surface: A mostly flat creekside trail of dirt, rocks, and mud, with a couple of difficult to navigate portions

Blaze: White

Seasons: Best mid-April through mid-October

Other trail users: Mountain bikers; horses on some sections

Canine compatibility: Leashed dogs permitted

Water: Available at the parking lot

Land status: State park

Nearest towns: Calcutta, Rogers

Fees and permits: No fees or permits required

Schedule: Trails open dawn to dusk daily

Maps: USGS quad: East Liverpool North; Maptech Terrain Navigator: Ohio Northeast/Cleveland/Canton

Trail contacts: Beaver Creek State Park, East Liverpool; (330) 385-3091; www.ohiodnr.com/parks/parks/beaverck.htm

Finding the trailhead: From East Liverpool, travel on State Route 7 north and U.S. Highway 30 west until they split. Turn north onto SR 7 and drive 2.3 miles to Bell School Road, marked with a brown state park sign. Turn east (right) and drive 1.2 miles to Echo Bell Road, also marked with brown state park signs. Turn north (left) and drive 1.5 miles. Pass the park office and the pioneer village on the left. Turn right into the parking lot. **Option:** To set up a shuttle, travel east on Bell School Road 2.8 miles to Cannon's Mill Road, marked only with a brown GROUP CAMPING AREA sign. Take a left and drive 2.1 miles to the group camp parking lot on the left. **DeLorme: Ohio Atlas and Gazetteer:** Page 53 C7.

The Hike

Begin the hike with a visit to Gaston's Mill and Pioneer Village, located near the trailhead. Built in 1830, Gaston's Mill was one of six mills constructed along this stretch of the Little Beaver Creek (and one of eighty in Columbiana County). During its heyday, the mill ground almost 200 barrels of flour daily. The mill operates today for visitors. Around the mill, visit the log cabin, chapel, one-room schoolhouse, blacksmith shop, trading post, and covered bridge.

The Vondergreen Trail in Beaver Creek Nature Preserve closely follows the edge of Little Beaver Creek.

From the pioneer village, walk by a restored lock on your way to the trailhead. This is the first of several locks and dams you will see along the hike, since the path also follows the route of the former Sandy and Beaver Canal. Following the construction of the Ohio-Erie Canal in 1825, a number of "feeder" canals were built to access this successful transportation route. The Sandy and Beaver, one of these feeder canals, enjoyed less success. Privately funded and not completed until 1848, the Sandy and Beaver had to compete with rail transport from the start. The canal operated for only four years until a reservoir dam broke upstream and the ensuing floodwaters ruined a large portion of the canal. The Vondergreen Trail is named after one of the canal's lock keepers.

Walk past the lock and then cross over the red steel bridge. Pick up the trailhead on the other side and begin walking downstream. As you hike, look for the different types of sedimentary rocks present here, predominantly sandstone, shale, and limestone. The area has abundant clay, which made it the ceramics capital of the country from the mid-1800s through the 1930s. This creek valley is unique in that it's the only one in the United States where geologists have found evidence of all

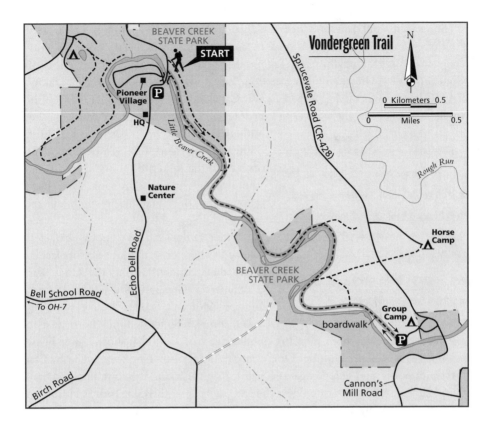

four major glaciations that have occurred in North America over the past two million years. This evidence is the distinctively different rock and mineral deposits left by the retreating glaciers.

From the vantage point of this rocky trail, it's hard to imagine that white-tailed deer and beaver were extirpated (driven out) from Ohio. Both species flourish here today, and black bears are being sighted more and more often. Also look for red fox, raccoons, and skunks. Overhead, keep an eye out for another comeback species, the bald eagle—two nests have been found within the park. Great blue herons, king-fishers, and ducks also make the creek their home. In the evening listen for screech, barred, and great horned owls. Walk quietly and you're likely to see and hear wildlife, especially around the edges of the day.

Toward the center of the trail, where there is a large bend in the creek, conditions get cozy. Understory plants tickle you as you walk by. Smell the spicebush when you disturb it, but also keep an eye out underfoot for poison ivy. In fact, it's best to wear pants along this trail. Touch-me-not (jewelweed), a poison ivy antidote, also grows thick here. Other common flowering plants include purple-flowering raspberry, cow parsnip, Canada violet, phlox, and daisy fleabane. Growing along the shores are water-loving sycamore and silver maple trees.

Some of the old dams and locks are becoming overgrown, but it's still clear what kind of craft and engineering it took to build the canal. Gretchen's Lock is identified with a sign along the trail. Take a short side trip to visit it and reflect on Gretchen's story: Gretchen Gill came from Europe with her mother and her father, E. H. Gill, who was the Sandy and Beaver Canal engineer. Her mother died on the voyage; Gretchen caught malaria and died during construction of the canal, and her father entombed her casket in the lock. When Gill decided to return to Europe, he excavated the casket to rebury at home. On the return trip, the ship sank. Gretchen's ghost is one of several said to still haunt the old canal.

▶ Extirpated species are those that are driven out of a certain place (such as the Ohio Valley) but still survive elsewhere. Once-extirpated species that have returned to Ohio include beaver, black bear, river otter, wild turkey, trumpeter swan, and osprey. Some of these came back on their own; others were reintroduced.

Other famous and infamous characters seemed to have chosen this beautiful place to meet their demise. During the Civil War, Confederate General John Hunt Morgan and his Morgan's Raiders beat a swath almost completely across Ohio from west to east before being captured near the present-day park. In 1934, shortly after being named "Public Enemy Number One," gangster Pretty Boy Floyd was killed by East Liverpool police and federal agents. There's a sign marking the spot, just upstream from Hambleton's Mill, located near the east trailhead of the hike. Today's visitors, in contrast, enjoy a safe and peaceful place to hike, fish, and canoe.

Miles and Directions

0.0 Start on the east side of the steel bridge spanning Little Beaver Creek. The trailhead is marked with signs for the Upper and Lower Vondergreen Trails. Take a right and descend to the creek to begin the Lower Vondergreen Trail. **Option:** For some diversity, turn left and walk up the road a couple hundred feet to the Upper Vondergreen Trailhead. Both trails meet up in about a mile.

0.6 Cross a horse trail. Continue straight.

1.1 Arrive at the junction with the Upper Vondergreen Trail. Continue straight.

1.4 Pass Grey's Lock on the right.

1.8 Cross straight over another horse trail and then a footbridge.

2.2 Walk past Vondergreen's Lock on the right.

2.3 Come to a five-way intersection. Take the first left, following the sign to check out Gretchen's Lock, then return to this spot. Continue downstream, on the trail blazed orange (horse trail). Pass an access trail to the creek on the right.

2.6 Pass a dam on the left.

2.7 The horse trail veers off to the right, down to the creek. Continue straight, picking up the white blazes again. Then pass another lock and hit a fork. Take the right fork, continuing downstream.

2.9 Walk past another lock. The trail narrows but is still fairly easy to follow. Look to the left for some towering rock walls.

3.4 The trail climbs a slope and reaches a shale outcropping. *Do not* walk down the shale talus slope to the creek. Rather, scramble up the steep, crumbling shale to firm ground again. (**FYI:** This is a difficult and somewhat dangerous spot; use caution.)

3.6 Come to an intersection with the bridle trail. Cross the bridle trail and continue on a faint, unmarked path that still parallels the creek.

4.1 Pass another lock and reach a T intersection. Turn left and approach an almost immediate fork. Take the right fork, picking up the white blazes again as well as blazes for the North Country Scenic Trail. Pass a sign on the left for the Vondergreen Trail (which, technically, you haven't been on for the past half mile).

4.4 Cross another bridle trail and continue straight along a wide path next to this straight stretch of creek.

5.0 Come to the end of the line at the group campground parking lot. **Option:** Set up a shuttle and end the hike here.

10.0 Return to the trailhead the way you came.

Hike Information

Local information

East Liverpool Chamber of Commerce; (330) 385–0845.

Columbiana County homepage: www.area living.com.

Local events and attractions

Gaston's Mill and Pioneer Village, in the park.

Beaver Creek Trail Rides, East Liverpool; (330) 853–5241.

The Museum of Ceramics, East Liverpool; (800) 600–7180; www.ohiohistory.org/ places/ceramics/indes.html.

Leetonia-Lisbon Greenway, Lisbon; (330) 424–9078.

Accommodations

Beaver Creek State Park campground; (330) 385–3091.

Lock 30 RV Campground; (877) 856–2530; www.ohioparks.net/lock30.

Organizations

Columbiana County Forest & Parks Council.

Sandy and Beaver Canal Association; (330) 332–1084.

North Country Scenic Trail; www.northcountry trail.org/gts/index.htm.

13 Hemlock Gorge to Lyons Falls Trail

Mohican State Park

Make a 9.3-mile lollipop to explore all the main attractions at Mohican State Park. Begin by walking the Hemlock Gorge Trail along the Clear Fork of the Mohican River, which runs through a glacial meltwater gorge that's 300 feet deep. Its natural features include sandstone outcroppings, hemlocks, sycamores, oaks, and rare virgin white pine stands. Continue on the Lyons Falls Trail and walk into a recess cave under Big Lyons Falls and then to the top of Little Lyons Falls, which pour into a box canyon. Return on this loop to the covered bridge, where you'll again meet the Hemlock Gorge Trail.

Start: From main campground trailhead for Hemlock Gorge Trail

Distance: 9.3-mile lollipop; optional 3.3- and 6.0-mile hikes

Approximate hiking time: 3.5 to 5 hours

Difficulty: Moderate due to length and a couple of steep sections

Trail surface: Dirt path; some spots often muddy

Blaze: Only Lyons Falls Trail is blazed, with yellow and blue spraypaint

Seasons: Best early May through late October

Other trail users: Hikers only

Canine compatibility: Leashed dogs permitted

Water: Available seasonally at campgrounds

Land status: State park and state forest

Nearest town: Loudonville

Fees and permits: No fees or permits required

Schedule: Open daily year-round from dawn to 11:00 P.M.

Maps: USGS quad: Jelloway; Maptech Terrain Navigator: Ohio Lima/Toledo/Northwest

Trail contacts: Mohican State Park, Loudonville; (419) 994-5125; www.ohiodnr.com/parks/parks/mohican.htm. Mohican Memorial State Forest, Perrysville; (419) 938-6222; www.ohioparks.net/Forests/Mohican-Memorial/.

Finding the trailhead: From I-71, south of Mansfield, take State Route 97 east about 20 miles to its dead end into State Route 3. Take a left (north) onto SR 3 and then an almost immediate left into the campground. *DeLorme: Ohio Atlas and Gazeteer:* Page 49, D7.

Option: You may want to set up a shuttle between the campground and the covered bridge. Travel 15.7 miles on SR 97. Just past the Mohican Memorial on the right, take a left turn onto State Forest Road 58 and travel 1.5 miles, following the signs for the covered bridge.

The Hike

The centerpiece of Mohican State Park is the Clear Fork of the Mohican River, which runs through a gorge more than 300 feet deep. The meltwaters from the edge of the last glacier helped to carve out this gorge. Its natural features include sandstone outcroppings, hemlocks, sycamores, oaks, and rare virgin white pine stands that have earned the area Registered National Natural Landmark status.

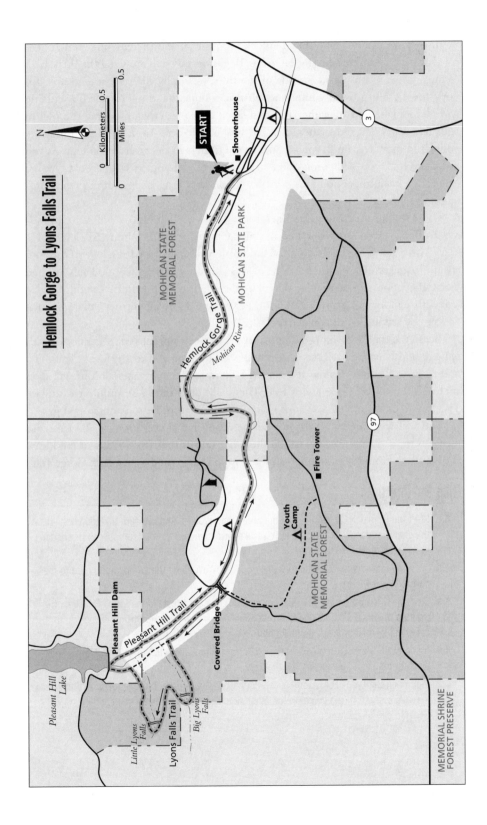

Hemlock Gorge to Lyons Falls Trail

N

Kilometers
0   0.5

Miles
0   0.5

START

Showerhouse

MOHICAN STATE
MEMORIAL FOREST

MOHICAN STATE PARK

Hemlock Gorge Trail

Mohican River

Pleasant Hill Dam

Pleasant Hill Lake

Pleasant Hill Trail

Covered Bridge

Little Lyons Falls

Big Lyons Falls

Lyons Falls Trail

Fire Tower

Youth Camp

MOHICAN STATE
MEMORIAL FOREST

MEMORIAL SHRINE
FOREST PRESERVE

3

97

Too many hikers bypass the Hemlock Gorge Trail and thereby miss some of the park's most rare and interesting offerings. Begin on this trail, noticing the thick layer of moss growing on the north side of the trees, especially the sycamores. Look up-slope for the old-growth white pines. Within a mile, the gorge broadens to a fairly wide floodplain, and then the river and slope come together, pinching the trail in between. Watch for spots where the trail washes out here. Trout and bass fishing are popular in the Clear Fork; you are sure to see anglers in the river as you hike. As you finish the trail, you will come upon an idyllic scene of anglers with an old covered bridge as a backdrop. Look for great blue herons and kingfishers, both of which frequent the gorge.

Cross the covered bridge and begin the Lyons Falls Trail. You will walk by waterfalls that were once frequented by John Chapman, a.k.a. Johnny Appleseed. He carved his name and the date on the sandstone walls of Lyons Falls, but his carvings are no longer visible. Some portions of this overused trail are considerably washed out. Other spots can be slick or may skirt the edge of drop-offs. Be careful if walking with children or in wet conditions. Take care to avoid further environmental damage by staying on designated trails.

Begin the trail by walking along the river in a forest dominated by hemlocks, with red oak and beech as well. Soon you will walk upslope and to Big Lyons Falls. The trail takes you into a shallow recess cave, behind a trickling waterfall. You will then approach the top of Little Lyons Falls. These falls drop into a beautiful box canyon. The trail returns to the Clear Fork Gorge, this time atop the rock outcroppings.

You will continue by skirting the earthen dam that creates Pleasant Hill Lake and then return to the covered bridge on the other side of the river by way of the Pleasant Hill Trail. From the bridge, return the way you came on the Hemlock Gorge Trail.

Miles and Directions

0.0 Start the Hemlock Grove Trail from the main campground; find the spur trailhead behind the showerhouse. Walk past the BICYCLES PROHIBITED sign and take a footpath to the wooden trailhead sign. Parallel the river.

2.5 Cross a footbridge and walk into Campground B. Walk along the campground road to the covered bridge.

3.3 Cross the covered bridge and take and immediate right (west) to the Lyons Falls Trail. The wooden trailhead sign may be obscured, but the trail itself is not. **Option:** If you set up a car shuttle, you can finish your hike here.

3.8 Come to an overly blazed (yellow spraypaint) junction. Take a left to go to Big Lyons Falls. Walk up the slope, paralleling the tributary.

4.2 Approach Big Lyons Falls, pouring over a shallow recess cave. The trail takes you behind the falls and out of the gorge on the other side. Look for the carved steps. Soon you will begin to see blue blazes.

4.5 Arrive at the top of Little Lyons Falls, which pour into a slot-like canyon. The path crosses the waterfall and parallels its drainage.

4.8 Come to a T intersection. Take a left and descend gradually.

5.0 Come to the end of the trail at the dam. Cross the grass below the dam and pick up the Pleasant Hill Trail. You can see the trailhead sign from the dam.

6.0 The Pleasant Hill Trail ends at the covered bridge. **Option:** If you set up a shuttle, end the trail here. Walk along the road again that serves Campground B. Return on the Hemlock Grove Trail.

9.3 Return to the campground trailhead.

Hike Information

Local information
Loudonville-Mohican Convention and Visitors Bureau, Loudonville; (800) 722–7588; www.loudonville-mohican.com.

Local events and attractions
Malabar Farm State Park; (419) 892–2784; www.ohiodnr.com/parks/parks/malabar.htm.
Clear Fork and Snow Trails ski resorts; www.skiclearfork.com and www.snowtrails.com.

Accommodations
Mohican State Park cottages; (419) 994–4290.

Restaurants
Malabar Inn Restaurant, Perrysville; (419) 938–5205.

DUCT TAPE IS THE ANSWER Blister prevention? Duct tape. Broken tent pole? Duct tape. Pack repair? Duct tape. Need a splint? Duct tape. Yes, a pack, water bottle, raincoat, and map are essentials for even a short day hike. But so is duct tape. Hailed as "the ultimate power tool," it's a versatile problem-solver you'll be glad you had. An easy way to carry duct tape with you is to wrap it around your water bottle.

Northeast Ohio Honorable Mentions

E Headlands Dunes State Nature Preserve

There are no official hiking trails, but walk along the many sandy paths in Headlands Dunes State Nature Preserve. Enjoy views of shifting sand dunes, unusual grasses and flowers, Lake Erie, and a scenic lighthouse. This preserve isn't just picturesque, it's also ecologically important. Headlands Dunes is one of the last sand dune plant communities along a river bay in the Great Lakes. This is also your chance to begin hiking from the northern terminus of the statewide Buckeye Trail. You can walk from here through Headlands Beach State Park (which is mostly a parking lot with a beach) to Mentor Marsh State Nature Preserve and keep going for about as long as you care to.

Trail contacts: Headlands Dunes State Nature Preserve, Painesville; (440) 632–3010; www.ohiodnr.com/dnap/location/headlands.html.

Finding the trailhead: From State Route 2 in Painesville, turn north onto State Route 44 and drive 2.6 miles until it ends at the Headlands Beach State Park entrance. Drive straight into the park and take the first right. Travel to the easternmost row in the parking lot. Walk to the northeast corner of the parking lot to the trailhead sign. *DeLorme: Ohio Atlas and Gazetteer:* Page 32 B1.

F Rocky River Reservation

Rocky River Reservation is part of the Cleveland Metroparks "Emerald Necklace" of greenspace surrounding the city. This long, narrow park is a buffer around the Rocky River as it flows north into Lake Erie. Starting from the nature center, hike south along the river, with views of its shale banks, and then up the steep wooden stairs to a good overlook of the valley below. Heading either north or south, walk the trail pinched between the river on one side and the bike path and road on the other. Like so many other Ohio hikes, this is nice year-round, but especially during spring wildflower and fall foliage seasons or after a winter snowfall. Park naturalists offer guided hikes year-round; contact the reserve for up-to-date information.

Trail contacts: Rocky River Nature Center, North Olmsted; (440) 734–6660; www.clemetparks.com/.

Finding the trailhead: From I–480 in North Olmsted, exit onto State Route 252 South. Travel 0.5 mile to Butternut Ridge Road and take a left (east). Drive 0.1 mile to Columbia Road and turn left (north). Drive 0.3 mile to Cedar Point Road and turn right. Descend to Valley Parkway in 0.6 mile and turn left (north). Drive 0.3 mile to the nature center parking lot on the left. *DeLorme: Ohio Atlas and Gazetteer:* Page 40 A4.

G Buckeye Trail: Frazee House to Bridal Veil Falls, Cuyahoga Valley National Park

If you're looking for a quality hike without the crowds in the Cuyahoga Valley, look no further than the Buckeye Trail from Frazee House to Bridal Veil Falls. Begin at Frazee House, built between 1825 and 1827, and check out the displays inside if it's open. Walk south along Canal Road to Sagamore Road, where you'll enter the woods. Follow an attractive creek upstream until you climb out of the creek valley and onto a ridge. Continue along the bridle trails to a scenic overlook of Tinkers Creek Valley, a National Natural Landmark. Parallel the valley until you arrive at Bridal Veil Falls, a scenic cascade of water over a shale bed surrounded by hemlocks and deciduous trees. Return the way you came for a 9.0-mile round trip hike. Another fun option is to set up a bicycle shuttle. Leave your bike at the parking lot for Bridal Veil Falls and ride back to the trailhead—downhill all the way!

Trail contacts: Cuyahoga Valley National Park, Brecksville; (216) 524–1497; www.nps.gov/cuva. Buckeye Trail Association, Worthington; (800) 881–3062; www.buckeyetrail.org.

Finding the trailhead: From the junction of I–77 and Rockside Road, turn east onto Rockside Road and drive 1.2 miles to Canal Road. Turn right (south) and drive 3.1 miles to Frazee House on the left. *DeLorme: Ohio Atlas and Gazetteer:* Page 41 B6.

H Eagle Creek State Nature Preserve

Only one thing stands between this being a featured hike and an honorable mention: mosquitoes! Go in dry or breezy or freezing weather, and be prepared for the mosquitoes. Then enjoy Eagle Creek's nearly 5 miles of trails through unpolluted beaver ponds, cranberry bogs, and swampland. This place is home to abundant wildlife, most noticeably beaver and deer (and mosquitoes). Two rare and endangered species also live here: the spotted turtle and the four-toed salamander. It's even home to two carnivorous plants: round-leaved sundew and pitcher plant. Located along the watershed divide in Ohio, Eagle Creek flows south toward the Ohio River, while the Cuyahoga River, just a few miles north, drains into Lake Erie. You can combine a day hike here with one at nearby Nelson-Kennedy Ledges State Park.

Trail contacts: Eagle Creek State Nature Preserve, Garretsville; (330) 527–5118; www.ohiodnr.com/dnap/location/eaglecreek.html.

Finding the trailhead: From State Route 82 east of Garretsville, turn north onto Parkman-Nelson Road and drive 0.6 mile to Hopkins Road. Take a left and drive 1.6 miles to the parking lot on the left. *DeLorme: Ohio Atlas and Gazetteer:* Page 42 B3.

Glens Trail, Gorge Metro Park

Straddling the cities of Akron and Cuyahoga Falls, Gorge Metro Park is a long narrow strip of greenspace that overlooks the Cuyahoga River. Head out on the 3.6-mile out-and-back Glens Trail and find yourself pinched between Sharon conglomerate sandstone outcroppings on one side and the dammed-up river on the other. Enjoy abundant spring wildflowers, and look for white-tailed deer. If you'd like, continue on the Gorge Trail to Mary Campbell Cave, named after a young white girl who lived as a child with her Delaware Indian captors. You can even hop on the Highbridge Trail and walk to Cascade Valley Metropark.

Trail contacts: Metro Parks, Serving Summit County, Akron; (330) 867–5511; www.neo.lrun.com/MetroParks.

Finding the trailhead: From State Route 8 in Cuyahoga Falls, turn west onto Broad Boulevard and take an immediate left (south) onto Front Street. Drive 1.1 miles to the Metro Park entrance and parking lot on the right. Pick up the GORGE TRAILHEAD sign next to boulders at the southwest end of the parking lot. Walk across Front Street and pick up the trail again on the other side. *DeLorme: Ohio Atlas and Gazetteer:* Page 41 D6.

Buckeye Trail, West Branch State Park

At West Branch State Park, a portion of the statewide Buckeye Trail makes a 9.0-mile loop around the western third of Michael J. Kirwan Lake (reservoir). Hike the entire loop with two sections on the road, or make it a 7.5-mile horseshoe with a shuttle. Beginning at the junction of State Route 14 and West Cable Line Road, follow the blue blazes as you make your way around the south side of the lake in a mostly young forest with beaver ponds along the runs that drain into the lake. The area is also home to glacial kettle lakes. Look for water-loving cattail, buttonbush, and swamp white oak, as well as the usual array of spring wildflowers. Cross the lake by walking along Rock Spring Road bridge. From here you'll get views of the anglers and boaters who throng to this park, named after the West Branch of the Mahoning River. On the north side of the lake is a picnic area that's perfect for a halfway-point lunch stop. Continue walking counterclockwise on the north side of the lake, where the forest floor is covered in ramps (wild leeks) in the springtime and several fern species year-round. Finish the trail at Knapp Road, where you can pick up your bike or car shuttle or continue walking back to OH 14.

Trail contacts: West Branch State Park, Ravenna; (330) 296–3239; www.ohiodnr.com/parks/parks/westbrnc.htm

Finding the trailhead: From the junction of State Route 59 and SR 14 in Ravenna, turn south onto SR 14 and drive 2.3 miles to West Cable Line Road on the left and a pullout on the right (west) side of SR 14. Park at the pullout and pick up the trail across the road. It enters the woods about 150 feet south of West Cable

Line. To shuttle, turn back 0.25 mile on SR 14 to Knapp Road and take a right (east—there is a gravel parking lot here, and this may be a preferred starting point). Travel 1.0 mile on Knapp Road to a pullout and the trail on the right, marked with a blue blaze. *DeLorme: Ohio Atlas and Gazetteer:* Page 42 C2.

K Butternut Nature Trail, Malabar Farm State Park

Malabar Farm, late author and conservationist Louis Bromfield's estate, is a working farm popular with literature and history buffs and equestrians more than with hikers. But if you're looking for a nice short hike, don't overlook Mohican State Park's next-door neighbor. Try the 1.8-mile out-and-back walk from the farm complex to the cave along the Butternut Nature Trail. Begin from the farm complex parking lot, across from the youth hostel. Walk west along Bromfield Road for a few hundred feet to a gravel driveway on the left. Walk along the driveway, under the shade of mature trees, to the Butternut Nature Trail trailhead on the right. Take in the mature forest, hemlocks, boulders, cabins, and ferns on your way to the cave. Don't forget your flashlight.

Trail contacts: Malabar Farm State Park, Lucas; (419) 892–2784; www.malabar farm.org.

Finding the trailhead: From I–71 and State Route 13 south of Mansfield, take Hanley Road east for 2.0 miles to Little Washington Road. Turn south (right) and travel 0.3 mile to a fork. Take the left fork and travel east on Pleasant Valley road 5.2 miles to Bromfield Road. The parking lot for the farm complex is the first one on the left. *DeLorme: Ohio Atlas and Gazetteer:* Page 49 C6.

L Deer to Red Fox Trail Loop, Tappan Lake Park

If you look at a map of Ohio, take note of the many sizable permanent reservoirs located in the Muskingum River Watershed, the result of fourteen flood-control dams built by the U.S. Army Corps of Engineers between 1933 and 1938. The Muskingum Watershed Conservancy District, a unique political entity, has a mission to oversee flood control, conservation, and recreation on the lakes and the entire 54,000 acres of land and water space it manages for public use. Tappan Lake in Harrison County is one of the more popular recreation areas in the district, for hikers as well as other users like boaters, anglers, and hunters. Beginning at the camp-ground amphitheater, combine the Deer, Pine Tree, and Red Fox Trails for a 5.8-mile loop hike that takes you by the lakeshore and into deciduous and pine forests. Look for old fencerows along the trail, which are now made up of stately old oak trees. Wildlife and wildflowers are plentiful. Nearby, the Buckeye and North Country Trails make their way through the park. Camping and cabins are available.

▶ A watershed is an area of land that drains into the same body of water, often a river. For example, the Muskingum River Watershed contains the Muskingum River as well as the tributaries that flow into it and the surrounding land.

Trail contacts: Tappan Lake, c/o Muskingum Watershed Conservancy District, New Philadelphia; (330) 343–6647 or (877) 363–8500; for park and campground call (740) 922–3649; www.mwcdlakes.com/.

Finding the trailhead: From I–77 in New Philadelphia, take U.S. Highway 250 east 24.4 miles to near the end of Tappan Lake. Turn south (right) onto County Road 55 (Tappan-Moravian Trail—it joins County Road 2), and drive 3.7 miles to the park entrance on the right. Turn into the park and drive 0.7 mile, just past the guard shack, and take a left at the sign that reads CAMP AREA/BOAT LAUNCHING RAMP/AMPHITHEATER/HIKING TRAILS. Drive about 150 feet to a stop sign and take a right into Campground 1. Drive on the campground road 0.2 mile to a stop sign, on the left side of the marina as you face it. Park at the boat launch parking lot and look for the amphitheater sign. That's the trailhead. *DeLorme: Ohio Atlas and Gazetteer:* page 62 B2.

M Buckeye Trail: U.S. 22 to Piedmont Marina Campground, Piedmont Lake Park

The little-used section of the Buckeye Trail that skirts the northwest edge of Piedmont Lake offers some of the best views in the region. You'll likely find solitude along this 8.0-mile out-and-back segment that skirts the water's edge. Expect to see and hear your watercraft neighbors, though. Try a late-afternoon hike to catch the good light casting its glow on the far side of the lake and the rolling hills off into the distance as you walk through a young deciduous forest and a few pine plantations. Stop at the campground and marina for a halfway-point water or lunch stop. If

▶ Two other Eastern forest trees are now experiencing blights: Unless a cure is found, flowering dogwood and eastern hemlock's numbers will continue to diminish, if not disappear altogether.

you're spending some time on the water, too, make your way to the rock that juts out of the lake near Indian Run, where you can see a fossilized snake. Piedmont Lake is one of ten permanent flood-control/recreation reservoirs in the Muskingum Watershed Conservancy District.

Trail contacts: Piedmont Lake, c/o Muskingum Watershed Conservancy District, New Philadelphia; (330) 343–6647 or (877) 363–8500; for the marina call (740) 658–3735; www.mwcdlakes.com/.

Finding the trailhead: From the junction of I–70 and I–77 near Cambridge, travel north on I–77 for 3.3 miles to U.S. Highway 22. Turn east and drive 22.0 miles to the trailhead on the right. Just after US 22 and State Route 800 split, continue down a hill with guardrails on both sides of the road. The trail starts at a break in the guardrail on the right side of the road. Just after that is a pullout. If you hit the rest area, you've gone too far. Look for the blue blazes. *DeLorme: Ohio Atlas and Gazetteer:* Page 62 C2.

The once-widespread American chestnut has all but disappeared from the landscape.

AMERICAN CHESTNUT (CASTANEA DENTATA)

Just when you start to feel that the world is coming to an end—global warming, clearcuts, huge forest fires, massive road-building projects, suburbs—take a minute to think about what it must have been like to live through the American chestnut blight.

Until the beginning of the twentieth century, fully one in every four trees in the central Appalachians and the eastern half of Ohio was an American chestnut. This was the dominant tree species in more than nine million acres in the East, most often found on dry ridge tops. These giants regularly grew to 5 feet in diameter and 100 feet tall, and many were bigger than that.

The American chestnut was easily the most important tree species in the forest. Wild animals, domesticated animals, and people near and far feasted on the large, meaty nuts. The lumber from the American chestnut was also very important. The trees grew tall and straight, and often the first branches were 50 feet from the ground (think of a mature tulip poplar in today's forest). Straight grained and fairly easy to work, the wood was used for just about everything—from furniture to musical instruments to railroad ties to pulp.

In 1904 an Asian fungus was discovered in New York that would turn out to be the American chestnut blight. Less than fifty years later, virtually every American chestnut tree was dead.

Dying trees were cut and milled for their usual lumber uses (check out the shelters and picnic tables at Fort Hill State Memorial, for example). You can sometimes see fallen chestnut logs along the trail today, long ago stripped of their bark. In fact, you can even see some American chestnuts growing in the forest, but these are mostly young stump sprouts that will succumb to the blight within a couple of decades, before producing nuts.

Researchers are now working on bringing back the American chestnut, mostly by breeding it with Asian chestnut varieties in an attempt to produce a blight-resistant strain. For more information, contact the American Chestnut Foundation at (802) 447–0110; chestnut.acf.org.

Central Ohio

Central Ohio is often overlooked as a hiking destination, but a handful of very nice trails are within an hour or two of the state's largest (by area and population) city. When Columbus was designated state capital of Ohio in 1812, it was not yet a city at all. In fact, it was pretty much a wilderness area. Several landowners donated the property near the confluence of the Olentangy and Scioto Rivers to the relatively new state, and by 1816 the capital was relocated from Chillicothe, a former Shawnee Indian settlement that lay farther south along the Scioto River. The Scioto Trail, a Native American north-south thoroughfare running between Lake Erie and the Ohio River, ran right through present-day Columbus.

Many public lands that have been preserved in this region center around Native American sites. Flint Ridge is one of the most important sites in Ohio's human his-

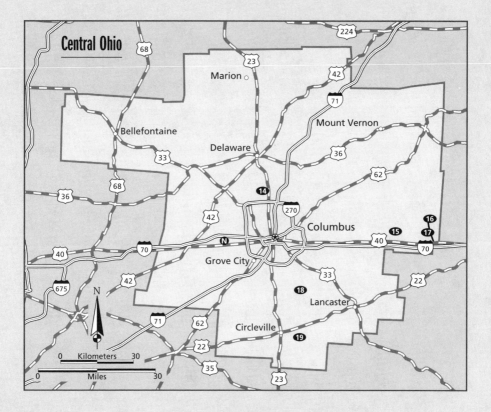

tory. Native Americans and, to a lesser extent, European settlers converged here to quarry flint, a highly prized and useful stone. Blackhand Gorge, located along the Licking River near Flint Ridge, served as a byway along another major Native American thoroughfare, this one east-west. Closer to Columbus, Highbanks Metro Park is home to a Cole Indian earthen embankment and an Adena Indian burial mound. The park overlooks the Olentangy, a state scenic river.

Slate Run and Clear Creek, two other featured Columbus Metro Parks, are just part of the fourteen parks operated by the Metro Parks System, which was established in 1945. Metro Parks operates 20,000 acres in seven central Ohio counties.

Prior to European settlement, the Till Plains region of Ohio was home to a vast beech-maple forest, with occasional prairie openings. The Till Plains are so called due to the thick layer of till, or debris, left by the Wisconsinan Glacier that retreated from Ohio about 12,000 years ago. Not only did the soils of these plains prove to be very fertile, but the flat landscape made the work of clearing and working the land easier than in Ohio's hill country. Today, 95 percent of the land in the Till Plains is cultivated or urbanized, a ratio that makes parkland all the more valuable.

Central Ohio's state parks all surround reservoirs of varying sizes. Hiking trails complement water sports at these parks, and lakeside hikes are a common feature.

14 Overlook and Dripping Rock Trails

Highbanks Metro Park

Highbanks gets its name from the towering shale riverbanks that rise on either side of the Olentangy, a state scenic river. Your best bet to see the unusual bowling ball–like rock "concretions" that jut out of the shale banks is in the park's nature center. Combine the Overlook and Dripping Rock Trails to get a 5.8-mile sampling of everything at this suburban park, including a fairly mature forest, prehistoric Native American earthworks, pioneer artifacts, a constructed wetland, and a river overlook.

Start: From Oak Coves Picnic Area

Distance: 5.8-mile trail network, including spur trails

Approximate hiking time: 2 to 3 hours

Difficulty: Moderate due to length

Trail surface: Dirt and gravel

Blaze: Overlook Trail, blue arrowhead; Dripping Rock Trail, woodpecker silhouette

Seasons: Best April through October

Other trail users: Pedestrian traffic only, but these trails are very popular with joggers, so expect to share the trail with them.

Canine compatibility: Leashed dogs permitted only on separate 3.7-mile Primitive Pet and Ski Trail

Water: Available in the picnic area

Land status: Columbus Metro Park

Nearest city: Columbus

Fees and permits: No fees or permits required

Schedule: Open 6:30 A.M. to 10:00 P.M. in summer, 6:30 A.M. to 8:00 P.M. in winter

Maps: USGS quad: Powell; Maptech Terrain Navigator: Ohio Columbus/Cincinnati/Southwest

Trail contacts: Columbus Metro Parks, Westerville; (614) 508–8000; www.metroparks.net

Finding the trailhead: From I-270 on the north side of Columbus, turn north onto U.S. Highway 23 (exit 23). Drive 3.0 miles to the park entrance on the left. Past the nature center on the right, continue to the second left into the Oak Coves Picnic Area. Park at the first lot, in front of the trailhead kiosk. *DeLorme: Ohio Atlas and Gazetteer:* Page 58, C1.

The Hike

Before you start hiking, stop by the attractive and informative nature center. There you'll find information on the park's natural features, including unusual rock "concretions," bowling ball–looking rocks that formed around organic materials 300 to 350 million years ago during the Devonian period. These concretions now protrude out of the sedimentary shale banks. A large window in front of bird feeders allows you to watch some of the sixty species of forest birds found here, including woodpeckers, jays, and finches. The nature center also features interpretive exhibits about local Native American and early European settler history.

Winter light casts long shadows in the forest at Highbanks Metro Park.

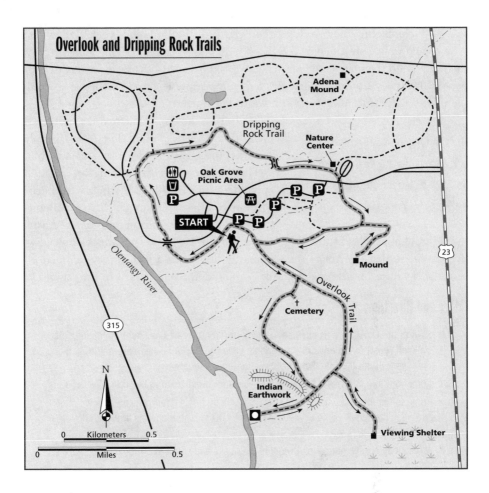

Start the hike with the Overlook Trail. Here you will walk by the Pool family gravestones, which were moved here from their original place. Next to the gravestones, notice the line of stately oaks that once served as a fencerow. Continuing on, you will walk beside a 1,500-foot horseshoe-shaped earthwork. An interpretive sign tells you that this earthwork, likely a fortification of an old village, was constructed by the Cole Indians of the Late Woodland period around A.D. 800 to 1300. This portion of the park is designated a National Natural Landmark.

Continue to an observation deck overlooking the Olentangy River, its high shale banks, sycamore trees, soaring birds, and encroaching development. Contact the park ranger for canoe-access information.

Soon you will come to the Wetland Spur Trail that takes you to a bird blind overlooking a pond. This is an excellent spot to see migrating ducks and geese. These constructed wetlands are important for wildlife, since Ohio has lost over 95 percent of its original wetlands to agriculture and development.

After completing the Overlook Trail, return to the Dripping Rock Trail, where you should notice an abundance of spiny honey locust trees. Walking along streams that drain into the Olentangy, you will get a better view of the shale banks that prevail in the area. At several points, this trail skirts a forest– meadow edge area. Look here for wildlife, including birds and white-tailed deer.

▶ According to a study sponsored by *Men's Fitness* magazine, Columbus is the nation's sixth fattest city. Need any more incentive to hit the trail?

Toward the end of the trail is a spur leading to an Adena mound. The Adena people settled the area around 800 B.C. to A.D. 100. They are best known as prehistoric mound builders. Some of these mounds were burial mounds; others are thought have been constructed for ceremonial purposes. The Adena lived throughout what is now Ohio and in parts of Kentucky and West Virginia. Evidence shows that the Adena were primarily hunters and gatherers who practiced some agriculture. Shortly after the Adena mound, the trail returns to the trailhead.

Miles and Directions

0.0 Start at the Oak Coves Picnic Area. Looking at the trailhead kiosk from the parking area, walk left (east) to the edge of the asphalt. Follow the woodpecker blaze and walk the wide, gravel path that parallels the shale-bottomed streambed.

0.1 Come to a fork. Stay right, following the blue arrowhead blaze to begin the Overlook Trail.

0.4 Come to another fork, where the Overlook Trail loop begins. You can go either way, but staying right you will come to a spur in about 100 feet. To the left is a relocated pioneer cemetery.

0.8 Walk along a long, narrow earthwork to your right and come to a T intersection. Take a right here and cross the earthwork.

1.0 Approach the observation deck overlooking the Olentangy River. Return the way you came to the junction at Mile 1.1.

1.2 Come to the Wetland Spur Trail. Turn right; walk a few hundred feet and look for a sign to the right for the Wetland Trail, Don't continue to the open field.

1.6 The Wetland Trail ends at a bird blind overlooking a pond. Return the way you came to the main trail at Mile 2.0.

2.4 Return to the original junction for the Overlook Trail. Continue straight.

2.7 Hit the Dripping Rock Trail again. Turn left.

2.8 Return to the parking area. To continue on the Dripping Rock Trail, simply keep walking past the parking on your right and back into the woods. **Option:** You can end your hike here or stop for lunch before continuing on the Dripping Rock Trail.

3.4 Approach the junction with the Big Meadows path on the left at Mile 0.7. Continue straight, follow the woodpecker blaze, and cross a bridge.

3.5 Come to a second junction. This time follow the blaze to the right to stay on the Dripping Rock Trail.

4.2 Pass a short side trail on the left to an observation deck overlooking the meadow.

4.6 Come to another fork. To the left is the nature center. Continue along the trail to the right and cross the park road. After crossing the road, you will see a picnic area to the right before you reenter the woods.

4.8 Cross a wooden bridge and come to a spur trail to the left that takes you to an Adena burial mound.

5.2 Return to the main trail and take a left.

5.4 Pass a spur on the right that takes you to a parking lot.

5.6 Come to a T intersection. Take a right.

5.8 Return to the trailhead.

Hike Information

Local information

City of Columbus: ci.columbus.oh.us.
Greater Columbus Convention and Visitors Bureau; (800) 354-COLS (2657); www.surpriseitscolumbus.com/visit.htm.
Ohio Historical Society; (614) 297-2300; www.ohiohistory.org/places/ohc/.

Local events and attractions

Olentangy Indian Caverns are just north of the park; (740) 548-7917; www.olentangyindian caverns.com/.

Accommodations

Alum Creek State Park campground, Delaware; (614) 548-4631; www.ohiodnr.com/parks/ parks/alum.htm.
Hosteling International Columbus; (614) 294-7157; hicolumbus@hotmail.com.

Organizations

Columbus Outdoor Pursuits; (614) 447-1006; www.outdoor-pursuits.org

15 Oak Trail with Japanese Garden Spur

The Dawes Arboretum

On this 2.9-mile ramble through a human-manipulated landscape, the trees and shrubs along the path are identified for you. Highlights include a Japanese garden, prairie wildflowers, collections of exotic and unusual trees, magnificent older trees, views of the surrounding landscape, and a small cypress swamp. If you're looking for a more traditional trail through a forest (or more seclusion), check out the 5.0-mile Arboretum East Trail, which features a mature beech-maple forest, an Adena Indian mound, and an overlook of a glacial terminal moraine.

Start: At the visitor center

Distance: 2.9-mile loop with spur loop

Difficulty: Moderate due to length and sun exposure

Approximate hiking time: 2 to 3 hours

Seasons: Best mid-April through mid-October

Trail surface: Wide and clearly marked grass, mulch, dirt, cement, and gravel path

Other trail users: Hikers only

Canine compatibility: Leashed dogs are permitted, but owners are expected to clean up after their dogs and to prevent dogs from urinating on the plants.

Water: Available at visitor center

Land status: Privately owned nonprofit arboretum

Nearest town: Newark

Fees and permits: No fees or permits are required, but the arboretum does accept donations.

Schedule: Open dawn to dusk daily except Thanksgiving, Christmas, New Year's Day, and during threatening weather

Maps: USGS quad: Thornville; Maptech Terrain Navigator: Ohio Columbus/Cincinnati/Southwest

Trail contacts: The Dawes Arboretum, Newark; (800) 44-DAWES; www.dawesarb.org

Finding the trailhead: From I-70 about 30 miles east of Columbus, turn north on State Route 13 (exit 132) and travel 2.6 miles to the Dawes Arboretum entrance on the left. Drive past the gate and continue straight past the visitor center to the parking lot. *DeLorme: Ohio Atlas and Gazetteer:* Page 69 A6.

The Hike

The trees and shrubs along the Oak Trail, compatible with central Ohio's climate zone, are identified for you. These identifications will help you better appreciate the forests you hike in afterward. This is an unusual Ohio hike in that it's not through a forest; rather it meanders through a human-manipulated landscape of many interesting plants and features.

The arboretum, a private not-for-profit enterprise, was established by Beman and Bertie Dawes in 1929. Beman Dawes was a successful businessman and an Ohio rep-

The Cypress Swamp at the Dawes Arboretum.

resentative. His brother, Charles, Vice President of the United States under Calvin Coolidge and recipient of the Nobel Peace Prize, also contributed to an endowment that set up a fund to operate the arboretum.

Wear a sun hat and head out on the Oak Trail. Begin by walking past mostly native trees that are identified along the path, such as serviceberry, shagbark hickory, hemlock, different maple species, and black walnut. Walk through some small patches of forest, both deciduous and evergreen. In about a half mile, take the Japanese Garden Trail on a cemented-grit loop path. Designed by Makoto Nakamura of Kyoto

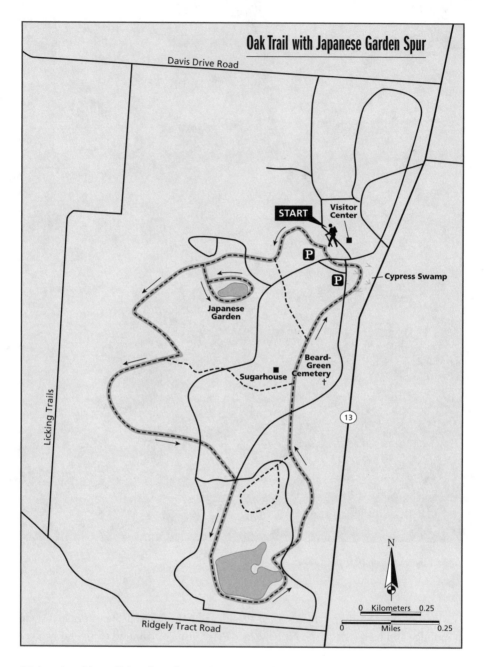

Oak Trail with Japanese Garden Spur

University, this traditional garden aspires to simplicity and harmony. Features include a "hide and reveal" element of landscape, a hill and pond, and a raked dry-landscape feature. Perhaps all the mowed grass is where the Japanese meets the American aesthetic. You can take a rest at a meditation house near the pond. No picnicking is allowed here.

After returning to the Oak Trail, continue on and skirt a meadow of native flowers, including wild sunflower, black-eyed Susan, and echinacea. Then walk through some woods again and out to Holly Hill, with an impressive collection of holly trees. Past Holly Hill are some of the most impressive trees in the arboretum, including a magnificent black maple. From this spot you get an expansive view of the landscape's rolling hills. Soon you will walk through a tunnel of trees and then circle around Dawes Lake, next to the 2,000-plus feet of hedge lettering. Much of the return trip is through a native forest. In late winter and early spring, enjoy the maple sugaring and the forest floor covered in ramps (wild leeks). The last segment of the trail winds through the striking bald cypress swamp. Walk over the boardwalk and enjoy not only the beautiful deciduous trees with needlelike leaves but also the abundant wildlife that lives in the small swamp, including frogs, salamanders, and dragonflies.

The 5.0-mile Arboretum East Trail starts at the Cypress Swamp and continues through a maintained prairie ecosystem and then into a mature beech-maple forest. An Adena mound is located within the forest. The trail also skirts the edge of a glacial terminal moraine before returning along the edge of the forest and open meadow/farmland. If you plan to do the Arboretum East Trail, first stop by the visitor center to get directions and a free permit.

Miles and Directions

0.0 Start at the visitor center. Walk out of the visitor center and take a right. Walk to the gazebo-like "outpost" where most hikes in the arboretum originate. From the outpost walk west, following the sign for the hiking trails and Japanese Garden. You will immediately begin to see the conspicuous brown posts blazed with a white oak leaf.

0.1 The trail forks. Take the right fork, following the blaze.

0.2 Cross the auto tour road and enter a pine forest.

0.3 Come to a four-way intersection with the Japanese Garden Trail. Take a left and walk a short loop trail through the Japanese Garden.

0.6 Return to the Oak Trail and take a left.

1.0 Come to a T intersection at a gazebo. Take a right, following the blaze for the Oak Trail.

1.4 Cross the auto tour road.

1.6 Cross straight over a traffic circle and walk due south through a "tunnel" of various trees. Then circle around the south side of Dawes Lake. (The benches around the lake might make a good lunch spot.)

2.0 Pass a junction on the right for the tower overlook.

2.1 Come to a T intersection next to the road. Take a right and cross the road.

2.5 Cross the auto tour road again.

2.6 Pass a side trail on the left and then a second side trail to the right for the cemetery. Continue straight.

2.7 Pass a side trail on the left that leads to an old log cabin/sugaring shack, and then pass another side trail coming in from the left. Emerge from the woods into a picnic area. Before the picnic shelter, turn right.

2.8 Cross the auto tour road again and enter the cypress swamp and a boardwalk trail. At the end of the boardwalk, turn right. Follow a mowed path that parallels the road.

3.0 Cross the road and head toward the visitor center.

3.1 Return to the visitor center.

Hike Information

Local information

Licking County Convention and Visitors Bureau; (800) 589-8224; www.lccvb.com.

Local events and attractions

The Dawes Arboretum celebrates **Arbor Day** the third Saturday in April.

Flint Ridge State Memorial, Glenford; (800) 283-8707; www.ohiohistory.org/places/flint/.

Longaberger Basket Company, Dresden; (740) 322-5900; www.longaberger.com.

Accommodations

Dillon State Park campground, Nashport; (740) 453-0442.

Pitzer-Cooper House (bed-and-breakfast), Newark; (740) 323-2680.

Restaurants

Cherry Valley Lodge, Newark; (740) 964-0056.

16 Blackhand to Quarry Rim Trail Loop

Blackhand Gorge State Nature Preserve

At this spot the Licking River cuts a striking gorge through this sandstone, creating a scenic byway that's been used by humans for countless generations. Begin on the multiuse Blackhand Trail and then take the Quarry Rim Trail out of the river valley and around an old quarry. Return by walking through the Deep Cut and by the river's edge.

Start: From the parking lot on Toboso Road (County Road 278)

Distance: 2.4-mile loop

Approximate hiking time: 1 hour

Difficulty: Easy; short and well worn, with stairs to help you up and down steep parts

Trail surface: Begin and end on an asphalt path; side dirt trails with a few difficult footings

Seasons: Best March through October and in winter after a snowfall

Other trail users: Bicyclists

Canine compatibility: Leashed dogs permitted on the Blackhand Trail only

Water: No potable water is available here; bring your own.

Land status: State nature preserve

Nearest towns: Zanesville, Newark

Fees and permits: No fees or permits are required

Schedule: Open daily a half hour before sunrise to a half hour after sunset

Maps: USGS quad: Thornville; Maptech Terrain Navigator: Ohio Columbus/Cincinnati/Southwest

Trail contacts: Blackhand Gorge State Nature Preserve, Newark; (740) 763-4411; www.ohiodnr.com/dnap/location/blackhand_gorge.html

Finding the trailhead: From I-70 in Zanesville, take State Route 146 west 17 miles to County Road 273, marked with a green sign for Toboso and Blackhand Gorge State Nature Preserve. Turn left (south) and travel 1.8 miles to the parking lot on the right. *DeLorme: Ohio Atlas and Gazetteer:* Page 60 D1.

The Hike

Blackhand sandstone gets its name from an image of a large hand carved into the sandstone walls of Blackhand Gorge. It's believed that this hand was engraved by Native Americans as a directional sign to the flint deposits at nearby Flint Ridge. The region beyond the black hand and around Flint Ridge is said to have been neutral territory for all tribes coming to access the valuable flint deposits. Today you won't see the black hand; it was destroyed when the Ohio and Erie Canal was constructed through the gorge. But you will see fantastic outcroppings of the namesake sandstone towering above the scenic Licking River.

This spot where the river cuts an east-west gorge has been used as a transportation route by humans for countless generations. Evidence of prehistoric Native American use includes petroglyphs and mounds. As is often the case with obvious

Yellow birch spreads its roots over sandstone outcroppings at Blackhand Gorge State Nature Preserve.

transportation routes, European explorers continued to use this passageway. In the 1820s the Ohio and Erie Canal was constructed through the gorge. You can hop on the Canal Lock Trail on the river's north side to get a look at the long-dry sandstone locks. As railroads replaced the less efficient canal system, the Central Ohio Railroad was built through the gorge and carried steam-powered engines. A newer elevated rail line now crosses over the gorge. Also early in the twentieth century, an electric railroad (trolley) was built through the gorge, this time by blasting a tunnel for its right of way. (The tunnel is now on private property.) Today, most travelers through Blackhand Gorge are here for recreation rather than to get from one place to another. Running along the river is the Blackhand Trail, a 4.3-mile multi-use path. Two hiking trails are accessible from the Blackhand Trail, and two others are nearby.

A 2.4-mile loop beginning from the main parking lot on the east end of the preserve allows you to take in the main attractions of the preserve. Begin on the asphalt Blackhand Trail. Shortly you'll come to an overlook spur that lets you view the buttonbush swamp, named for the plant's round flowers. Return to the main trail and then hop on the Quarry Rim Trail, a 1.0-mile side path that, as the name implies,

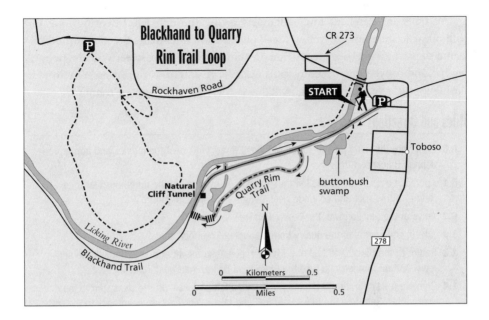

takes you around the lip of an old sandstone quarry that was in operation from the 1870s to the 1920s. From this trail you get good views of tall sandstone walls jutting out of the old quarry, now filled with water. The Quarry Rim Trail ends farther down the Blackhand Trail. From here, take a right and return by immediately walking through the "Deep Cut," blasted out by the Central Ohio Railroad in the winter of 1850–51. Reportedly the project consumed more than 1,200 kegs of gunpowder. The Deep Cut measures approximately 330 feet long, 65 feet deep, and 30 feet wide.

On your return trip be sure to take the Blackhand Stone Spur Trail to the river's edge, where you'll be across from sandstone outcroppings towering 100 feet over the meandering Licking River. Across the way are the sandstone block walls that were part of the Ohio and Erie Canal towpath. At the time, dams were also constructed at both ends of the gorge, creating a lake where the river now runs. Atop the rocks hemlocks grow, and out of the soil grow cottonwoods and sycamores. As you return to the trailhead, see the roots of yellow birch trees that extend like tendrils over the large sandstone rocks.

This short loop is just the beginning of all the hiking you can do at Blackhand Gorge. Continuing westward along the Blackhand Trail, hop on the 2.3-mile Chestnut Trail, another spur on the south side of the river. From there you can continue to the end of the multiuse path and return for a 10.0-mile round trip walk. For a footpath that gets away from the crowds, hop on the Marie Hickey and Oak Knob Trail loop, above the gorge on its north side. This is a spectacular trail in springtime when the dogwoods are flowering—while they last, that is, since they are succumbing to a fungal blight.

All trails are excellent for wildflowers spring through fall. In spring look for trillium, wild geranium, solomon's seal, phlox, and Dutchman's breeches on north-facing slopes near the Blackhand Trail. In summer wingstem, sweet William, bouncing bet, and oxeye grow in sunny spots near the river. This is a great preserve to visit throughout the year for walking, wildflower viewing, canoeing, or fishing.

Miles and Directions

0.0 Start from the main parking lot off of Toboso Road. Walk past the latrines and hop on the asphalt Blackhand Trail.

0.1 Approach a spur trail on the left that leads to an overlook of the buttonbush swamp. Return to this spot and continue west along the Blackhand Trail.

0.2 Arrive at the junction with the Quarry Rim Trail. Take a left.

1.0 Take in good views of the quarry from a couple of overlook spots.

1.3 Return to the Blackhand Trail at a T intersection. Take a right and walk through the narrows. **Option:** Turn left and take the Blackhand Trail to the Chestnut Trail.

1.4 Come to a sign for the Blackhand Rock. Take a left and walk on the short spur to the river's edge. Return to the Blackhand Trail and take a left (east) to head back to the trailhead.

2.4 Return to the parking lot.

Hike Information

Local information
Licking County Convention and Visitors Bureau; (800) 589-8224; www.lccvb.com.

Local events and attractions
Flint Ridge State Memorial, Glenford; (800) 283-8707; www.ohiohistory.org/places/flint/.
Dawes Arboretum, Newark; (800) 44-DAWES; www.dawesarb.org.
Longaberger Basket Company, Dresden; (740) 322-5900; www.longaberger.com.

Accommodations
Dillon State Park campground, Nashport; (740) 453-4377; www.ohiodnr.com/parks/parks/dillon.htm.

Restaurants
Cottage Restaurant, Hanover; (740) 763-3636.

17 Flint Ridge to Creek Trail Loop

Flint Ridge State Memorial

Flint Ridge is the eponymous site where prehistoric and historic Native Americans came to quarry the Midwest's highest quality flint. On this 2.0-mile hike, it won't take long to notice the flint itself—a sometimes translucent, sometimes multicolored, hard, jagged rock. This is in sharp contrast to the soft sandstone that is found throughout most of central and southeastern Ohio. The protected site is home to a mature forest with excellent spring wildflowers and impressive fall foliage.

Start: From museum trailhead
Distance: 2.0-mile loop, including a spur
Approximate hiking time: 1 hour
Difficulty: Easy; short and flat
Trail surface: Winding dirt path
Seasons: Best April through October
Other trail users: Hikers only
Canine compatibility: Leashed dogs permitted
Water: Available at the museum
Land status: State memorial
Nearest town: Zanesville
Fees and permits: No fees or permits are required for hiking. The museum entrance fees are $3.00 for adults (free for Ohio Historical Society members) and $2.00 for students.
Schedule: Trails are open daily 9:30 A.M. to dusk year-round. The museum is open Wednesday through Sunday, Memorial Day weekend through Labor Day and on weekends only through October. The museum is closed the rest of the year.
Maps: USGS quad: Glenford; Maptech Terrain Navigator: Ohio Columbus/Cincinnati/Southwest
Trail contacts: Flint Ridge State Memorial, Glenford; (800) 283-8707; www.ohiohistory.org/places/flint/

Finding the trailhead: From I-70, west of Zanesville, eastbound, turn north on State Route 668 (exit 141) and travel 3.7 miles to Flint Ridge Road. Turn right into the state memorial grounds.

Westbound, take exit 142 and follow the signs for Flint Ridge. Turn right (north) onto Rankin Road to U.S. Highway 40, where you will turn left (west) to State Route 668. Turn right (north) and travel 3 miles to Flint Ridge Road. Turn right into the state memorial grounds. ***DeLorme: Ohio Atlas and Gazetteer:*** Page 69 A7.

The Hike

Flint Ridge was a neutral zone where all Native American tribes could come and peacefully access this important natural resource. The flint, workable but very durable, was primarily used to fashion arrowheads and implements for hunting, cutting, and fire-making. Archaeologists have found flint artifacts from this ridge as far away as Vermont and the Chesapeake Bay.

Geologists believe that Flint Ridge (or Vanport) flint was formed during the Pennsylvanian period, about 290 to 320 million years ago. At that time, a sea

Flint pits serve as vernal pools at Flint Ridge State Memorial.

covered what is now Ohio, and sediment piled up on the sea floor, including colonies of sponges. These sponges contained support structures made of silica, which crystallized into a hard stratum of flint. The flint was heaved up into a ridge about 200 million years ago, and then the long process of weathering began. The flint eventually became exposed and was discovered by prehistoric humans. It was mined by generations of Native Americans and then by European settlers, who prized it for making high-quality millstones.

▶ **Flint is the official gemstone of Ohio.**

Beginning from the visitor center, it won't take long to notice the flint itself. Flintstones as large as several feet across are scattered near the museum and all around the site, most of which have probably been moved several times from their original location. The trail then takes you around several flint pits, which also serve as vernal pools.

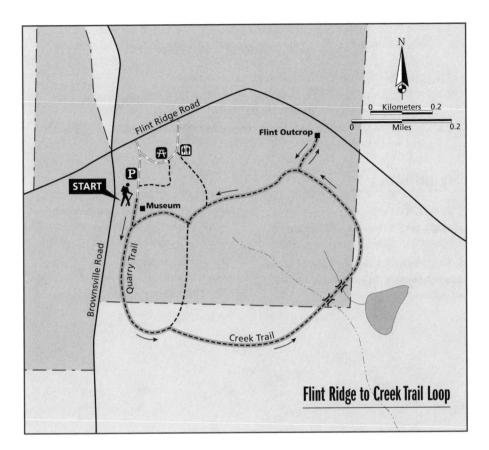

Flint Ridge to Creek Trail Loop

Although the flint deposits are the main attraction at Flint Ridge, the forest here is mature, with the usual beech and maple in the bottomlands and oaks and hickories upslope. In springtime look for wildflowers on the forest floor, including trillium, phlox, bloodroot, and mayapple. In fall the forest is ablaze with color.

A spur trail takes you up a short but steep slope. At the top you will walk on what could be described as flint gravel. After checking this out, return to the main trail and walk around the flint pits again and back to the museum.

Miles and Directions

0.0 Start at the trailhead in front of the museum. Walk to the end of the asphalt and onto the dirt trail. In about 100 feet come to a fork. Take a right, following the sign that reads MAIN PATH DEEP FLINT PIT, and walk counterclockwise around a flint pit. (**Note:** To the right are informal trails that peter out. Be sure to walk around the pit to stay on the trail.)

0.2 Come to the junction with the wagon shortcut trail. Continue straight.

0.3 Come to the junction with the Creek Trail. Take a right.

1.3 Arrive at the spur trail to the flint outcrop. Take a right and ascend the slope. This trail ends at an open field. Return the way you came to this junction at Mile 1.7, and take a right.

1.8 Pass a spur trail from the right that leads to the picnic area.

1.9 Return to the junction for the Creek Trail loop. In about 50 feet, reach the Wagon Trail shortcut. Take a right onto the shortcut trail.

2.0 Return to the first junction near the trailhead in front of the museum. Take a right and walk back to the museum.

Hike Information

Local information

Licking County Convention and Visitors Bureau; (800) 589-8224; www.lccvb.com.

Local events and attractions

Dawes Arboretum, Newark; (800) 44-DAWES; www.dawesarb.org.

Blackhand Gorge State Nature Preserve, Newark; (740) 763-4411; www.ohiodnr. com/dnap/location/blackhand_ gorge.html.

Accommodations

National Schoolhouse Inn, Brownsville; (740) 787-1808; www.brownsvilleschool.com.

18 Five Oaks to Kokomo Wetland Trail

Slate Run Metro Park

Slate Run Metro Park is an outstanding example of environmental restoration. Just ten years ago, most of this park was a cornfield. Today, it combines 6.6 miles worth of park trails through an oak forest surrounding the shale-bottomed (and misnamed) Slate Run and a restored prairie that's home to ground-nesting bobolinks and to a glacial outwash bank that provides an excellent view of the park's restored wetlands. This is a good bird-watching spot as well. While here, visit Slate Run living historical farm.

Start: From the Shady Grove picnic area
Distance: 6.6-mile trail system
Approximate hiking time: 2.5 to 3.5 hours
Difficulty: Moderate due to length and grassy/muddy trail conditions
Trail surface: Dirt, gravel, grass, wetlands, and boardwalks
Blaze: None, but trails are well worn. Look for blazes at junctions.
Seasons: Best April through October
Other trail users: Hikers only
Canine compatibility: Leashed dogs allowed only on pet trails in the park (Covered Bridge

and Shagbark Trails, 0.5 mile each)
Water: Available at picnic area
Land status: Columbus Metro Park
Nearest towns: Lithopolis, Canal Winchester
Fees and permits: No fees or permits required
Schedule: Open daylight hours year-round
Maps: USGS quad: Canal Winchester; Maptech Terrain Navigator: Ohio Columbus/Cincinnati/Southwest
Trail contacts: Metroparks, Westerville; (614) 508-8000; www.metroparks.net

Finding the trailhead: From U.S. Highway 33 about 7 miles southeast of I-70, turn south onto State Route 674 and follow signs 7.0 miles to the park's main entrance. Turn right (west) into the park and travel past the ranger station on the right, taking the first left toward Shady Grove picnic area. Park at the picnic area and pick up the trailhead at the far west end of the area, next to the rest rooms. *DeLorme: Ohio Atlas and Gazetteer:* Page 68 B3.

The Hike

Based on soil and groundwater conditions, park naturalists believe that the land now comprising Slate Run Metro Park was originally a meadowy wetland. In 1995 and 1996 the park reverted a portion of its lands to grasslands. Species you'll see growing here include Kentucky bluegrass, short fescue, ashy sunflower, purple bergamot, and butterfly milkweed. In 1999, with the help of the Wetlands Foundation, the park constructed a 135-acre wetland. Since then, more than thirty new species of birds have been observed as well as six new species of toads and frogs.

Just a few years ago, this was a cornfield. Today it's a restored wetland at Slate Run Metro Park.

Begin hiking on the Five Oaks Trail, a wide, flat gravel path winding through young woods and paralleling Slate Run on the right. This shale-bottomed stream was misnamed by European settlers, who mistook the shale for similar-looking slate. The bedrock of the park is Ohio black shale, laid down about 300 to 350 million years ago during the Devonian period. You'll find yourself walking in a predominantly oak-hickory forest, but also look for beech, maple, pawpaw, buckeye, cherry, and hackberry. Keep an eye out for woodpeckers and hawks.

Begin the Bobolink Grasslands Trail by entering into the grassland and following a mowed path. Look for here bobolinks in spring through fall. This is one of the few areas in central Ohio where you can reliably see this ground-nesting bird species. Also look around for glacial erratics, pieces of granite left by retreating glaciers. This trail begins by paralleling an old fenceline marking the boundary for Slate Run Farm. This is a "living historical farm," operating as it did in the 1880s. Volunteers work the farm using period tools and equipment. Plan time to visit Slate Run Farm during your visit. As you walk in the grassland, keep an eye out for a resident herd of white-tailed deer.

Take the spur to the overlook for the Kokomo Wetland Trail. You'll be rewarded with an expansive view of the restored wetland and beyond. You'll also have the chance to get up close and personal with a hundred-year-old osage orange tree. The spot you're standing on is a glacial outwash bank, made up of sediment deposited by a melting glacier.

Continuing on to the Kokomo Wetland Trail, walk along the boardwalks and through the wetlands. You might glimpse nesting and migrating birds, including pipe-billed grebes, American bitterns, and blue-winged teals. This trail can be very muddy, so wear appropriate footwear. Return on the Bobolink Trail to the Sugar Maple Trail and the wooded section of the park. Complete the loop made by the Sugar Maple and Five Oaks Trails. Toward the end of the hike, you'll see some of the most mature trees in Slate Run, including several species of the trail's namesake oaks. Park gates are locked at dusk, so plan to return to your car by then.

▶ **Five Oaks Trail is an understatement. The nine oak species found in Slate Run Metro Park include white, swamp white, red, black, chinquapin, burr, shingle, chestnut, and pin.**

Miles and Directions

0.0 Start at Shady Grove picnic area.

0.1 Come to the first junction that begins the Five Oaks Trail loop. You can travel it in either direction, but staying right, pass the observation deck and descend to two bridges that cross the stream.

0.7 Come to the junction with the Sugar Maple Trail. Continue straight. **Option:** You can return directly on the Five Oaks Trail for a 1.5-mile hike by turning left.

1.0 Pass a spur trail to the right that takes you to another parking area and the trails around Buzzard's Roost Lake. The trail here turns south and crosses Slate Run again.

1.2 Arrive at the junction with the Bobolink Grassland Trail. Take a right. **Option:** You can continue straight and return directly for a 2.5-mile loop, but at least a short foray onto the Bobolink Trail is recommended.

2.1 Reach the junction with a spur trail to an overlook deck. Continue straight to the overlook. Return to this junction at Mile 2.5 and take a left.

2.9 Come to the junction with the Kokomo Wetland Trail. Take a left.

3.1 Cross a lengthy boardwalk.

3.9 Pass a spur trail coming in from the left.

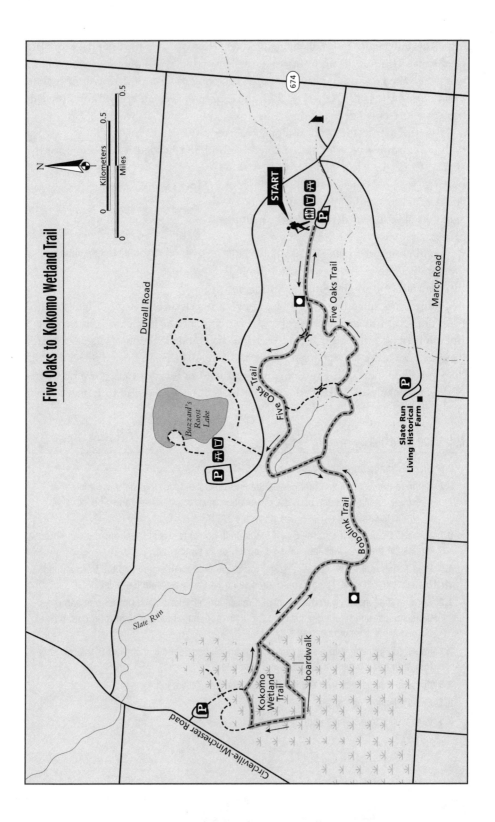

Five Oaks to Kokomo Wetland Trail

N

0   0.5   Kilometers   0.5
0   Miles

674

START

Duvall Road

Buzzard's Roost Lake

Five Oaks Trail

Five Oaks Trail

Bobolink Trail

Slate Run Living Historical Farm

Marcy Road

Slate Run

Kokomo Wetland Trail

boardwalk

Circleville-Winchester Road

4.0 Pass another spur trail on the left.

4.2 Come back to the Bobolink Grassland Trail. Turn left, returning the way you came.

5.5 Return to the junction with the Sugar Maple Trail. Turn right.

5.9 Return to the junction with the Five Oaks Trail. Take another right.

6.4 Return to the first junction, by the viewing platform. Take a right.

6.6 Finish at the parking lot and trailhead.

Hike Information

Local information

City of Columbus; www.ci.columbus.oh.us.
Greater Columbus Convention and Visitors Bureau; 800–354–COLS (2657); www.surprise itscolumbus.com/visit.htm.
Ohio Historical Society; (614) 297–2300; www.ohiohistory.org/places/ohc/.

Local events and attractions

Slate Run Living Historical Farm is part of the metro park. Nearby Canal Winchester boasts the largest Labor Day parade in the state of Ohio.

Accommodations

Central House Bed & Breakfast, Canal Winchester; (614) 837–0932.
A. W. Marion State Park campground, Mt. Sterling; (740) 869–3124.
Hosteling International Columbus; (614) 294–7157; hicolumbus@hotmail.com.

Organizations

Columbus Outdoor Pursuits; (614) 447–1006; www.outdoor-pursuits.org; e-mail: hiking@ outdoor-pursuits.org.

19 Hargus Lake Trail

A. W. Marion State Park

Take on this easy 4.4-mile lakeside loop around the 145-acre Hargus Lake, complete with views of a couple of small islands. On the west side of the dammed-up reservoir, hike in the sun and watch boaters, anglers, and Canada geese. On the east side hike along a small but noticeable ridge in the shade of a deciduous forest as you look out for turtles and white-tailed deer.

Start: From the picnic area south of the marina

Distance: 4.4-mile loop

Approximate hiking time: $1^1/_2$ to $2^1/_2$ hours

Difficulty: Easy; flat and fairly short

Trail surface: Mostly flat dirt trail; sometimes muddy

Blaze: Blue

Seasons: Best April through October

Other trail users: Hunters (in season); you might find yourself in the midst of a high school cross-country meet during fall.

Canine compatibility: Leashed dogs permitted

Water: Available near the pit toilets at the trailhead and in the campground

Land status: State park

Nearest town: Circleville

Fees and permits: No fees or permits required

Schedule: The park is open daily until 11:00 P.M.

Maps: USGS quad: Ashville; Maptech Terrain Navigator: Ohio Columbus/Cincinnati/Southwest

Trail contacts: A. W. Marion State Park, c/o Deer Creek State Park, Mount Sterling; (740) 869-3124; www.ohiodnr.com/parks/parks/awmarion

Finding the Trailhead: From U.S. Highway 23 in Chillicothe, turn east onto U.S. Highway 22 and drive 3.2 miles to Bolender-Pontius Road, marked with a brown STATE PARK sign. Turn left (north) and drive 1.5 miles to Warner-Huffer Road. Take a right (east) and drive 0.4 mile to a T intersection. Take a right, still on Warner-Huffer Road, and drive 0.2 mile to the park entrance, marked with a sign. Turn left into the parking lot. *DeLorme: Ohio Atlas and Gazetteer:* Page 68 D2.

The Hike

The Till Plains ecoregion, in which A. W. Marion State Park lies, is named after the thick layer of debris (till) left behind by retreating glaciers. The flat, well-drained soil of this region is perfect for agriculture. Indeed, 84 percent of the native forests and wetlands in this ecoregion were converted to farmland. A. W. Marion State Park is an oasis of water and trees in this broad, flat landscape.

A small but noticeable ridge that used to be called the Devil's Backbone rises along the east side of the lake. Hargus Lake was created when an earthen dam was built on Hargus Creek, beginning in 1948. This 145-acre body of water is a popular spot for fishing, evidenced by the many fishing access trails. When hiking, keep

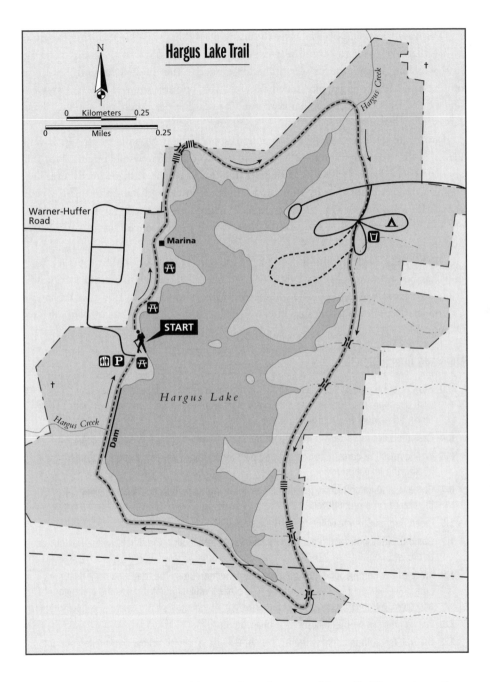

Hargus Lake Trail

parallel to the water's edge and bypass these frequent side trails. The main trail on the west side of the lake affords views of the water, anglers, and two little islands in the middle of the lake. On the east side of the lake, walk along the ridge and in a forest of oak, hickory, maple, and beech trees.

This easy lakeside loop trail is partly sunny, partly shady. Tackle it during the time of day that suits your sun- and heat-exposure preferences. Watch the many resident turtles basking in the sun for warmth or digging into the mud to cool off. Look for other critters, including white-tailed deer, red fox, and fox squirrel. The grassy west side of the lake is a popular hangout for Canada geese—watch out for the "land mines" they leave!

European settlers weren't the first to discover the rich soils of the Pickaway Plains. Prehistoric Adena Indians settled the land. Nearby Circleville is named for the circular Adena earthworks found there. Later the Shawnee Indians lived here. The area was much sought after by European settlers, who cleared and cultivated the rich soils. A Revolutionary War cemetery here is maintained by the local historical society. Until the early twentieth century, there was a picket-fence factory on what is now park land.

Most of the land surrounding the park today is in cultivation, but the park land itself has been protected since 1950, so some mature forest exists within its boundaries. The park was named after A. W. Marion in 1962 to honor this Pickaway County native, who was the first director of the Ohio Department of Natural Resources.

Miles and Directions

0.0 Start at the trailhead sign, between the picnic shelter and the lake. Walk north, in a clockwise direction. The "trail" here is the patch of grass between development and water. Look for an occasional blue blaze on a tree.

0.4 Pass the boat rental, again walking on the grass between the water and the asphalt.

0.5 Walk across the cement boat ramp and pick up another trailhead. Continue straight, paralleling the lakeshore.

0.7 Come to a junction just as private homes come into view. Turn right here, looking for a blue blaze on a redbud tree.

1.5 Cross Hargus Stream, which feeds Hargus Lake.

1.7 Come to what looks like a junction by another stream. Follow the blazes as the trail curves to the left.

1.9 Arrive at the campground, just past the amphitheater. Cross the road and walk past the park office, keeping an eye out for the blue blazes. Walk straight through the campground and pick up the trail again behind Site 24.

2.1 Pass a junction on the right for the Squawroot Trail.

2.2 The trail forks. To the right is the Squawroot Trail again, blazed yellow. Take the left and follow the blue blazes about 200 feet to the first of two stream crossings.

2.8 The trail forks again. To the right is a trail that leads to the lake. Take a left and descend a few wooden stairs.

4.1 Come to a T intersection. Take a right and cross over the dam.

4.4 Return to the parking lot where you began.

Two small islands stand in the middle of Hargus Lake at A.W. Marion State Park.

Hike Information

Local information

Pickaway County Visitors Bureau, Circleville; (888) 770–7425; www.circleville.com/visitors.html.

Local events and attractions

Check out the annual **Circleville Pumpkin Show,** held the third week in October; www.pumpkinshow.com.

Stages Pond Nature Preserve, Ashville; (740) 420–3374; www.ohiodnr.com/dnap/location/stages.html.

Accommodations

A. W. Marion State Park campground; (740) 869–3124.

Restaurants

Get pumpkin doughnuts at **Lindsey's Bakery,** Circleville; (740) 474–3871.

Goodwin's Family Restaurant, Circleville; (740) 474–1238.

Hike tours

Ranger-led hikes take place every Saturday, Memorial Day through Labor Day.

Organizations

Pickaway County Historical Society; www.rootsweb.com/~ohpickaw/gen.html.

Central Ohio Honorable Mention

N Batelle-Darby Creek Metropark

The Nature Conservancy has labeled this one of the "last great places" in the Western Hemisphere. The central feature of this metropark is, of course, Big Darby Creek. This State and National Scenic River is known for its intact, clean ecosystem that harbors healthy aquatic life, including several species of threatened or endangered mussels. In fact, 100 of the 166 fish species found in Ohio live in the Big Darby. But just becasue this metropark is known for its well-protected watershed doesn't mean it's a slouch when it comes to hiking. Begin hiking from the ranger station, and walk to the confluence of Little and Big Darby Creeks. You can hike the entire 6.0-mile trail system, which leaves the water's edge and takes you to a remnant of the Darby Plains tallgrass prairie near the Indian Ridge Picnic Area before returning to the ranger station.

Trail contacts: Columbus Metro Parks, 1069 West Main Street, Westerville 43081; (614) 508–8000; metroparks.co.franklin.oh.us/batelle.htm.

Finding the trailhead: From I–270 on the west side of Columbus, take U.S. Highway 40 West (West Broad Street) and travel 5.2 miles to Darby Creek Drive. Turn south (left) and travel 3.1 miles to the park entrance. Turn right (west) onto the park road. Pull into the huge parking lot on the right. The ranger station is located in the middle of the parking lot. There are trailheads on either side of the ranger station. *DeLorme: Ohio Atlas and Gazetteer:* Page 67 A7.

Southwest Ohio

Southwest Ohio is an area defined by both physical and political features, and a label can only just begin to provide a description. Native Americans inhabited southwest Ohio long before Europeans came to North America and started drawing straight lines and right angles. North of the Ohio River and west of the Scioto River, prehistoric Native Americans lived and built earthen embankments that today serve as mysterious reminders of their presence on this land long ago. Most famous of these is Serpent Mound, a quarter-mile-long earthwork in the image of a snake opening its mouth around an egg-shaped object. Fort Ancient and Fort Hill are two other well-known sites where hiking trails take today's visitors around and through the earthen embankments. The Hopewell Indians are credited with most of the mound building, but other prehistoric peoples, such as the Adena, Cole, and Fort Ancient Indians also inhabited and built up their cultures in southwest Ohio.

When Europeans arrived here, the Shawnee Indians claimed the southern portion of the state as their hunting grounds and, to a lesser extent, their permanent home. Lower Town, near the confluence of the Scioto and Ohio Rivers (today Portsmouth, Ohio), was the home of a Shawnee settlement. Now just west of Portsmouth lies Shawnee State Park and Forest. By far the state's largest state forest, Shawnee is home to Ohio's only wilderness area, and the park and forest combined host 60 miles of hiking trails. Southwest Ohio was also home to the Miami Indians at the time of European settlement.

Downstream on the Ohio River, Cincinnati grew to become the state's most important river city. In the midst of rapid industrialization, the Cincinnati Park Board in 1911 had the foresight to embark on the country's first urban reforestation project. Today Mount Airy Forest lies at the heart of Cincinnati's popular metropolitan park system. Cincinnati's Eden Park hosts the southern terminus of the statewide Buckeye Trail.

While Native American paths were becoming roads wide enough to haul Conestoga wagons, a young nation embarked on canal- and road-building projects. The National Road, designed to link state capitals, continued west past Columbus and bypassed Dayton by just a few miles to the north. Dayton's leaders and citizens

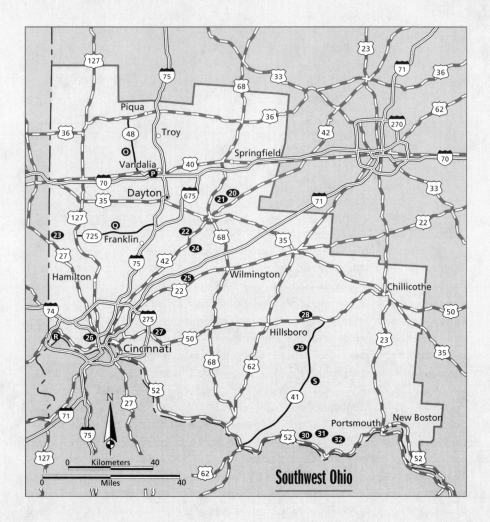

Southwest Ohio

pulled together to make possible the construction of the Dayton Cutoff, an alternate spur that became the preferred route for travelers and settlers moving west. The city of Dayton grew, and when the largest recorded flood hit the Great Miami River in 1913, hundreds were killed and thousands were displaced from their homes. In the process of building flood-control dams, the city of Dayton set aside the river and creek valleys for metropolitan parks. Today's Five Rivers MetroParks provide ample quality hiking opportunities.

More or less paralleling the Great Miami River to the east, the Little Miami River became the first State and National Scenic River in Ohio, designated in 1969. Running alongside the river from Springfield to Milford is the Little Miami Scenic Trail, a 70-mile shared-use asphalt path. The Little Miami River Valley serves as a natural greenway that connects excellent hikes in John Bryan State Park, Clifton Gorge

State Nature Preserve, Glen Helen Preserve, Caesar Creek State Park, and Fort Ancient State Memorial, among others.

Ecologically, most of southwest Ohio lies in the Till Plains region, atop rich soils left by the last glacier. The original forests were cleared for today's landscape of agriculture and cities. Hueston Woods State Nature Preserve, however, is home to a footpath exploring nearly 200 acres of virgin and near-virgin beech-maple forest. Surrounding that is the popular Hueston Woods State Park, with full amenities and many more miles of hiking trails. Jutting up from Kentucky across the Ohio River and into Brown and Adams County is the state's smallest ecoregion—the Interior Low Plateau, or Bluegrass region. The Nature Conservancy's Edge of Appalachia Preserve contains a few public access hiking trails that allow you to check out globally rare plant and animal communities.

20 Little Miami River Loop and Spur Trail

Clifton Gorge State Nature Preserve and John Bryan State Park

Located along the Little Miami Scenic River, Clifton Gorge is best known for its rushing waters through a striking narrow gorge. The gorge was cut by glacial melt-waters some 10,000 years ago, and its geologic history is largely the reason this 269-acre preserve is home to 347 plant species and 105 tree species. Start from John Bryan State Park and walk upstream and then back down for a 9.0-mile loop along the Little Miami in a gorge with dolomite walls, slump blocks with stands of cedar, and an upland chinquapin oak forest. Visit the adjoining preserve and learn about the natural and human history of the gorge from interpretive signs.

Start: From the trailhead in the campground

Distance: 9.0-mile loop with spur

Approximate hiking time: 3 to 4$^{1}/_{2}$ hours

Difficulty: Moderate due to length and the climb out of the gorge

Seasons: Best mid-April through mid-October and after a winter snowfall

Trail surface: Dirt, with some boardwalks

Other trail users: Hikers only

Canine compatibility: Leashed dogs are permitted in the state park but not permitted in the state nature preserve. It's easy to make a 5.0-mile loop hike with pets.

Water: Available at the campground

Land status: State park and state nature preserve

Nearest town: Yellow Springs

Fees and permits: No fees or permits required

Schedule: Open daylight hours year-round

Maps: USGS quad: Clifton; Maptech Terrain Navigator: Ohio/Cincinnati/Southwest

Trail contacts: John Bryan State Park, Yellow Springs; (937) 767-1274; www.john bryan.org.
Clifton Gorge State Nature Preserve, Yellow Springs; (937) 767-7947; www.ohiodnr.com/dnap/location/clifton.html.

Finding the trailhead: From I-70 in Springfield, turn south onto State Route 72 (exit 54) and drive 6.6 miles to State Route 343. Turn west (right) and travel 2.3 miles to State Route 370. Turn south (left) and drive 1.0 mile to the entrance to John Bryan State Park on the left. Turn into the park and drive to the first parking lot on the right. *DeLorme: Ohio Atlas and Gazetteer:* Page 66 B2.

The Hike

When you hike along this portion of the Little Miami Scenic River, the strong forces of natural and human history make themselves known. Begin the hike downstream from Clifton Gorge. As you walk upstream, notice the way the water has carved out layers of rock. The uppermost layer of rock in the gorge is Cedarville dolomite, which is resistant to weathering. Below that are two thin layers of other dolomites and then a thick layer of massie shale. This shale weathers easily, and eventually its undercutting leads to "slump blocks," where the upper layers of rock have tumbled down into the gorge, sometimes into the middle of the river. Below the layer of shale is brassfield limestone, also weather-resistant, and then elkhorn shale. Due to the types of rock present, the river is now mostly widening rather than deepening the gorge.

The relatively unusual geology of Clifton Gorge has contributed to its biodiversity. Naturalists have identified 347 species of wildflowers and 105 species of trees and shrubs within the 269-acre preserve. Along the river, water-loving sycamore and cottonwood trees thrive. Maple grows abundantly in the gorge, and a chinquapin oak forest dominates the upland area. Growing on the slump blocks is white cedar. In the spring, look for such wildflowers as spring beauty, trillium, hepatica, and jack-in-the-pulpit. Some rare species that grow here include the mountain maple, identifiable by its striped bark, as well as red-berried elder and Canada yew.

▶ John Bryan, inventor and conservationist, bequeathed 500 acres of his "Riverside Farm" to the state of Ohio in 1924. His offer had been previously rejected by three governors because he required that no religious worship could take place on the land. He also took matters into his own hands to ensure that the trees in the campground would never be cut—he spiked them!

This area has long been inhabited by humans. Nearby earthworks provide evidence that prehistoric peoples, probably the Hopewell culture, lived here. More recently, the Shawnee Indians made this region their home. One of the most famous incidents at Clifton Gorge occurred between the Shawnee and European frontiersmen. As the story goes, Daniel Boone and members of his party, including Cornelius Darnell, were captured by Shawnee Chief Black Fish in 1799. During their escape, Darnell outpaced his Shawnee pursuers by leaping 22 feet across the upper gorge to safety. More detailed accounts say that Darnell didn't quite make it across, but he was able to grab hold of tree branches and still make his way to the other side.

As Europeans continued to settle the area, gristmills, a textile mill, and a sawmill popped up along the gorge, all using the natural power of the rushing waters. The Clifton Mill, built in 1802, is still in operation today. Plan time to visit the mill on your trip. Clifton was home to more than 300 people in the mid-1800s. A railroad was never built here, but the Pittsburgh-Cincinnati Stagecoach Road was, and you will walk along this old road on your return trip downstream.

The preservation of this area has a history of nearly missed opportunities and narrowly avoided development. In 1924 the state of Ohio accepted 500 acres of land around the river, bequeathed by John Bryan. Hugh Taylor Birch later donated another 161 acres. But the upper portion of Clifton Gorge was still in private hands. In 1963 the Ohio chapter of The Nature Conservancy raised enough money to buy some of the upper gorge area, saving it from private recreation development. In 1968 The Nature Conservancy came through again and bought the rest of today's preserve land before a private housing development could be built.

A century-old tulip tree flowering near the trailhead in John Bryan State Park.

The hike begins and ends at the campground area in John Bryan State Park. A 5.0-mile loop takes you up the south bank and down the north bank of the Little Miami Scenic River. If you have pets, you can do this loop. But the most spectacular part of the trail, overlooking the narrow gorge, is the 4.0-mile out-and-back spur that begins at the turnaround for the loop hike. Plan accordingly.

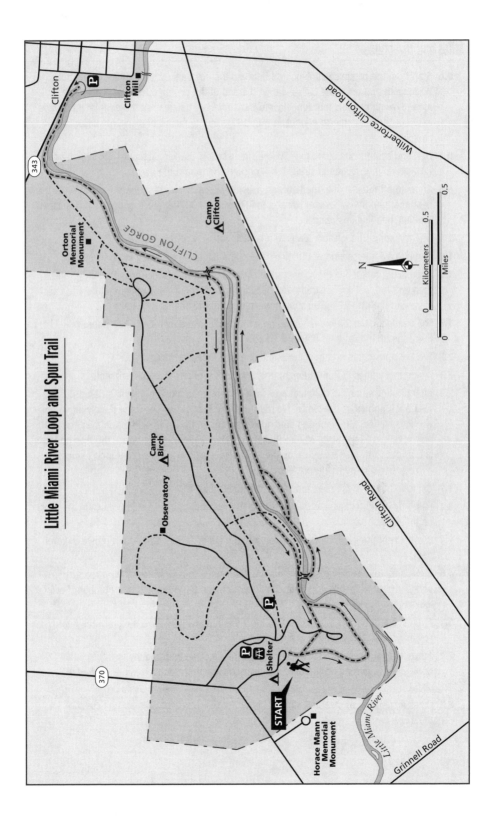

Little Miami River Loop and Spur Trail

Clifton

Clifton Mill

343

Orton Memorial Monument

CLIFTON GORGE

Camp Clifton

Wilberforce Clifton Road

Camp Birch

Observatory

P

370

P

Shelter

START

Horace Mann Memorial Monument

Little Miami River

Grinnell Road

Clifton Road

N

Kilometers   0.5

Miles   0.5

0   0.5

Miles and Directions

0.0 Start from the picnic shelter, located between the day parking lot and the campground. Walk south and cross the cul-de-sac at the end of the campground road. Look for a mowed swath of grass that funnels into the unmarked trailhead at the edge of the woods. In about 50 feet come to a junction with a side trail to the lower picnic area. Continue straight.

0.4 Descend some stone stairs to a five-way intersection, marked with only one sign, reading CAMPGROUND TRAIL. Continue straight, still descending toward the river.

0.5 Come to a T intersection, marked with a sign that reads CAMP TRAIL/LOWER PICNIC AREA. Take a right and then an immediate left at a fork. In about 100 feet reach another T intersection. Turn left, heading upstream.

1.0 The trail forks. The left fork leads to a parking lot. Stay right/riverside.

1.1 Come to a T intersection at the picnic area. Turn right, staying along the river's edge.

1.2 Approach a footbridge that crosses the Little Miami Scenic River. Cross the bridge and then turn left, walking upstream on the south side of the water. Continue along the trail closest to the river whenever you encounter formal or informal side trails.

1.6 The trail forks; the left branch stays near the river and the right crosses a boardwalk. Either fork ends up in the same place.

2.3 The two forks rejoin and become one trail again. Continue straight.

2.5 A side trail comes in from the right. This is private property. Continue straight.

3.1 After passing some tall dolomite rock faces, come to a fork. To the right is Camp Clifton. Take a left and cross the footbridge back over the river. Cross and immediately hit a four-way intersection. Turn right and continue upstream on the north side of the river. You are now in Clifton Gorge State Nature Preserve. (**FYI:** If you have a pet, cross the river and turn left, as pets are not allowed in the preserve. This is also a good spot for lunch, since picnicking isn't allowed in the preserve, either.)

3.7 Come to a pool in the river, marked as the Blue Hole.

4.1 Pass Amphitheater Falls on the left and then Steamboat Rock (a slump block in the river) on the right.

4.4 Climb out of the gorge by way of steep wooden stairs. Take a right onto a crushed gravel path.

4.5 Cross a footbridge over a side waterfall and continue to a sidewalk along a roadway bridge. Cross the bridge and then continue along the trail, stopping at a number of overlooks along the way.

5.1 Approach a three-way intersection; to the left is a parking lot. Take a right to the final gorge overlook. Return the way you came.

7.1 Arrive back at the footbridge at the edge of the preserve and a four-way intersection. Continue straight, picking up the old Pittsburgh-Cincinnati Stagecoach Road, marked with a sign.

8.2 Cross a stream over stepping-stones. Check out the top of the falls and an overlook for the river.

8.4 Come to a fork with an unmarked side trail to the left. Take this to rejoin the river's edge. You've passed this side trail if you see a fading orange arrow spraypainted on a tree.

8.6 Rejoin the stagecoach road (see another orange arrow), and in about 200 feet pass the footbridge you crossed toward the beginning of the hike. About 20 feet past the footbridge, take a left where the trail leaves the road again.

8.8 Arrive at the lower picnic area where the trail curves to the left, hugging the riverbank. At this junction go straight, leaving the river and walking through the picnic area.

8.9 Ascend the stone steps to a shelter house. Turn right and cross the road, staying to the right of the rest rooms. Pick up the trail again at a sign for the campground. Walk to the top of the ridge and a T intersection. Turn right.

9.0 Return to the trailhead.

Hike Information

Local information
Greene County Convention and Visitors Bureau; (800) 733-9109; www.greenecounty ohio.org.

Local events and attractions
In John Bryan State Park, go rock climbing or check out the observatory, a decommissioned Air Force satellite tracking station. Nearby attractions include the **Little Miami Scenic (shared-use) Trail** (937–376–7440) and **Antioch University's Glen Helen Preserve** (937–767–7375; www.antioch.edu/glenhelen. html).

Restaurants
Eat pancakes from locally milled flour at the **Clifton Mill's Millrace Restaurant;** (937) 767-5501; www.cliftonmill.com.

Accommodations
John Bryan State Park campground; (937) 767-1274.

Hike tours
Ranger-led hikes are offered between Memorial Day and Labor Day. Get the specifics from the park bulletin board.

21 Glen Helen Loop Trail

Glen Helen Nature Preserve

Glen Helen is Antioch College's very own land laboratory. Like nearby Clifton Gorge, the Glen was created by glacial meltwaters 10,000 years ago. On a 4.4-mile loop that takes you downstream and then back up the other side, take in some of the Glen's most well-known attractions: Yellow Spring, after which the town is named, dolomite cliffs and Pompey's Pillar, a beautiful waterfall known as the Cascades, excellent wildflowers, a relocated covered bridge, mature trees, and glacial erratic rocks strewn across the field near the museum.

Start: At the museum
Distance: 4.4-mile loop with a short spur
Difficulty: Easy; mostly flat and fairly short
Trail surface: Dirt
Blaze: None
Seasons: Best April through October and after a winter snowfall
Other trail users: Hikers only
Canine compatibility: Leashed dogs permitted
Water: Available at museum when it's open
Land status: Owned by Antioch College, open to the public

Nearest town: Yellow Springs
Fees and permits: Groups of more than ten persons must obtain a permit before hiking at the glen.
Schedule: Open daily year-round from dawn to dusk
Maps: USGS quad: Yellow Springs, Maptech Terrain Navigator: Ohio/Cincinnati/Southwest
Trail contacts: Glen Helen Nature Preserve, Antioch University, Yellow Springs; (937) 767-7375; www.antioch.edu/glenhelen.html

Finding the trailhead: From State Route 68 in Yellow Springs, turn east onto Corry Drive (on the north side of town) and travel 0.4 mile to the parking area on the left, marked with a sign. Park and then walk about 50 feet to the museum. *DeLorme: Ohio Atlas and Gazetteer:* Page 66 B2.

The Hike

Glen Helen Nature Preserve is a 1,000-acre land lab for Antioch University, replete with a State and National Scenic River, rock formations, waterfalls, and a pine forest. The land was donated by Antioch alumnus Hugh Taylor Birch in 1929 and has been mostly left alone since then to allow ecological processes to carry on undisturbed.

Like nearby John Bryan State Park and Clifton Gorge Nature Preserve, the valleys here were cut by glacial meltwaters. Begin the hike by stopping in at the museum to learn more about the natural features of Glen Helen. In the field by the museum, check out the large glacial erratic granite boulders. Then descend into the Yellow Springs Creek Valley and walk upstream. This upstream portion of the preserve features a high collection of attractions in the glen. Walk past Pompey's Pillar, a solitary column of dolomite. Then arrive at the famous Yellow Spring, from which

The famous Yellow Spring from which the town gets its name is a calling card at Glen Helen Preserve.

the town gets its name. Flowing at a rate of sixty to one hundred gallons per minute, the spring looks more orange than yellow, due to high concentrations of iron. The glen was home to a nineteenth-century resort that drew visitors to the believed healing qualities of the spring.

Past the Yellow Spring is the Cascades, one of the most scenic and well-known spots in the glen. A waterfall pours into a large pool, which then feeds a series of cascading waterfalls. After checking out the Cascades, head downstream. The creek is

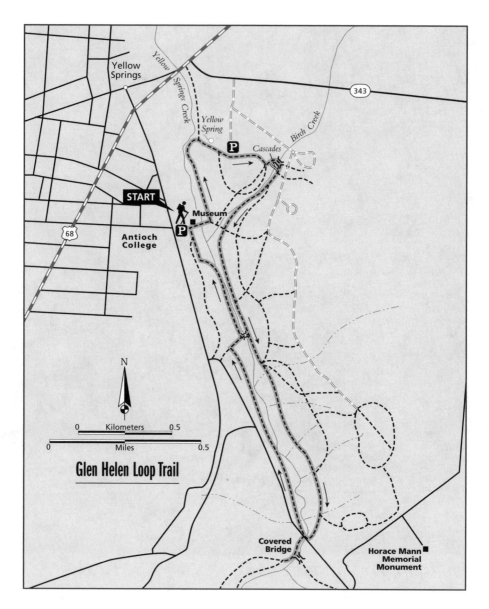

small and attractive, bordered in some spots by dolomite cliffs and a forest that includes chinquapin oak, hickory, ash, tulip poplar, and maple. Underfoot, look for the many species of flowering plants, including broad waterleaf, phlox, twinleaf, trillium, jack-in-the-pulpit, giant bellwort, and solomon's seal. By now you may have noticed a number of invasive exotics taking hold, including garlic mustard and honeysuckle. As you walk streamside, you'll see a number of side trails. These lead to upland portions of the preserve, including the pine forest, planted in the 1920s by the Ohio Division of Forestry.

The turnaround point on the hike is at Grinnell Road. It's worthwhile, however, to continue downstream a couple hundred feet and explore a relocated covered bridge, more than a hundred years old. Past the bridge, come to the confluence of Yellow Springs Creek and the Little Miami Scenic River. This is a nice spot to rest and wait to see some of usual inhabitants, including ducks, geese, great blue herons, and kingfishers. Preserve property and trails continue downstream on either side of the river if you're looking to add a few more miles to your hike.

When you begin the return trip from Grinnell Road, look for a giant hollowed-out sycamore tree near the road bridge. Five adults could stand inside it. Then walk up the trail along the water's edge, taking in new views along the same stretch of creek. Pass the tallest dolomite rock cliffs in the preserve just before returning to the trailhead by the museum.

Miles and Directions

0.0 Start at the museum. Walk down a few stairs to a junction. Continue straight down the stairs.

0.1 Cross a footbridge over Yellow Springs Creek; in about 150 feet come to a T intersection. Take a left.

0.2 A side trail to the right takes you to Pompey's Pillar. Continue straight.

0.4 Pass a footbridge on the left and approach an old cement bridge foundation, also on the left. A waterfall is on the right. Continue straight.

0.5 An access trail comes in from the left. Continue straight to the famous Yellow Spring. About 100 feet past the spring, come to a junction. Continue straight, passing a side trail on the right.

0.6 Pass an informational kiosk that details the life history of an oak tree. Past this kiosk, another access point comes in from the left.

0.7 Pass a monument on the left (a plaque affixed to a glacial erratic stone) and come to a fork. Look left and see the footbridge you will cross. But first take a short side trip to the right and down the stairs to check out the Cascades on Birch Creek. Return to this junction and take a right.

0.8 Cross the footbridge over the Cascades. Take the first trail off to the right. Slowly descend toward the creek, crossing a tributary along the way.

1.0 Come to a fork. Take a right and finish the descent into the valley.

1.2 Come to a four-way junction. Continue straight. **Option:** Turn right and cross the creek over stepping-stones to return directly to the museum.

1.5 A side trail comes in from the left. Continue straight.

1.7 Pass a footbridge over the creek on the right.

1.8 The trail turns away from the creek, crosses a tributary over stepping-stones, and then forks. Take the right fork, staying near the creek. Over the next 0.5 mile, various formal and informal trails crisscross. Stay always near the creek.

2.5 Come to Grinnell Road. Take a right and cross over the creek on the road. On the other side of the bridge, cross the road, heading downstream, and pick up the trail again.

2.7 Come to an old covered bridge. Continue downstream for about 200 more feet to the confluence of Yellow Springs Creek and the Little Miami Scenic River. (**FYI:** You can explore more trails and dirt roads on either side of the river here before beginning the return trip.)

3.0 Return to Grinnell Road. Cross the road and look to the left for a huge hollowed-out sycamore tree. Pick up the trail again, now on the west side of the creek, heading upstream.

3.5 Cross a footbridge over a cascading tributary, then almost immediately come to a fork. Take a right to stay near the creek.

3.8 Approach a fork. Take a right and descend to the creek. Walk over a boardwalk and then a bridge, then come to a four-way intersection. Turn left, continuing upstream on the west side of the creek.

4.1 A side trail joins from the left. Look across the creek for cascading water and dolomite rock shelves.

4.3 Ascend to a T intersection. Take a right. Check out the dolomite cliffs to the left, but keep generally below the rocks to stay on the trail.

4.4 Reach the stone stairs where you began the hike. Walk up and return to the museum.

Hike Information

Local information
Greene County Convention and Visitors Bureau; (800) 733-9109; www.greenecounty ohio.org.

Local events and attractions
John Bryan State Park; (937) 767-1274; www.johnbryan.org.
Little Miami Scenic (shared-use) Trail; (937) 376-7440.

Accommodations
John Bryan State Park campground; (937) 767-1274.

Restaurants
The Winds, Yellow Springs; (937) 767-1144; www.windscafe.com.
Sunrise Cafe, Yellow Springs; (937) 767-7211; www.sunrisecafe.com.

Organizations
The Glen Helen Association provides monetary and volunteer support for the Glen Helen Ecology Institute. Call for membership information; (937) 767-7375.

22 Three Sisters to Sycamore Ridge Loop

Sugarcreek MetroPark

The features of this park explain its popularity: a restored tallgrass prairie, a beech-maple forest, limestone-lined creeks, 550-year-old oak trees known as the Three Sisters, Sycamore Ridge, and an Osage orange "tunnel" that is the result of a fencerow planted long ago. Combine the trails that include these features for a fun 4.6-mile loop around Sugarcreek MetroPark.

Start: From the parking lot trailhead located off Conference Road
Distance: 3.7-mile loop
Approximate hiking time: $1^1/_2$ to $2^1/_2$ hours
Difficulty: Easy; short, flat, and well-worn
Seasons: Best April through October
Trail surface: A short asphalt section gives way to wide and mostly flat grass-and-dirt trail.
Other trail users: Cross-country skiers in winter
Canine compatiblity: Leashed dogs permitted; owners are expected to clean up after their dogs.

Water: Available at trailhead
Land status: Dayton MetroPark
Nearest town: Centerville
Fees and permits: No fees or permits required
Schedule: Open 8:00 A.M. to dusk year-round except Christmas and New Year's Day
Maps: USGS quad: Waynesville; Maptech Terrain Navigator: Ohio Columbus/Cincinnati/Southwest
Trail contacts: Sugarcreek MetroPark, Dayton or Centerville; (937) 433-0004; www.metroparks.org

Finding the trailhead: From I-75 south of Dayton, exit onto I-675 North and travel 7.2 miles to Wilmington Pike Road (exit 7). Turn south (right) and drive 2.9 miles to the junction with Conference Road at a stop sign. Continue straight on Conference Road 0.2 mile to the parking lot on the left, marked with a Sugarcreek MetroPark sign. *DeLorme: Ohio Atlas and Gazetteer:* Page 65 C7.

The Hike

The Five Rivers MetroParks are actually named after three rivers and two large creeks that converge in the Dayton metropolitan area. On Easter Sunday 1913, a giant flood hit Dayton, killing 361 persons and rendering thousands homeless. It has been called the worst disaster in Miami Valley history. City officials responded by building a series of dams to prevent such flooding again.

▶ **The Great Miami, Mad, and Stillwater Rivers plus Twin and Wolf Creeks inspire the Five Rivers MetroParks name.**

What's unusual about the dams is that they do not all create large, permanent reservoirs. Thus the river valleys are intact, and most of the Dayton MetroParks are located in these attractive river valleys.

Due to heavy use, Sugarcreek's trails are almost wide enough to drive on, but the features along the trails make up for it. Begin by following an asphalt handicap-

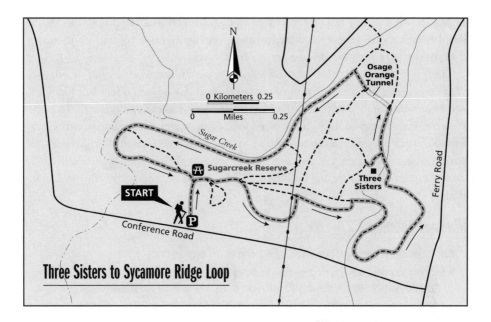

Three Sisters to Sycamore Ridge Loop

accessible path to the picnic area. Then hit the yellow-blazed trail, which weaves its way through a tallgrass prairie, home to such species as thistle, sunflower, echinacea, brown-eyed Susan, bergamot, clover, and numerous grasses. These plants require a lot of sun and have deep roots to weather dry spells. The MetroParks organization planted this prairie as a way to restore some of the former landscape of western Ohio, where natural prairie openings occurred within the forest.

The prairie section of the trail gives way to a green-blazed path in a beech-maple forest and attractive stream crossings atop quarried limestone. Take a minute to look at fossils in the limestone. The forest is also home to plentiful wildlife. Listen for the tapping of resident woodpeckers, and keep your eyes open for white-tailed deer along the prairie's edge in the evening.

Make a side trip off the green trail and up the slope to the Three Sisters. The name refers to three giant white oak trees estimated to be 550 years old. In the 1960s scientists took core samples from one of the trees and determined that it began growing around 1440, a full fifty years before Columbus set foot in the New World.

Instead of continuing around the perimeter trail in Sugarcreek, take a shortcut through the orange-blazed Osage orange "tunnel." Here and elsewhere in the park, former homesteaders planted Osage orange fencerows. What remains of these old fencerows are long straight stretches of path where the arcing branches of the Osage orange trees create a living tunnel to walk through. On the ground you may see the

◀ *The trail walks you through an Osage orange "tunnel" at Sugarcreek MetroPark.*

orange-colored roots of the trees. The orange-size green fruits are known to kids as monkeyballs and to farmers as effective spider repellents. Look off trail in other sections of the park for more Osage orange fencerows.

The trail then joins the edge of Sugar Creek, an attractive byway lined with sycamores and a good population of spiny honey locusts. Look underfoot for nettle and hoary mountain mint, identified by its square stem and minty smell. The trail stays creekside but rises above it for nice views of the water. The trail then turns away from Sugar Creek and rises to red-blazed Sycamore Ridge, named after these white-barked, water-loving trees. When you find sycamores at the ridgetop, it usually indicates the presence of a spring. End the trail where you began, shortly after Sycamore Ridge.

Miles and Directions

0.0 Start at the parking lot trailhead. Walk north on an asphalt trail.

0.1 Come to a four-way intersection next to a picnic shelter. Take a right and continue on the asphalt until it forks in about 100 feet. Take a left and walk on the gravel path.

0.2 Arrive at a junction marked with a wooden post and the number 2. Take a right and walk into the prairie on a mowed path (marked yellow).

0.6 Come to a T intersection under the power lines at Post 3. Take a right.

0.8 Approach a T intersection at Post 4. Take a right.

1.7 Come to a junction. Take a left to check out the Three Sisters.

1.8 Return to the green trail and take a left (north).

2.0 Approach a junction at Post 8. Take a left and walk on the orange trail through the Osage orange tunnel.

2.1 Come to a junction at Post 11. Continue straight to Sugar Creek.

2.2 The trail forks at Post 10. Take a left and parallel the creek.

2.5 The trail forks at Post 15. Take a right, staying near the creek.

2.8 Come to the junction with the Big Woods Trail on the right. Continue straight. **Option:** Take the 1.1-mile Big Woods Trail loop, which is illegally used by equestrians and very, very muddy.

3.0 Come to a junction at Post 17. Continue straight to finish along Sycamore Ridge. To the left is the red trail, which is a bit of a shortcut.

3.4 Come to the second junction with the red trail. Continue straight.

3.5 Return to the first junction of the trail. Take a right and head back to the parking lot on the asphalt path.

3.7 Finish at the parking lot trailhead.

Hike Information

Local information

Dayton Convention and Visitors Bureau, Dayton; (800) 221-8235, ext. 281; daytoncvb.com.

Local events and attractions

The 26-mile **Dayton River Corridor Bikeway;** (937) 223-1278.

Cox Arboreum and Gardens MetroPark, Springboro Pike; (937) 434-9005; www.metroparks.org.

Dayton Aviation Heritage National Historic Park; (937) 225-7705; www.nps.gov/daav/.

Dayton Art Institute; (800) 296-4426; www.daytonartinstitute.org.

Accommodations

John Bryan State Park, Yellow Springs; (937) 767-1274; www.johnbryan.org.

Restaurants

Amar India, Centerville; (937) 439-9005.

Organizations

Buckeye Trail Association, Worthington; (800) 881-3062; www.buckeyetrail.org.

Hike tours

MetroParks Trail Trekker Program; (937) 836-1888. Naturalist-led hikes and walks are offered throughout the year; contact Dayton MetroParks at (937) 275-PARK.

23 Big Woods and Sugar Bush Trails

Hueston Woods State Nature Preserve

Hike the 2.6-mile Big Woods and Sugar Bush trail system to see a virgin beech–maple forest in Ohio's western Till Plains region. The Hueston family homesteaded this spot and farmed most of it but kept some woods for maple sugaring. Thanks to that and the work of conservationists, you can now head to Hueston Woods State Park and take a trail through this spectacular bit of forest.

Start: From the trailhead located off the nature preserve parking lot
Distance: 2.3-mile lollipop
Approximate hiking time: 1 to 1½ hours
Difficulty: Easy; short and flat
Trail surface: Dirt trail, with a short section on the road
Blaze: None
Seasons: Best April through October
Other trail users: Hikers only in the nature preserve
Canine compatibility: Dogs not permitted in state nature preserve

Water: Available at Scenic 1 Picnic Area, north of the trailhead on Main Loop Road
Land status: State nature preserve, surrounded by state park
Nearest town: Oxford
Fees and permits: No fees or permits required
Schedule: Open daily year-round from dawn to dusk
Maps: USGS quad: College Corner; Maptech Terrain Navigator: Ohio/Cincinnati/Southwest
Trail contacts: Hueston Woods State Nature Preserve, Yellow Springs; (937) 767-7947; www.ohiodnr.com/dnap/location/hueston_woods.htm

Finding the trailhead: From State Route 177 north of Oxford, turn south onto State Route 732 and travel 0.5 mile to the Hueston Woods State Park entrance on the right. Follow Loop Road 5.0 miles to the Hueston Woods State Nature Preserve parking lot on the left, marked with a preserve sign. *DeLorme: Ohio Atlas and Gazetteer:* Page 64 D1.

The Hike

It's said that when Europeans first set foot on North American soil, a squirrel could climb into the forest canopy at the Atlantic Ocean and not touch the ground again until it hit the Mississippi River. The ensuing years have seen great change in the natural landscape. Today almost every tree that was growing in Ohio when the Europeans arrived has been cut. Hueston Woods contains a 200-acre tract of virgin and "near virgin" (lightly and selectively timbered) forest, a rarity in Ohio's western Till Plains region, where 95 percent of the original forests are now agricultural fields or urban areas. Enjoy a short hike along the Big Woods Trail for both a respite from modern day life and a look into the former landscape of this region.

The ancient history of this area begins, geologically, more than 400 million years ago, during the Ordovician era. What is now Ohio was under a sea that laid down many layers of sediment containing marine invertebrates such as corals, clams, snails,

A "near-virgin" beech and maple forest is protected in Hueston Woods State Nature Preserve.

trilobites, and brachiopods. The remains of these sea creatures are seen today as fossils. In fact, there's now a designated fossil collection area in Hueston Woods State Park. The seas drained away about 200 million years ago and the erosion process began. Then a series of four major glaciers advanced over this region beginning two million years ago and continuing until only about 15,000 years ago, leaving behind the rich soils on which vast beech–maple forests grew.

The history of the park and preserve is somewhat shorter. Matthew Hueston came to this region in the last years of the eighteenth century as a soldier under the leadership of American General "Mad" Anthony Wayne. He later bought land for a farm but also preserved a forested portion of his homestead. He and his descendants tapped the maple trees to make syrup—probably a major reason the woods were

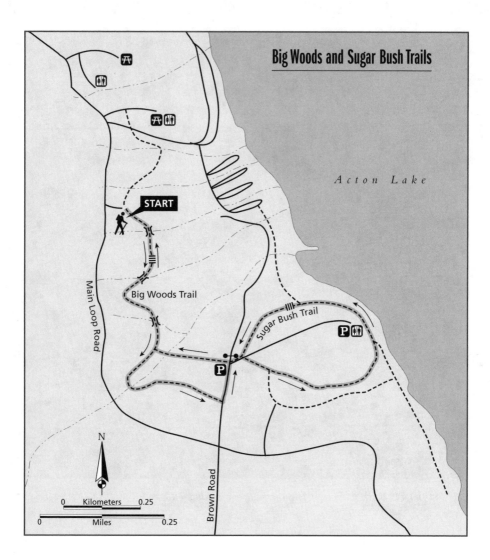

Big Woods and Sugar Bush Trails

Acton Lake

START

Main Loop Road

Big Woods Trail

Sugar Bush Trail

N

0   Kilometers   0.25

0   Miles   0.25

Brown Road

spared the saw. When the last of the Hueston descendants passed away in the 1930s, a local conservationist purchased the land and held it in trust until the state of Ohio was able to buy it in 1941. Preble County Legislator Cloyd Acton proposed the purchase to the state legislature. The Oxford Honor Camp was established in 1952, and Acton Lake was created with the completion of an earthen dam in 1957.

Today Hueston Woods State Park is an expansive compound with recreational opportunities for all tastes. Hiking, equestrian, and mountain biking trails surround Acton Lake, a popular fishing and boating destination. The park also features a lodge, cottages, a campground, and an eighteen-hole golf course. Before your hike, check out the nature center to learn more about the natural history of the area. The Big Woods and Sugar Maple Trails are located within Hueston Woods State Nature Preserve, which is within the state park.

The Big Woods Trail begins by winding through virgin beech-maple forest. The beech trees (which could be called graffiti trees—please don't add to their scars) tower above, casting shade on the understory. Naturally hollow beech trees provide habitat and food for such critters as squirrel, deer, and large birds, including turkey, bobwhite, pheasant, and ruffed grouse. Listen and look for the pileated woodpecker (North America's largest), which thrives in these forest conditions. Understory trees and shrubs are mostly pawpaw and spicebush. On the fairly clear forest floor look for lots of fungi (able to thrive on the many logs left here to rot) and a variety of fern species, including the black-stemmed maidenhair. Cross a number of streams and drainages over footbridges, and look for fossils in the streams. If you see some, it's because folks who were here before you did not collect any. You should do the same. (There is an official fossil collection area in adjacent Hueston Woods State Park.)

At the end of the Big Woods Trail, pick up the Sugar Bush Trail. This is also a magnificent forest, and in late winter/early spring, you'll see buckets hanging from the maple trees to collect sap. If you're not hiking during sugaring season, look on the trunks of the sugar maples along the trail. You'll see the telltale holes in the bark drilled to access the sap. This loop returns in part along the banks of Lake Acton before rejoining the Big Woods Trail.

Miles and Directions

0.0 Start the Big Woods Trail at the trailhead kiosk. (**FYI:** Look for a chickadee nest in the kiosk.) Walk straight into the woods (on the other side of the parking lot, a portion the Big Woods Trail heads into the state park). You'll walk over a couple of footbridges within the first half mile of trail.

0.5 Come to a junction with an informal side trail just before the stream. Cross over the stream and pick up the trail, which switches back downstream. Look for the American Discovery Trail blaze.

0.7 Come to Sugar Camp Road. Take a left and walk along the road. (**FYI:** Water is available right here. You can turn back for a 1.6-mile out-and-back hike. The American Discovery Trail branches off.)

0.8 Pass another trailhead on the left and follow the road as it curves to the right. In about 75 feet, hop onto the Sugar Bush Trail to the right, marked with a sign.

0.9 Reach a junction with the Blue Heron Trail. Continue straight.

1.2 Come to a fork. Take the left fork.

1.3 Approach the Sugar Camp parking lot. Walk to the other side of the parking lot and pick up the trail again, marked with a sign for the Sugar Bush and West Shore Trails.

1.4 Reach an unmarked four-way intersection. Take a left to return on the Sugar Bush Trail.

1.5 Come to a fork. Again, stay to the left.

1.6 Come to another fork. Again, stay left.

1.7 Return to Sugar Camp Road. Take a right and in about 75 feet come to a trailhead kiosk for the Big Woods Trail. Walk straight past the trailhead and back into the woods.

1.8 Cross the stream and come to a T intersection with the original trail. Take a right and return the way you came.

2.3 Return to the trailhead.

Hike Information

Local information

Oxford Visitors and Convention Bureau, Oxford; (513) 523-8687; www.oxfordchamber.org/vcbhome.html.

Local events and attractions

Hueston Woods State Park, College Corner; (513) 523-6347; www.ohiodnr.com/parks/parks/huestonw.htm. The park is host to 10 miles of hiking trails, a fossil collection area, horse rentals, mountain biking trails, an eighteen-hole golf course, and a paintball range. Boating, fishing, and swimming are popular on the 625-acre Acton Lake. Nearby Oxford is home to Miami University and the McGuffey House and Museum of William McGuffey of *McGuffey Readers* fame.

Accommodations

Hueston Woods State Park Campground; (513) 523-6347.
Hueston Woods Lodge; (800) 282-7275.

Restaurants

Hueston Woods Lodge dining room; (513) 523-6381.
Bagel and Deli, Oxford; (513) 523-2131; www.bagelanddeli.com/.
Pedro's Cactus Cantina, Oxford; (513) 523-7529.
DiPaolo's, Oxford; (513) 523-1541.

Organizations

Friends of Hueston Woods State Park, Inc.; http://huestonwoods_friends.tripod.com/friends.htm.

Hike tours

Naturalist-led hikes are offered year-round. Contact the park for up-to-date information; (513) 523-6347.

24 Flat Fork Ridge Trail to Pioneer Village

Caesar Creek State Park

More than 50 miles of developed trails circle 10,000-acre Caesar Creek Lake. The 6.0-mile out-and-back segment from Flat Fork Picnic Area to Pioneer Village offers a little bit of everything at Caesar Creek: fossil hunting, lake views, forest, a rocky-bottomed river, shale cliffs, a small waterfall, and a restored pioneer village. Stop by the visitor center to learn more about the natural and human history of this area before hitting the trail.

Start: At the Flat Fork Ridge Picnic Area
Distance: 6.0-mile out-and-back with optional 3.0-mile point-to-point
Approximate hiking time: 2 to 3 hours
Difficulty: Moderate due to length
Seasons: Best April through October
Trail surface: Dirt, grass, and gravel trail
Blaze: Yellow
Other trail users: Hunters (in season)
Canine compatibility: Leashed dogs permitted
Water: Available at picnic area
Land status: State park
Nearest town: Waynesville

Fees and permits: No fees or permits required for hiking; a free permit is required for fossil collection. The Pioneer Village suggests a donation.
Schedule: Open daylight hours year-round
Maps: An excellent Friends of Caesar Creek map and guide is available at the visitor center for $2.00.
USGS quads: Oregonia, Waynesville; MapTech Terrain Navigator: Ohio Columbus/Cincinnati/Southwest
Trail contacts: Caesar Creek Lake Visitor Center, Waynesville; (513) 897–1050; www.lrl.usace.army.mil/ccl

Finding the trailhead: From I-71 north of Wilmington, turn west onto State Route 73 (exit 45) and drive 7.7 miles to Clarksville Road, past Caesar Creek Lake. Turn south (left) onto Clarksville Road and drive 2.9 miles to the Flat Fork Picnic Area on the left, past the visitor center and the dam. *DeLorme: Ohio Atlas and Gazetteer:* Page 75 A7.

The Hike

Caesar Creek State Park's 50-plus miles of developed hiking, mountain biking, and bridle trails make it difficult to choose just one route. But the Flat Fork Picnic Area to Pioneer Village trail segment offers a little bit of everything at Caesar Creek: fossil hunting, lake views, forest, a rocky-bottomed river, shale cliffs, a waterfall, and a restored pioneer village.

Trails in the park surround Caesar Creek Lake, which was the town of New Burlington until 1978, when the Army Corps of Engineers created the 10,000-acre lake as part of an overall Miami Valley flood-control project. Caesar Creek flows into the Little Miami River just downstream from the dam.

Caesar Creek gets its name from a slave who was adopted by the Shawnee Indians after his party's capture in 1776. A contemporary of Shawnee War Chief Blue

The blacksmith shop at the Pioneer Village at Caesar Creek State Park.

Jacket, Caesar often hunted along the banks of the creek that eventually bore his name. At this time, the west side of the Little Miami River served as a portion of the Bullskin Trace (Native American) Trail, along which many Shawnee villages existed. The valley was home to other cultures before the Shawnee, including the Fort Ancient culture around 600 B.C. and, before that, prehistoric Mound Builders.

From the Flat Fork Picnic Area, you'll walk through some forest along the edge of Caesar Creek Lake and then into the spillway, whose construction essentially excavated a long escarpment of shale in

▶ **The trilobite is the official Ohio state fossil.**

front of you. Everywhere you look (if you look closely), there are fossils. Caesar Creek is home to one of the world's most renowned fossil beds. These fossils were created during the Ordovician period, roughly 445 to 510 million years ago, when a sea existed here. The prehistoric sea animals were laid down on the sea floor and materials accumulated into what is today's sedimentary rock. The ones that most resemble seashells are brachiopods. The ice cream cone–shaped fossils are

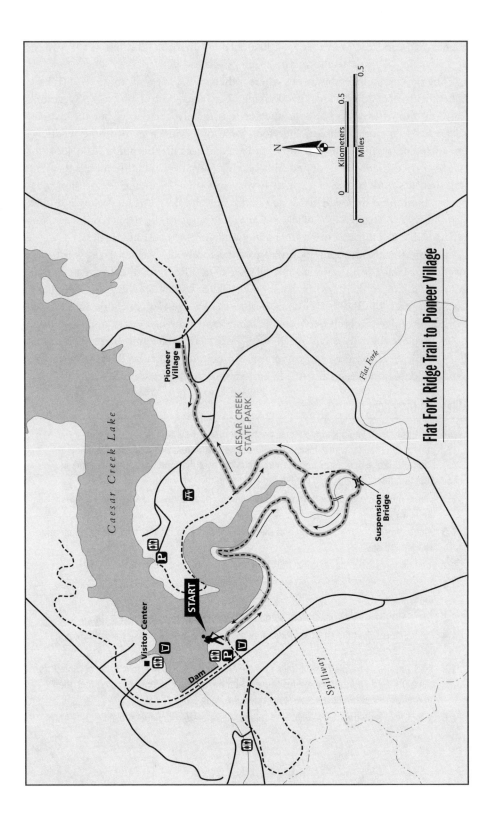

Flat Fork Ridge Trail to Pioneer Village

cephalopods, and the ones that look like coral are byrozoa. Thistle favor this rocky area near the lake, and swallows dart around overhead.

The trail soon enters the woods where it then stays. First walk above the Flat Fork Valley, with occasional views overlooking this rocky-bottomed creek. Sycamores grow up from the valley; upslope the forest is mainly deciduous, but the fragrant cedars have a strong foothold. Underfoot, look for a wide array of spring wildflowers, including spring beauty, trillium, ginger, and jack-in-the-pulpit. Also look for spleenwort on the forest floor and fruit-bearing pawpaw trees in the understory. The trail then descends to the creek, which you cross on a "swinging" suspension footbridge. From here there are good views both up- and downstream. Below is a thick stand of willow. This is a spot where you may find some of the many reptiles and amphibians that call the area home, including salamanders, toads, and turtles.

Be sure to take the spur loop trail past the footbridge, which takes you to the river's edge near a small waterfall and tall shale cliffs. After returning to the main trail, continue hiking in the forest, crossing other tributaries that feed Caesar Creek Lake, until you reach the Pioneer Village. The Pioneer Village is a collection of relocated log homes and shops built between 1797 and 1860, now in a circle around a village green. Explore the village (an interpretive guide is available) and then return to Flat Fork Picnic Area the way you came. You can continue past the Pioneer Village for about as long as you want if you'd like to tack on some more miles.

Miles and Directions

0.0 Start from the Flat Fork Ridge Picnic Area. Pick up the trailhead at the east end of the parking lot, marked with a hiker sign and two yellow blazes. Descend the stairs and in about 70 feet reach a junction. Continue straight over the footbridge and hit a fork in about another 50 feet. Take the left fork, following the yellow blaze.

0.2 Come out of the woods into a rocky prairie area. Follow the well-worn path that parallels the lakeshore.

0.5 Where the exposed shale seam and the water meet, the trail forks. Take the right fork and walk up the stairs.

0.7 The trail forks. Take the right fork, following the yellow blazes.

1.1 A short spur on the left leads to an overlook of the rocky-bottomed Flat Fork. Continue straight.

1.3 Cross Flat Fork on a suspension footbridge. Take a left at the other side of the bridge.

1.4 The trail forks, and the Flat Fork Ridge Trail continues to the right. Take the left fork and pick up the spur trail.

1.5 After passing a couple of side trails to the creek on the left, come to a T intersection. The trail turns right here and continues to parallel the creek. In a couple hundred feet, reach an overlook boardwalk. Take the stairs up to the right.

1.6 Pass a faint side trail to the right with a faint yellow blaze. Continue straight.

1.7 Come to a junction with a footbridge on the right. Cross over the footbridge, and then take an immediate left at a fork. Climb to the top of the stairs and reach a T intersection with the Flat Fork Ridge Trail. Take a left.

2.0 Pass a side trail and footbridge on the left and continue straight, following the yellow blaze.

2.2 Come to a junction. Take a right and walk through a stand of cedar trees, following the yellow blaze.

2.4 Cross Wellman Meadows Road.

2.6 Pass an access trail to a picnic area on the left.

2.8 Come to a junction with a footbridge to the left. Either direction takes you out to an open field, and then the two trails converge.

3.0 This section of the trail ends at the Pioneer Village.

6.0 Return the way you came to the trailhead.

Hike Information

Local information
Warren County Convention and Visitors Bureau; (800) 791-4FUN; www.ohio4fun.org.

Local events and attractions
The park offers a "stargazer campout" on the beach about once a year during a major meteor shower. Contact the park for up-to-date information.
Caesar's Creek Pioneer Village; (513) 897-1120.
Little Miami Scenic (shared-use) Trail; (937) 376-7440.
Blue Jacket outdoor drama; (877) 465-BLUE www.bluejacketdrama.com.
Caesar Creek State Nature Preserve, Oregonia; (513) 934-0751; www.ohiodnr.com/dnap/location/caesar_creek.html.

Accommodations
Caesar Creek State Park Campground; (937) 488-4595.

Restaurants
Angel of the Garden, Waynesville; (513) 897-7729; www.angelofthegarden.com.
Cobblestone Cafe, Waynesville; (513) 897-0021; www.waynesvilleshops.com/cobblestonevillage.

Organizations
Friends of Caesar Creek; (513) 897-1050; www.lrl.usace.army.mil/ccl/focc.htm.

Hike tours
Ranger-led walks are available in season. Contact the park for up-to-date information.

NATIVE AMERICAN TRAILS
Roads existed in Ohio long before the Ohio Department of Transportation was formed. The first roads were broad trails beat by Native Americans and their animal brethren, including rather imposing species, such as the wood bison. These transportation routes were the most practical way of getting from one place to another and usually followed water routes in order to stay on relatively flat terrain and to access the water. Today highways and roads have replaced most Native American trails (think U.S. 50 and U.S. 23). Generally, today's hiking trails exist to take you away from these roads. The result is that you are most often *not* hiking along ancient Native American Trails.

25 Earthworks Trail to Sun Serpent Effigy

Fort Ancient State Memorial and YMCA Camp Kern

Take a 3.4-mile out-and-back trail beginning at the earthworks constructed by the prehistoric Hopewell Indians. Follow the earthworks and then descend a forested slope down to the Little Miami Scenic Trail, a 70-mile multiuse path. Continue across the Little Miami Scenic River and along a farm field to the Sun Serpent Effigy, built by Native Americans to mark the summer solstice. Don't forget to stop by the excellent museum that will help you interpret what you see along the trail.

Start: From the Earthworks trailhead

Distance: 3.4-mile out-and-back

Approximate hiking time: 1 to 2 hours

Difficulty: Moderate due to a steep ascent on the return trip

Trail surface: The path is mostly dirt with a section on the asphalt bike path and then the road. There is a steep descent and then ascent out of the river valley.

Blaze: None for Fort Ancient Trails, but junctions are marked; Buckeye Trail is blue blazed.

Seasons: Best mid-April through mid-October

Other trail users: Only hikers on footpaths; the Little Miami Scenic Trail is a multiuse trail.

Canine compatibility: Leashed dogs permitted

Water: Available at the museum when it's open; otherwise bring your own.

Land status: State memorial, private camp

Nearest town: Lebanon

Fees and permits: You must get permission from YMCA Camp Kern to take the spur trail to the effigy. Since it is a youth camp, trespassing laws are strictly enforced. For permission call (513) 932-3756. Admission to Fort Ancient State Memorial is $6.00 for adults and $2.00 for students.

Schedule: Fort Ancient State Memorial is open 10:00 A.M. to 5:00 P.M. daily, May through September; open 10:00 A.M. to 5:00 P.M. Wednesday to Sunday and holidays, March through April and October through November. The gate is locked at all other times.

Maps: USGS quad: Oregonia; Maptech Terrain Navigator: Ohio/Southwest/Cincinnati; Buckeye Trail Association Section map: Loveland

Trail contacts: Fort Ancient State Memorial, Oregonia; (800) 283-8904; www.ohiohistory.org/places/ftancien. YMCA Camp Kern, Oregonia; (513) 932-3756; www.CampKern.org.

Finding the trailhead: From I-71 east of Lebanon, turn east onto Wilmington Road (exit 36) and then take an immediate right onto Middleboro Road. Drive 1.9 miles to a stop sign at State Route 350. Turn right (west) and drive 0.7 mile to the entrance on the left. Drive past the guard shack and take the first left to the museum. To get to the trailhead, drive straight (south) 0.5 mile past the guard shack to a large parking lot. Pick up the trailhead at the southern end of the parking lot. **DeLorme: Ohio Atlas and Gazetteer:** Page 75 A7.

A Native American mound at Fort Ancient State Memorial.

The Hike

Situated on a wooded ridgetop 235 feet above the Little Miami Scenic River in Warren County is an earthen embankment that snakes around for 3.5 miles, enclosing the hilltop with walls from 4 to 23 feet in height. Built by the prehistoric Hopewell culture, the earthwork retains for the most part the same form it had when it was constructed some 2,000 years ago. But as time undeniably marched on, the Hopewell culture and later the Fort Ancient culture ceased to exist as the mound builders and traders they once were. Some of these peoples eventually became known as Shawnee Indians, who were hunting and growing crops here when European settlers arrived. Today contemporary Ohioans drive to the site and stare, impressed at the achievements of people who conducted a large earth-moving project with little more than hand tools.

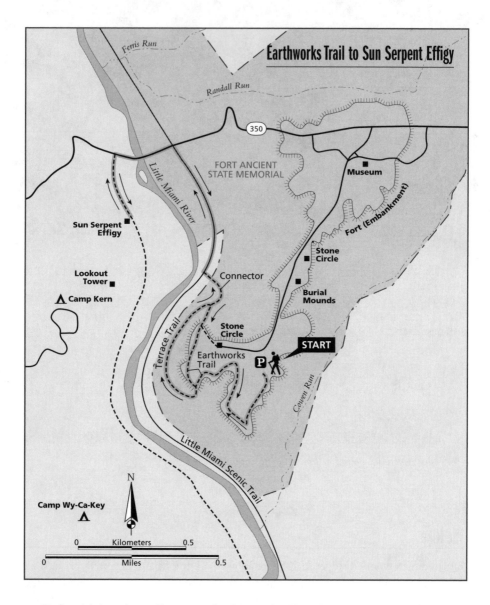

Earthworks Trail to Sun Serpent Effigy

Before hitting the trail, stop at the impressive Fort Ancient museum that raises and then answers just about any question you could have about the region's human history. It even takes a look at the discipline of archaeology and the scientific method. Archaeologists figure that the first humans to reach the Ohio Valley were Paleo-Indian hunters and gatherers about 15,000 years ago. The Hopewells added horticulture to their hunting and gathering lifestyle. This non-nomadic life allowed the Hopewells to construct their now-famous mounds and earthworks. They inhabited the Ohio Valley from approximately 100 B.C. to A.D. 400, and no one knows exactly what happened to their culture after that.

The Fort Ancient culture then occupied this region from about A.D. 900 to the time of "historic" contact. The site was named after the Fort Ancient Indians because it was originally thought that they built the earthworks. The Fort Ancient people did inhabit the site sometime between A.D. 1200 and 1600. They practiced full-fledged agriculture, and behind the museum today is a nice demonstration garden that features heirloom varieties of the "three sisters" common to Native American agriculture: corn, beans, and squash. When Europeans arrived here by 1700, they found 400- to 600-year-old trees growing out of the earthworks. Excavations have turned up innumerable artifacts, mainly tools and implements such as arrowheads, drills, and knives.

▶ **By some estimates, there were once more than 10,000 Native American mounds in the Ohio Valley.**

Today younger trees grow atop the still recognizable earthworks. Begin a hike on the Earthworks Trail and follow along the inside of the enclosure. Interpretive signs tell you that the embankment was originally thought to be a fort. Archaeologists today, however, believe this theory is false. They cite the fact that sixty-four openings in the walls would have been difficult to defend, and that most of the domestic sites excavated are outside the earthworks, not inside. This has led archaeologists to theorize that the enclosed earthwork was built primarily for social and/or ceremonial purposes.

Continue from the Earthworks Trail to the Terrace and then Connector Trails. Walk down the steep slope in a forest of oak, hickory, maple, tulip poplar, and cherry in the canopy with understory species such as pawpaw, redbud, and spicebush. In the springtime, look for ramps (wild leeks) and wildflowers. Descend all the way to the Little Miami Scenic Trail, a 70-mile all-purpose asphalt path stretching from Milford in Hamilton County to Springfield in Clark County. This also serves as a portion of the statewide Buckeye Trail. Get permission from YMCA Camp Kern to walk as far as the Sun Serpent Effigy (also known as the Kern Effigy), a snake-shaped collection of flagstones with a tall wooden pole at one end (and, inexplicably, a line of Buddhist prayer flags). Archaeologists have studied several of these effigies around the site and conclude that they were constructed to mark solar solstices. From here you can return basically the way you came to the trailhead. If you like, when you hop on the Little Miami Scenic Trail, you can add a few more miles in either direction.

Miles and Directions

0.0 Start at the trailhead off of the southernmost parking lot. It's marked with a sign that reads TO SOUTH OVERLOOK. This is the Earthworks Trail. Walk along the edge where the field meets the woods.

0.1 Reach a fork on a mowed path. Take the right fork, staying on the edge of the field.

0.2 Come to the overlook. Take the stairs to the overlook patio, then continue clockwise around the edge of the field.

0.3 Come to a junction. Take a left and walk into the woods.

0.4 Hit a junction just before wooden steps. Continue straight and over the steps to walk the Terrace Trail.

0.9 Arrive at the junction with the Earthworks and Connector Trails. Take a left and descend the steps on the Connector Trail.

1.0 Reach a T intersection with the Little Miami Scenic Trail (bike trail). Take a right and walk north.

1.4 Come to SR 350. Turn left (west) and cross the Little Miami River. You will pick up white blazes for the Silver Moccasin Trail.

1.5 On the other side of the bridge, look left for a farm lane that follows the edge of a field. Turn left onto the lane.

1.7 Arrive at the Sun Serpent Effigy on the right.

2.5 Return the way you came to a T intersection with the Terrace Trail. Take a left to finish the Terrace Trail.

2.6 Approach a wooden overlook platform that provides a nice view of the Little Miami Valley below. Walk down the steps on the other side of the platform and back onto the Earthworks Trail. In about 50 feet the trail forks. Take a right and walk back into the woods.

2.8 Walk straight through a four-way intersection underneath a magnificent white oak tree.

2.9 Reach a fork just before the steps where you began the Terrace Trail. Take a left and return the way you came on the Earthworks Trail.

3.4 Arrive back at the trailhead.

Hike Information

Local information
Warren County Convention and Visitors Bureau; (800) 791-4FUN; www.ohio4fun.org.

Local events and attractions
The annual **Fort Ancient Celebration** is held the second weekend in June; (800) 283-8904.

Morgan's Canoe Livery offers trips down the Little Miami Scenic River; (800) WE-CANOE; www.morganscanoe.com.

Accommodations
Morgan's Fort Ancient Canoe Livery and Riverside Campground; (513) 932-7568 or (800) 283-8904; www.morganscanoe.com.

Restaurants
Golden Lamb Inn (at 197 years old, Ohio's oldest restaurant and inn), Lebanon; (513) 932-5056.

Other resources
Fort Ancient: Citadel, Cemetery, Cathedral, or Calendar by Jack Blosser and Robert Glotzhober (Ohio Historical Society; Columbus: 1995).

Organizations
Ohio Historical Society, Columbus; (800) 297-2332; www.ohiohistory.org/index.html.
Buckeye Trail Association, Worthington; (800) 881-3062; www.buckeyetrail.org.

Hike tours
An annual Night Hike is held in August. Contact the museum for up-to-date information at (800) 283-8904.

26 Beechwood to Red Oak Trail Loop

Mount Airy Forest

One of the few hikes in Ohio accessible by public transportation, Mount Airy Forest is an oasis of greenspace within the heart of greater Cincinnati. Combine several trails to make a 3.9-mile loop around the oval picnic shelter. A flat, well-worn footpath makes its way around the ridge in a maturing deciduous forest—all thanks to the Cincinnati Park Board, which embarked on the first municipal reforestation project in the United States, beginning in 1911.

Start: From the Oval Open Shelter
Distance: 3.9-mile loop
Approximate hiking time: 1$\frac{1}{2}$ to 2$\frac{1}{2}$ hours
Difficulty: Easy; fairly short, flat, and well-maintained
Trail surface: Mostly flat dirt trail with many intersections
Blaze: An occasional white blaze; an E blaze for most of the trail; some junctions are marked.
Seasons: Best April through October
Other trail users: Cross-country skiers (in season), park bridle trails are separate but you may run into an errant equestrian

Canine compatibility: Leashed dogs permitted
Water: Available next to shelter house
Land status: Cincinnati park
Nearest city: Cincinnati
Fees and permits: No fees or permits required
Schedule: Open daily year-round from dawn to dusk
Maps: USGS quad: Cincinnati West; MapTech Terrain Navigator: Ohio Columbus/Cincinnati/Southwest
Trail contacts: Cincinnati Parks, Cincinnati; (513) 352-4080; www.cincy-parks.org/

Finding the trailhead: From the junction of I-74 and I-75 in Cincinnati, take I-74 west to Colerain Avenue (one-way only) and drive 1.5 miles to the Mount Airy entrance on the left. Take the first left onto Trail Ridge Road and drive 0.5 mile to the oval. *DeLorme: Ohio Atlas and Gazetteer:* Page 74 C3.

For public transportation, use Metro Routes 18 and 19 (and Route 74 on weekdays only).

The Hike

Take a break from the noise and crowds of the city, step onto a trail, and find solitude within minutes in Mount Airy Forest. This is all due to the forethought of the Cincinnati Park Board, which in 1911 bought 168 acres of abused farmland around the top of Colerain Hill and embarked on the first municipal reforestation project in the United States.

As the Queen City became more urbanized and industrialized, the Cincinnati Park Board continued planting trees and acquiring more land. In the 1930s African-American crews employed by the Civilian Conservation Corps (CCC) planted more than a million trees and built the shelters that are still in use. Today's Mount Airy

A mature oak tree grows along the trail at Mount Airy Forest.

Forest comprises nearly 1,500 acres of native hardwoods, evergreens, open space, and a popular arboretum that boasts more than 1,600 species of trees and shrubs.

Begin your hike from the Oval Open Shelter, which was built in 1931 and has the telltale characteristics of the structures erected during that period: stone floor and foundation, cedar-log framing, and wooden roof shingles. From the shelter, located on Trail Ridge Road, pick up the Beechwood Trail, toward Sunset Ridge. Begin a counterclockwise loop that takes you around Trail Ridge on a flat, even footpath. Soon you will cross the first of many attractive drainages while hiking in a forest of maple, beech, and hemlock. The understory is full of spicebush and fruiting pawpaw trees. In springtime look for such flowers as trillium, jack-in-the-pulpit, and common blue violet.

The trail crosses many side paths to and from picnic shelters, but as long as you stay straight and level, you should remain on course, where you will soon pick up the Furnas Trail and an E blaze for La Trainee de L'Explorateur Boy Scout Trail, which joins for a while. You may also notice orange boxes on some trees. These are orienteering geocaches, used by groups who put together recreational orienteering

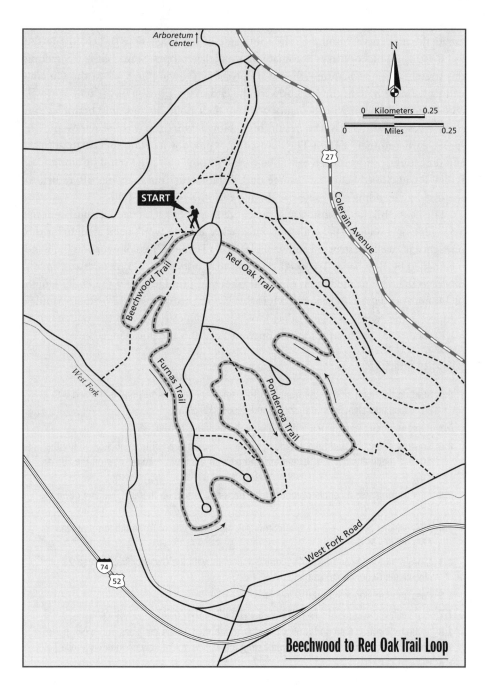

Beechwood to Red Oak Trail Loop

courses. You may also notice some small fenced-in areas in the park. These are deer exclosures, designed to keep deer out of small patches of the forest. The use of exclosures allows the park to monitor the damage deer are doing to the forest understory; the park sometimes uses these exclosures to protect patches of wildflowers.

As the trail curves around to the south side of the ridge, note the change in the forest. Oak and hickory trees dominate on these drier slopes. Some of the trees along this stretch are quite mature—they were probably growing here when the Cincinnati Park Board bought the land. Toward the end of this portion of the trail, you will come upon an opening in the canopy where light pours in and only brambles and small trees grow. This is the result of a blowdown from strong winds in late spring/early summer of 1993. The devastating winds downed countless mature trees, and the cleanup effort took weeks. The park left some oak snags standing along Oak Ridge Road. Shortly after La Trainee de L'Explorateur Trail branches off, return to the oval by ascending alongside the drainage up the Red Oak Trail.

The classic hike at Mount Airy is the entire length of La Trainee L'Explorateur for a 5.0-mile one-way or 10.0-mile out-and-back walk. You won't need a guide for this one, since it's well constructed and well blazed. La Trainee L'Explorateur was built and maintained by Boy Scout Troop 83, and you may notice the old metal blazes in addition to the new painted ones. This trail takes you through nearly the entire length of Mount Airy Forest. Access it at McFarlan Woods, on Westwood Northern Boulevard. Near the Maple Ridge Lodge, look for a trailhead sign and the trademark E blazes. The other trailhead is located on West Fork Road below Lingo Woods.

Miles and Directions

0.0 Start on the north side of the oval, next to a small shelter. The trailhead is marked with a BEECHWOOD TRAIL sign. Enter the woods and descend slightly.

0.1 Come to a fork. Take the left fork, following the drainage downstream.

0.4 Arrive at a junction and take a right. In about 50 feet take a left at a junction. In another 50 feet, reach another fork. Take a left and pick up the E blaze. You're now on the Furnas Trail.

0.8 After walking over a couple of footbridges, pass a side trail on the right, leading down the hill.

1.0 After walking over a couple more footbridges, pass two side trails on the left that lead to Area 21 picnic shelter.

1.3 Cross a footbridge and come to a marked junction with the Overlook Trail to Area 23 picnic shelter. Continue straight.

1.5 Pass another side trail to the picnic area.

1.7 Approach a four-way intersection with a sign for the Overlook Trail. Go straight.

1.8 Come to a grassy field and a picnic shelter to the right. Cross the grass and pick up the unmarked trail on the other side, reentering the woods. You're now on the Ponderosa Trail.

1.9 The trail forks. Take a right.

2.3 Hit another fork. Take a right and in about 25 feet come to the junction with the Quarry Trail. Continue straight.

2.5 Walk past a side trail on the left. Look ahead for the E blaze.

2.8 Come to a four-way intersection. To the right are the stone steps that lead down from Stone Steps Ridge. Continue straight.

3.1 Approach a fork. Take a right and walk over the footbridge

3.2 Approach a second fork. Again, go right.

3.4 Come to a fork. Take the left fork and immediately hit a second fork. Take the right fork this time, keeping an eye out for a white blaze and then the E blaze.

3.6 Cross a footbridge and in about 20 feet hit a fork. The Boy Scout Trail turns off to the right. Take the left fork, and begin a gentle ascent on the Red Oak Trail.

3.9 Return to the oval.

Hike Information

Local information
(800) CINCY-USA; www.cincyusa.com.

Local events and attractions
Mount Airy Arboretum and disc golf course; (513) 352–4080.

Restaurants
Myra's Dionysus, Cincinnati; (513) 961–1578.

Accommodations
Winton Woods Campground (Hamilton County Park District), Greenhills; (513) 851–CAMP. **Park House Bed-and-Breakfast,** Cincinnati; (513) 579–8236.

Hike tours
Cincinnati Parks offer regular naturalist-led nature walks in the park system. Call (513) 352–4080 for more information.

Organizations
Friends of Cincinnati Parks/Cincinnati Parks Foundation, Cincinnati; (513) 357–2619; www.cinci-parks.org.

Other resources
Cincinnati Park produces a parks newsletter; the Nature Education Section puts out quarterly program guides. Call (513) 321–6070 for more information.

JOHN JAMES AUDUBON For most of us, the name Audubon is synonymous with birds and birding. Of course this is because the Audubon Society and Audubon field guides bear the name of the first person to put together an exhaustive catalog of North American birds, complete with detailed paintings. Less known is John James Audubon's connection to Cincinnati. Born in French colony Santo Domingo (now Haiti) in 1785, Audubon was raised and educated in France. He left for the United States in 1803 to escape conscription in Napoleon's army. The itinerant Audubon lived first on the East Coast and then in Kentucky, where he was jailed for debt in 1819. In 1820 he moved his family to Cincinnati, where he took a job as a taxidermist at the Western Museum while also working as a portrait artist and teacher. It was during this time that he began in earnest to catalog and paint North American birds. *Birds of America* was published in 1827.

27 Rowe Woods Trails

Cincinnati Nature Center

Rowe Woods, operated by the Cincinnati Nature Center, is home to 14 miles of trails. Combine several trails to view many of the most distinguishing features of the preserve, including old-growth woods, open fields, small waterfalls, vistas, and a lotus pond. Hikes and programs here are popular with kids.

Start: From the Rowe Interpretive Building

Distance: 6.7-mile trail system

Approximate hiking time: $2^{1}/_{2}$ to $3^{1}/_{2}$ hours

Difficulty: Moderate due to length

Trail surface: A well-maintained gravel, wood chip, and dirt trail system

Blaze: None; most junctions are marked with numbered posts.

Seasons: Best April through October

Other trail users: Hikers only

Canine compatibility: Dogs permitted on a 6-foot leash; pet owners are expected to pick up after them.

Water: Available at Rowe Interpretive Building when it's open; also available at rest rooms, which are open year-round

Land status: Private, nonprofit nature preserve

Nearest town: Milford

Fees and permits: Admission for adults is $3.00 Monday to Friday and $5.00 Saturday and Sunday. Admission for children ages 3 to 12 is $1.00. Annual memberships are available.

Schedule: Grounds are open daily year-round from sunrise to sunset. Rowe Interpretive Building is open Monday to Saturday 9:00 A.M. to 5:00 P.M. and Sunday 1:00 to 5:00 P.M.

Maps: A large map of all trails is available at the Rowe Interpretive Building; USGS quad: Batavia; Maptech Terrain Navigator: Ohio Columbus/Cincinnati/Southwest.

Trail contacts: Cincinnati Nature Center, Rowe Woods, Milford; (513) 248–9868; www.cincy-nature.org

Finding the trailhead: From I–275 on the east side of Cincinnati, take exit 59B east to a T intersection with U.S. Highway 50 east. Turn right and drive 2.0 miles to Roundbottom Road. Take a right and drive 0.4 mile to Tealtown Road. Turn left and continue 0.7 mile to the entrance to Rowe Woods on the right. Stop at the guard shack and then continue to the parking lot on the left. *DeLorme: Ohio Atlas and Gazetteer:* Page 75 C6.

The Hike

When young Carl Krippendorf came down with typhoid in the late 1800s, his family doctor recommended that Carl get out of Cincinnati and recuperate in the fresh air of the countryside. Carl's well-to-do father, founder and president of the Krippendorf-Dittman shoe company, sent him to live with a doctor in Perintown, east of the city. Carl Krippendorf grew to love the land so much that he bought ninety-seven acres of it in 1898 and built a house for himself and his wife, Mary. What was then known as "Lob's Woods" is today known as Rowe Woods, operated by the Cincinnati Nature

A boardwalk overlooks Spring Pond at Rowe Woods.

Center. Home to 14 miles of trails, Rowe Woods can satisfy those who are looking for both quantity and quality of hikes, all in the fresh air of the countryside.

In the 1950s and 1960s there was a small but significant trend toward preserving the diminishing wild places in Ohio. A series of nature preserves were founded at this time, including the Cincinnati Nature Center's original site in 1965. Stanley Rowe Sr. was part of a group of environmentalists who established Rowe Woods on the Krippendorf land. (The Cincinnati Nature Center now has two other sites: Gorman Heritage Farm and Long Branch Farm.)

A good starting point for any hike in the preserve is the Rowe Interpretive Building. This is home to the CNC's nonprofit educational center and hosts lots of programs, mostly for children, but there are ample programs for adults as well, including nature, bird, and full-moon hikes. Permanent and revolving exhibits feature nature interpretation as well as photography and art shows.

From the interpretive center, the Edge Trail skirts Powel Crosley Lake, the largest of several ponds you will see on your hike. Overhead, look for squirrel nests in the black walnut and pine trees. These critters are most active in fall but are conspicu-

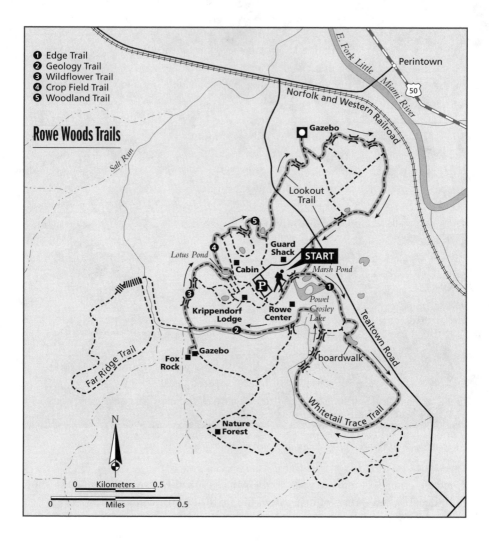

ous at all times. Continue to walk around Crosley Lake and then turn away as you enter a forest of maple, ash, elm, and hackberry on the Whitetail Trace Trail. Walk by Spring Pond and then a couple of fields. This area was farmed before the Cincinnati Nature Center purchased it, and the process of succession from farm fields to forest is happening in front of your eyes. Look in the morning and evening for bird and deer activity along the edges where field meets forest.

Pick up the Geology Trail and parallel Avey's Run, an attractive, rocky-bottomed creek. The drainages here are steep, and the water rushes downstream, tumbling over limestone and shale bedrock. There are even several small waterfalls, one clearly visible from a footbridge that crosses the creek. The trail itself crosses the creek over large stepping-stones, making this route a popular one with kids. Take a steep side trip to Fox Rock outcropping. Return to complete a loop through a relatively young forest on the Far Ridge Trail before beginning the Wildflower Trail through a mature forest. Look for magnificent specimens of maple, oak, beech, and sycamore in this sixty-five acres of old-growth forest. Several benches allow you to rest and take in your forest surroundings.

As you exit the mature forest, approach the Lotus Pond, full of water lilies. Listen for that satisfying plop! sound of bullfrogs jumping in. Walk around the pond and then briefly take the Crop Field Trail as you pass an old log cabin in the distance. Then return to the woods and follow the short Woodland Trail to the longer loop Lookout Trail. The Lookout Trail includes a spur to an overlook of the Little Miami River Valley. On the last leg of the hike, before returning to the Rowe Interpretive Building, walk through the Daffodil Planting. This grove of daffodils is maintained in honor of the legacy of Carl and Mary Krippendorf, who planted daffodil and other bulbs. It's said that every visitor to this place left with a bulb in hand. After your hike, you'll surely leave with something, too—perhaps plans for your next visit.

Miles and Directions

0.0 Start from the Rowe Interpretive Center. Walk out the front doors and onto the Edge Trail, the first trail to the right.

0.1 Come to a fork before a footbridge. Take the right fork and cross the footbridge, then keep straight on the woodchip-covered trail, passing mowed side trails.

0.2 Come to another fork. Take a right and walk on the boardwalk over a small pond. Rejoin the main trail again in about 50 feet.

0.3 At Post 3, come to a junction. Walk straight to a boardwalk overlooking Powel Crosley Lake, and then return to this post.

0.4 Back at Post 3, take a right and begin the Whitetail Trace Trail.

0.6 Dead-end into a prairie at Post 29. Take a left and walk around the prairie's edge.

0.8 At a V junction marked by Post 30, take a left. Walk past a side trail on the left and continue to a boardwalk overlooking Spring Pond.

1.2 Come to a junction at Post 31. Take a right and ascend to a wooded ridge.

1.7 Take a left at Post 32.

1.9 Come to a T intersection at Post 4. Take a left.

2.0 Reach a fork at Post 5 and take a left. The trail narrows here.

2.1 Descend to a bench where the trail curves to the right and begins to parallel East Branch Avery Run. You'll come to a bridge. Don't cross the bridge but instead continue downstream on the same (north) side of the creek.

2.2 Walk past a side trail at Post 7. (**FYI:** In a few hundred feet look for somewhat obscured steps down to the water's edge, where you can view the shale and limestone banks.)

2.5 Come to a four-way intersection. Take a left and walk down the stone steps to the creek. Continue to parallel the creek downstream. The trail crosses the stream twice.

2.8 Hit a fork at Post 9. Take a left and walk past a bench. On the other side of the bench, make a sharp left turn onto the Fox Rock Trail. Cross the creek and begin ascending the wooden steps. **Option:** If a 0.2-mile walk straight up stairs is too much for you right now, take a right at the fork and bypass this spur.

3.0 There's a junction just before the gazebo. Take a right and descend the stairs to the boardwalk that takes you out to the rock outcropping and gives you a good view of the valley below.

3.2 Return the way you came to Post 9. Take a left and walk along the edge of the field and forest. You are now on the Wildflower Trail and will soon enter the mature forest.

3.5 Hit a junction at Post 12. Take a left and hop onto the Buckeye Trail.

3.7 Come to a junction at Post 13. Take a right. In about 200 feet come to Post 14, just in front of the Lotus Pond. Walk counterclockwise around the pond; just before returning to Post 14, take a right onto Crop Field Trail, which follows the edge of the woods.

4.0 Pass a side path that leads to the log cabin, and approach a T intersection at a sign for the Wildwood Center. Take a right. In about 75 feet come to another junction and take a left.

4.1 Reach a junction at Post 20. Take a left and begin the Woodland Trail in a nice forest. (**FYI:** Note the upland sycamore trees. Perhaps there's a spring around here.)

4.3 Come to a T intersection at Post 21. Take a left and begin the Lookout Trail by walking past a small pond.

4.6 The trail crosses Tealtown Road. On the other side of the road is a fork; take the left fork.

4.8 Cross a stream and come to Post 22. Take a left to follow a spur trail to an overlook.

4.9 Hit a T intersection and take a left.

5.0 Arrive at a gazebo and an overlook. After exploring this spot, turn around and head back. In about 250 feet reach a fork and take the left one.

5.1 Pass a side trail on the left and rejoin the main trail at a junction next to a bench. Take a left; in about 30 feet hit a T intersection (Post 23).

5.3 Reach a fork at Post 24 and take a left.

5.7 Come to a junction at Post 25 and continue straight. Pass a less than stunning overlook on the left.

6.1 Come to a junction at Post 27 and continue straight.

6.2 Return to Tealtown Road and the entrance road to the Cincinnati Nature Center/Rowe Woods. Walk across Tealtown Road and continue along the park road for about 50 feet. Take a left and enter the woods.

6.4 The trail comes out in a grassy clearing. Turn right and in about 20 feet the trail reenters the woods. In about 150 feet hit a fork at Post 28. Take a left.

6.5 Return to the Edge Trail at a T intersection. Take a right.

6.7 Finish back at the Rowe Interpretive Center.

Hike Information

Local information

Clermont County Convention and Visitors Bureau; (513) 732–3600; www.clermont cvb-ohio.com.
City of Milford; (513) 831–4192; www.milford ohio.org/.

Local events and attractions

The Spring into Nature Celebration is an annual spring event at Rowe Woods. Call (513) 248–9868 for more information.

Restaurants

Freeport Attractions, Milford; (513) 831–8464.
Everyday Cafe, Milford; (513) 248–1717.

Accommodations

East Fork State Park, Bethel; (513) 734–4323; www.ohiodnr.com/parks/park/ eastfork.htm.

Hike tours

Every Saturday morning there is a bird walk, rotating among the three Cincinnati Nature Center Sites.
Every second Saturday there's a nature hike at Rowe Woods.
Full-moon and old-growth hikes are offered; call the Rowe Interpretive Building for up-to-date information; (513) 831–1711.

Other resources

The Rowe Interpretive Building is home to the William Whitaker Memorial Library.

PASSENGER PIGEON (ECTOPISTES MIGRATORIUS)

Cincinnati, the state of Ohio, and much of the Eastern United States were home to one of the most tragic events in North American natural history. In the early to mid-1800s, passenger pigeon flocks were measured in *miles* and in *billions*. The flocks would reportedly darken the sky for hours, and a single arrow or gunshot skyward would guarantee a successful hunt. No one could have predicted that by September 1, 1914, the last passenger pigeon in the world, named Martha, would die at the Cincinnati Zoo.

How did this happen? Many factors contributed to the extinction of what had been one of the most abundant bird species in the world. The primary culprit, however, was unregulated overhunting. Passenger pigeons bred in colonies where a mating pair would both care for the single egg. Tens of thousands were killed at a time at their nesting sites. Also, since passenger pigeons did not always return to the same nesting place every year, most people didn't worry when they didn't see the birds each year, nor were they aware of how rapidly the numbers were declining. Captive breeding programs were generally unsuccessful, and soon the numbers of passenger pigeons fell below recoverable levels.

28 Barrett's Rim Trail

Highlands Nature Sanctuary

If you're looking for solitude, here's your trail. There is a daily limit of twelve hiking permits on this private preserve, and you need to call in advance to get yours. Highlands Nature Sanctuary is the result of dedicated individuals who have put their money where their mouths are. The result is a 1,200-acre (and growing) private preserve that's the beginning of a "wilderness east" vision for this part of southwest Ohio. Begin with the preserve's most outstanding trail, the 2.0-mile Barretts Rim Trail, which takes you along the rock-lined Rocky Fork Creek and through a sea of spring wildflowers, including some rare and endangered species. Then head out to the Big Beech Woods Trail to see something you may have thought didn't exist: unscarred virgin beech trees.

Start: From the trailhead pullout off Taloden Woods Campground access road
Distance: 2.0-mile loop
Approximate hiking time: 2 hours
Difficulty: Moderate due to some steep sections
Trail surface: Dirt trail that is faint at times
Blaze: Orange flags
Seasons: April is the best month for wildflowers
Other trail users: Hikers only
Canine compatibility: Dogs are not permitted.
Water: Available in the campground

Land status: Private sanctuary
Nearest town: Bainbridge
Fees and permits: Reserve the $12 per day wilderness hiking permit at least a week in advance.
Schedule: Open daily from 9:00 A.M. to 6:00 P.M.
Maps: Sanctuary maps; USGS quad: Rainsboro
Trail contacts: Highlands Nature Sanctuary, Bainbridge; (937) 365-1935; www.highlandssanctuary.org

Finding the trailhead: From U.S. Highway 50 west of Bainbridge, turn south onto Cave Road (there's a big billboard for 7 Caves) and travel 2.6 miles to the sanctuary entrance on the left, marked with a small sign. When you call ahead for a hiking permit, you will receive a gate code. Punch in the code, then drive through the gate and park next to the green office building on the right. *DeLorme: Ohio Atlas and Gazetteer:* Page 77 C6.

The Hike

Barrett's Rim has been called the jewel of the Rocky Fork Gorge. Indeed, it contains quite a few gems: a beautiful creek, towering limestone walls, and an abundance of wildflowers, including state endangered species. But perhaps the most outstanding feature this trail has to offer is solitude. Because of the daily permit limit, you are unlikely to see other hikers on the trails.

Jack-in-the-pulpit flowering at Highlands Nature Sanctuary.

Highlands Nature Sanctuary was established in 1995 when Larry and Nancy Henry bought forty-seven acres of land surrounding 7 Caves, a longtime area tourist attraction. They helped raise the money for the original purchase by distributing flyers to customers at their Columbus bakery. Today the sanctuary encompasses just under 1,200 acres. The money for land purchases came from donations and conservation easements. The Henrys have a vision of a "Wilderness East" that could grow as large as 50,000 acres. The goal is to buy the land and then stand back and watch what happens. Nearby lands that are already protected include Fort Hill State Memorial, Serpent Mound, Seip Mound, and Miller State Nature Preserve.

Highlands Nature Sanctuary is located where three distinct bioregions meet. Glacial plains lie to the west, the Western Allegheny Plateau rises to the east, and the Bluegrass Region sweeps up from the south. The bedrock here varies and shifts among limestone, sandstone, and shale, helping produce a high concentration of caves, springs, and sinkholes. These edge areas provide habitat for a large diversity of plant and animal species.

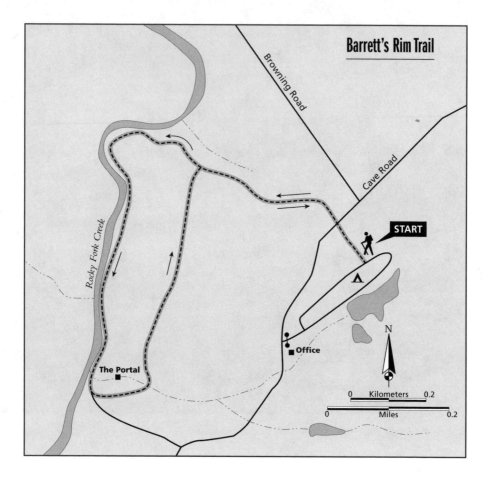

The sanctuary contains more than 12 miles of trails, including the Big Beech Loop Trail, which features virgin beech trees that have never been marked by graffiti. All trails are lined with small logs and marked with orange flags. Follow both of these cues closely; some former trails may look like the current trail, but they're not!

Begin the Barrett's Rim Trail from the Taloden Woods Campground. You will begin by walking through a young but nice-looking forest of tulip, cherry, beech, sassafras, hackberry, and ash trees, with the forest floor dominated by mayapples in spring. Understory trees and shrubs include pawpaws and spicebush. Descend gradually, soon paralleling Kellogg's Branch, an attractive rocky-bottomed stream to your right.

Then the trail switches back and forth, following closely along dolomite rock walls as you make your way down to Rocky Fork Creek. Growing out of these undisturbed rocks are showy flowers, including columbines and shooting stars in April and May. On the forest floor it's a riot of wildflowers in spring. These include snow trillium, a state endangered species, as well as large trillium, celandine poppy, solomon's seal, waterleaf, Dutchman's breeches, and wild geranium. The rare evergreen Canada yew also grows here.

The trail then continues between dolomite walls as tall as 40 feet to your left and the Rocky Fork Creek to your right. This relatively clean body of water supports a dozen freshwater clam species. Without the din of other visitors, you will find it easy to listen for the calls of thrushes and warblers.

The trail leaves the creekside and ascends the ridge, bringing you around to the top of the portal, where water rushes through a narrowly cut opening in the rock. Return on the trail above the gorge in a young maple-beech forest.

Miles and Directions

0.0 Start from the trailhead off the Taloden Woods Campground. The trailhead is marked with an orange flag. Walk along the mowed swath for about 20 feet and then cross Cave Road. Angle off to the left and pick up another orange flag across the road at an old driveway.

0.5 Come to a four-way intersection. To the right is Kellogg's Branch and a PRIVATE PROPERTY sign. Continue straight.

0.6 Descend by switchbacks to Rocky Fork Creek.

1.0 Cross a tributary to the Rocky Fork, using some stone steps. In about 100 feet reach a T intersection. Take a left, ascending an old road away from the creek for about 200 feet. The trail then veers off the road to the left, marked with orange flags.

1.5 Descend back to the four-way intersection. Take a right and return the way you came.

2.0 Finish at the trailhead.

Hike Information

Local information
Highland County Convention and Visitors Bureau; (937) 393-4883; www.highland county.com.

Local events and attractions
Fort Hill State Memorial, Hillsboro; (800) 283-8905; www.ohiohistory.org/places/fthill/.
Serpent Mound State Memorial, Peebles; (800) 752-2757; www.ohiohistory.org/places/serpent/index.html.

7 Caves, Bainbridge; (937) 365-1283; www.7caves.com.
The Dental Museum; (740) 634-2246; www.bainbridgedentalmuseum.com.

Accommodations
Highlands Nature Sanctuary runs a campground and two lodges; call (937) 365-1935.

Hike tours
Highlands Nature Sanctuary offers monthly guided hikes March through November.

29 Gorge to Fort Trail Loop

Fort Hill State Memorial

Fort Hill is the site of an ancient stone-and-earth embankment that encloses the top of the hill and was likely built by the prehistoric Hopewell Indians. But for a nature lover, this is a secondary attraction. Walk in a healthy, beautiful (and in places virgin) forest while skirting the edge of Baker Fork, an attractive rippling creek that has undercut the dolomite rock faces that line its edge. Spring wildflowers are incredible, especially when complemented by numerous rock features, including a natural bridge, and a cascading waterfall. Take a 4.0-mile loop that parallels Baker Fork and then climbs the hilltop enclosure.

Start: From the parking lot
Distance: 4.0-mile loop
Approximate hiking time: 2 hours
Difficulty: Moderate due to a lot of ups and downs
Trail surface: An up-and-down dirt path with some close drop-offs
Blaze: Gorge Trail, yellow disk; Fort Trail, red disk
Seasons: Best from mid-April through mid-October
Other trail users: Hikers only
Canine compatibility: Leashed dogs permitted
Water: Available at museum when open
Land status: State memorial
Nearest town: Hillsboro

Fees and permits: No fees or permits are required for hiking. Museum admission is $3.00 for adults and $1.50 for children ages 6 to 12.
Schedule: Trails are open dawn to dusk year-round. The museum is open Wednesday through Sunday, Memorial Day weekend through Labor Day, and weekends only through October.
Maps: State memorial brochure; USGS quad: Sinking Spring; Buckeye Trail Association Section map: Sinking Spring
Trail contacts: Fort Hill State Memorial, Hillsboro; (800) 283-8905; www.ohiohistory.org/places/fthill/

Finding the trailhead: From U.S. Highway 32 at Peebles, turn north on State Route 41 and drive 14.6 miles to Fort Hill Road. Turn left and drive 0.7 mile to the entrance on the left.

From State Route 50 east of Hillsboro, turn south on State Route 753 and drive 7.0 miles to SR 41. Turn right (south) onto SR 41 and continue 0.6 mile to Fort Hill Road. Turn right (west) and drive 0.7 mile to the entrance on the left.

From the entrance road, the museum is on the right and the parking lot is straight ahead, past the museum. ***DeLorme: Ohio Atlas and Gazetteer:*** Page 77 D5.

The Hike

Fort Hill State Memorial is a place rich in both archaeological and natural history. The name comes from the memorial's central feature, a prehistoric Native American hilltop enclosure that covers forty acres. All trails encircle Fort Hill, and the Fort Trail

The trail is constructed to go right through an old log cabin at Fort Hill State Memorial.

takes you over and into the ancient stone and earthen embankment, now largely overgrown but still recognizable. The wall ranges from 6 to 15 feet tall and is 40 feet wide at its base. Burrow pits within the enclosure may have been dug for wall materials, and they are now hilltop ponds. It's not certain who built Fort Hill and for what purposes, but it was possibly the Hopewell Indians (100 B.C. to A.D. 400), who are also credited with building nearby Serpent Mound.

To the nature lover, the forest itself is the main attraction. Ecologically, Fort Hill is an exceptionally biodiverse region, situated along the edge of the Appalachian Plateau where it meets the glaciated plains of central Ohio. Due to this edge topography, Fort Hill is home to some locally rare and endangered species, including Sullivantia and Canada yew—plants found here that normally grow only in more northern climes. They likely migrated south more than 12,000 years ago, keeping ahead of the advancing glaciers.

Begin on the Gorge Trail—which also serves as the Deer Trail, Buckeye Trail, and North Country Scenic Trail. These trails all eventually break off the Gorge Trail. One of the first things to notice is a healthy, mature forest. In fact, some sections of this forest are virgin or nearly so. When the chestnut blight came through in the first half of the twentieth century, American chestnut trees were cut and the wood was used to construct some of the buildings, shelter houses, and picnic tables still in use today. The forest canopy consists of large tulip, beech, and maple trees along the slopes and oaks and hickories on the ridgetop. Understory species include witch hazel, paw-paw, spicebush, and sourwood. On the forest floor there's no shortage of showy wild-flowers, including trillium, wild ginger, solomon's seal, wild yam, wild geranium, dwarf larkspur, celandine poppy, spiderwort, Canada violet, and wood sorrel, to name just a few. In springtime no other trail in the state is more beautiful.

More than half the Gorge Trail runs alongside Baker Fork, a beautiful, winding creek that has undercut the dolomite rocks along its banks. You will walk right along the water's edge and under recessed overhangs and then climb atop columbine-covered rocky overlooks on this up-and-down trail. The scenery is ever unfolding and fantastic, including views of cascading waterfalls and a natural bridge. There are a number of rocky overlooks along the trail. Footing can be dangerous at times, so walk with care and keep an eye on children. At one point the trail even walks right through an old log cabin.

▶ **The Hopewell were a prehistoric people, so we don't know what they called themselves. The name we use today for this culture comes from an 1893 excavation of twenty-eight mounds on Captain Mordecai Hopewell's Ross County farm.**

The trail eventually turns away from the creek and ascends about 400 feet to the top of Fort Hill, where you will join the Fort Trail. The bedrock changes from dolomite to shale and then sandstone. You will walk around the southern end of the fort and then over the embankment and into it. Look to your left for a long, distinctive embankment with occasional openings. After walking along the length of the fort, descend steeply to the parking lot, just a few hundred feet from where you began.

Miles and Directions

0.0 Start by picking up the trailhead on the far side of the small meadow between the parking lot and the museum. You will pass a trailhead sign and walk on a mowed path. The path forks; take the left fork, cross the stream and see another set of trailhead markers. Continue straight.

0.5 Come first to a sign and then a T intersection. The Deer Trail goes off to the right. Turn left to continue on the Gorge Trail. Ascend slightly and walk through a restored log cabin.

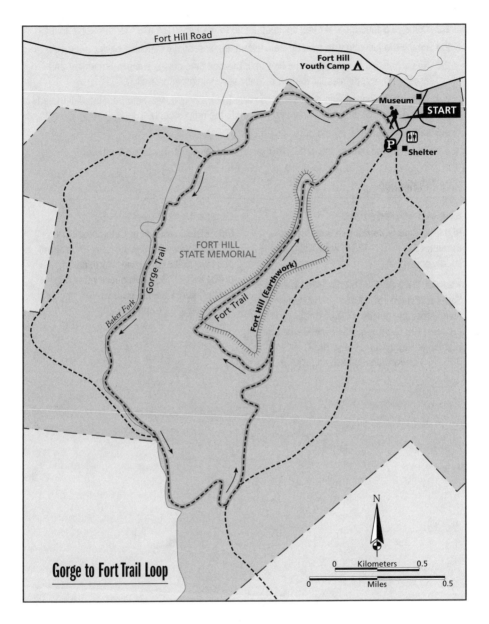

Gorge to Fort Trail Loop

1.3 Approach a sign that indicates the halfway point on the Gorge Trail. The Deer Trail comes in from the right and joins the Gorge Trail again. Turn left to continue on the Gorge Trail, following the sign.

1.7 Come to a T intersection. Take a left, following the sign for the Gorge Trail.

2.1 Ascend to a junction. Take a left to continue along the Gorge Trail toward Fort Hill. The Buckeye Trail turns off to the right.

2.2 Come to a fork. The Deer Trail splits off again to the right. Take a left for the Gorge Trail.

2.4 Reach the junction with the Fort Trail. Take a left, essentially switching back.

2.7 See a red sign to the left for the Fort Trail. The trail here curves sharply to the right and ascends the slope steeply. You are actually ascending the fort wall.

3.4 Come to a wooden sign that reads VIEWPOINT. There's only a view here from late fall to early spring. The trail turns right here and descends the ridge steeply.

3.5 Cross straight over an old access road.

4.0 Return to the parking lot, about 100 yards south of where you began the trail.

Hike Information

Local information

Highland County Convention and Visitors Bureau; (937) 393-4883; www.highland county.com.

Local events and attractions

Serpent Mound; (800) 752-2757; www. ohiohistory.org/places/serpent/index.html.
7 Caves; (937) 365-1283; www.7caves.com.
Highlands Nature Sanctuary; (937) 365-1935; www.highlandssanctuary.org.

Organizations

Ohio Historical Society, Columbus; (800) 297-2332; www.ohiohistory.org/index.html.
Buckeye Trail Association, Worthington; (800) 881-3062; www.buckeyetrail.org.
North Country Scenic Trail; www.northcountry trail.org/gts/index.htm.

30 Trail to Buzzardroost Rock

Edge of Appalachia Preserve

Atop Buzzardroost Rock, you're more than 300 feet above Ohio Brush Creek, with an expansive view of the creek valley and the ridges beyond. This 3.5-mile out-and-back hike is a prominent feature in this 13,000-acre preserve, home to globally rare species of plants and animals as well as cedar barrens or glades, miniprairies that have been carefully preserved by The Nature Conservancy.

Start: From the parking lot on Weaver Road
Distance: 3.5-mile out-and-back
Difficulty: Moderate due to elevation gain
Trail surface: Dirt
Blaze: None
Seasons: Best mid-April through mid-October
Other trail users: Hikers only
Canine compatibility: Leashed dogs permitted
Water: None available; bring your own
Land status: Private preserve
Nearest Towns: West Union and Lynx

Fees and permits: No fees or permits required
Schedule: Open daily sunrise to sunset
Maps: USGS quad: Lynx; Maptech Terrain Navigator: Ohio Columbus/Cincinnati/Southwest
Trail contacts: The Nature Conservancy Ohio Chapter, Dublin; (614) 717-2770; nature.org/wherewework/northamerica/states/ohio/.
Edge of Appalachia Preserve, Lynx; (513) 544-2880.

Finding the trailhead: From State Route 125 in West Union, travel east on SR 125 for 6.7 miles to the second junction with Weaver Road. Turn left (north) and cut back 0.1 mile to a small gravel parking lot on the left. *DeLorme: Ohio Atlas and Gazetteer:* Page 84 B1.

The Hike

The view from Buzzardroost Rock is the hiker's reward for more than 1.7 miles of hiking up, up, up. Atop the overlook, take a few minutes to notice what makes this place unique—not only to Ohio but also to the world. You are standing in the middle of the Interior Low Plateau/Blugrass ecoregion of Ohio, which shoots up from Kentucky into only Adams and parts of Brown and Highland Counties. You may have already noticed that the hills are taller and steeper here than elsewhere in the state. This ecoregion is also characterized by barrens and glades, which are small patches (up to ten acres) of prairie communities. These miniprairies are found in only a few places in the U.S. Midwest and are globally rare.

The Edge of Appalachia Preserve, operated by The Nature Conservancy and the Cincinnati Museum Center, is home to more than 135 species of rare plants and animals. Well-known Ohio ecologist E. Lucy Braun first studied this area in the 1920s and took note of its ecological significance, particularly the remnant prairie plant species found along edge areas with calcium-rich dolomite as a bedrock. Globally rare plant species include ear-leafed foxglove and juniper sedge. Endangered animals

The rewarding view from atop Buzzardroost Rock overlooks the Brush Creek Valley.

found here include green salamanders and eastern woodrats. The biodiversity of this preserve is largely a result of diverse underlying bedrock, which includes two types of shale (Estill and Ohio Black) and two types of dolomite (Lilly Bisher and Peebles).

Begin the hike by walking down from the parking lot through some trees and crossing OH 125. Just past the road, look to the left of the trail to see a big patch of lily of the valley and, back farther, wisteria, which is evidence of an old homesite. The shale bedrock supports a mixed mesophytic forest, and the understory is full of pawpaw and spicebush. Cross the stream over a footbridge and sign in at the trail register. As you continue hiking, look on the forest floor for a wide variety of plant species, including bloodroot, hepatica, black cohosh, twinleaf, hog peanut, trillium, and wild ginger.

Soon you will notice a change as you walk through a somewhat barren spot of nutrient-poor Estill shales dotted with naturally occurring cedar trees. Continue hiking up the slope and notice more changes in your surroundings: Dolomite cliffs jut out of the hillside in an Appalachian oak forest. Stairs and switchbacks help you to the top of the steep slope, while mayapple and Virginia creeper are underfoot. At the top of the ridge, the trail curves sharply to the right, joining an old doubletrack road.

The anticipation mounts as you approach Buzzardroost Rock, because you can see that a good view is likely coming up. From the rock outcrop take in the valley and farmland below as well as the ridges folding into the distance. Look around closely. Cedar and redbud trees grow out of the dolomite rock outcropping, as do showy columbine flowers and the state-endangered great-plains muhlenbergia grass. Below, look upon a forest dominated by chinquapin oak. On the ridge above is chestnut oak, whose leaves are reminiscent of the bygone American chestnut. Across the valley, see

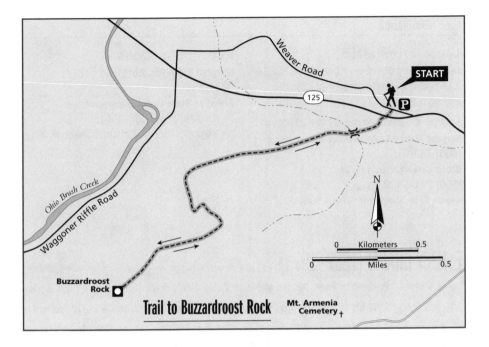

Trail to Buzzardroost Rock

slopes covered in deciduous trees with the occasional patch of cedar. Overhead, you are sure to see the buzzards for which this rock is named. More often called turkey vultures in these parts, these large black birds sport a distinctive dihedral wingspan.

Buzzardroost Rock, Wilderness Trail, and Lynx Prairie are the three public access points in the preserve. Everywhere else in this 13,000-acre protected area is accessible by permission only. The Nature Conservancy made the first land purchase here in 1959, and since then the holdings have grown to eleven preserves along 12 miles of the Ohio Brush Creek, making this one of the largest private nature preserves in the East. Portions of the preserve are registered National Natural Landmarks, including Buzzardroost Rock. Threats to the plant communities here include forests encroaching upon the grasslands, invasive exotic species, poaching, and illegal off-road-vehicle use. Contact the preserve for volunteer information if you're interested in helping maintain the ecological integrity of the protected area.

Miles and Directions

0.0 Start from the parking lot. Walk down the stone steps onto the trail. Walk downhill, past the trailhead sign. In about 200 feet cross Route SR 125.

0.2 Cross a footbridge and sign in at the trail register.

1.1 At the top of the ridge, the trail curves sharply right, joining an old doubletrack road.

1.8 Reach Buzzardroost Rock overlook.

3.5 Return the way you came to the parking lot.

Hike Information

Local information

Adams County Chamber of Commerce; (888) 223-5454; www.adamscountyohchamber.org/main.htm.

Local events and attractions

Serpent Mound State Memorial, Peebles; (800) 752-2757.
Brush Creek Excursions, West Union; (800) 941-5400.
Adams Lake State Park; (740) 858-6652.

Accommodations

Murphin Ridge Inn, West Union; (877) 687-7446.
Shawnee State Park campground, West Portsmouth; (740) 858-4561; www.ohiodnr.com/parks/parks/shawnee.htm.

E. LUCY BRAUN (1889-1971)

E. Lucy Braun reportedly logged 65,000 miles hiking, but this is not her claim to fame. Rather, she is probably Ohio's most accomplished plant ecologist. Braun spent her life in Cincinnati, growing up the daughter of schoolteachers. She earned a Ph.D. in botany in 1914 from the University of Cincinnati and went on to become a full professor of plant ecology at her alma mater. She was a prolific researcher and writer, with 180 works to her credit. Her seminal piece is *Deciduous Forests of Eastern North America,* published in 1950. *The Woody Plants of Ohio* (1961) is used today as a textbook for aspiring plant ecologists.

Braun was the first woman president of the Ohio Academy of Science and the Ecological Society of America. Her work went beyond studying single plant species to studying the ecology of entire regions. Her research led her to identify some of the forests found in southeast Ohio and elsewhere in the Appalachian region as "mixed mesophytic." In a mixed mesophytic forest, twenty to twenty-five tree species are common, such as oak, hickory, tulip, buckeye, and maple, but no single species dominates the canopy. Most commonly found on north- and east-facing slopes, mixed mesophytic forests are also identified as highly biodiverse, made up of thousands of species of plant and animal life.

Devoted to conservation, Braun is credited with helping to preserve more than 10,000 acres of Ohio land. Two of her students, Richard and Lucile Durrell, helped lead the effort to create the Edge of Appalachia Preserve.

Lucy Braun was often accompanied by her sister, Annette, an entomologist. Old photos show the two women in the field wearing full-length skirts, as expected of them during the early years of the twentieth century.

31 Lynx Prairie Loop
Edge of Appalachia Preserve

Get out your wildflower guide and head to Lynx Prairie for a one-of-a-kind hiking adventure in Ohio. This is The Nature Conservancy's oldest Ohio preserve, acquired in an effort to protect the rare glades, or miniprairies, that naturally occur in this thin-soiled landscape that sits atop dolomite bedrock and is home to deciduous and cedar forests. The 1.5-mile loop trail takes you through several of these beautiful glades, which are at their flowering peak between late July and September.

Start: From the East Libety Church cementery
Distance: 1.5-mile loop
Approximate hiking time: 1hour
Difficulty: Easy; short and flat
Seasons: Praire flowers peak late July through September
Trail surface: Dirt and grass
Blaze: None, all junctions are marked
Other trail users: Hikers only
Canine compatibility: Leashed dogs permited
Water: There is no potable water available along he hike; bring your own.

Land status: Private preserve owned by The Nature Conservancy and Cincinnati Museum Center
Nearest town: West Union
Fees and permits: No fees or permits required
Schedule: Open daily sunrise to sunset
Maps: USGS quad: Lynx; Maptech Terrain Navigator: Ohio/Cincinnati/Southwest
Trail contacts: Edge of Applachia Preserve, West Union; (937) 544-2880 or (937) 544-2188; nature.org/wherewework/northamerica/states/ohio/

Finding the trailhead: From West Union, take State Route 125 for 7.8 miles to Tulip Road in the sparsely populated town of Lynx. Turn south (right) and drive 1.0 mile to the East Liberty Church driveway on the left. Pass the church and drive through the cemetery to a white fence. Facing the fence, turn right and walk to the tree line. When you hit the tree line, turn right and walk along its edge to the trailhead, marked with a green metal sign. *DeLorme: Ohio Atlas and Gazetteer:* Page 84 B1.

The Hike

Located in the small Bluegrass region of Ohio, the main feature at Lynx Prairie is the presence of small prairie openings in the forest that are less than ten acres in size. In late summer expect to see countless prairie flowers blooming here, including echinacea (purple coneflower), yellow coneflower, brown-eyed Susan, blazing star (*Liatris*), rattlesnake master, lobelias, butterfly weed, and prairie dock. Even more dominant are the many grass species that grow here, such as big and little bluestem, Indian grass, and side-oats grama grass. These are tough plants that can thrive on thin soil and can weather drought conditions, using their deep roots and narrow leaves to adapt.

Begin by walking in a forest of oak and hickory as well as Virginia pine and cedar. The hike winds through forest and about a half dozen picturesque prairies.

One of several miniprairies open the canopy at Lynx Prairie.

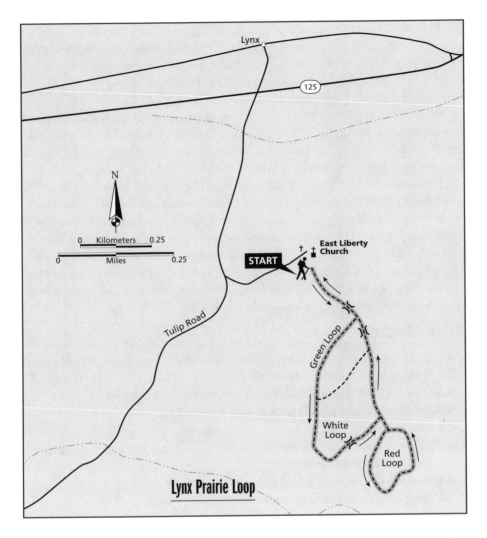

Lynx Prairie Loop

These prairies are also known as cedar barrens due to the high presence of cedar trees, which also do well on the thin soil atop the dolomite bedrock. And these are the real thing—the prairies of Lynx Prairie are native remnants of what the land looked like hundreds of years ago when Europeans arrived, and probably long before that. You can really sense the wildness of this place when you're in it.

Although no one is certain how these prairies originated or continued to thrive, it's most likely that they were established after the Wisconsinan Glacier retreated about 12,000 years ago. Any number of natural "disturbances" probably occurred in the forest—fire, tree blowdowns, erosion—and prairie species moved in. Scientists theorize that human disturbances helped maintain the prairies. Native Americans are known to have managed the landscape with fire. Old photos from the 1930s, as well as fence wire, show that Lynx Prairie was more recently a farm.

Today the Nature Conservancy manages these miniprairies through a combination of burning and cutting, which keeps the forest from encroaching. Because most of their plant mass is in the root system, prairie species not only withstand fire but flourish in its presence. Most prairie species are long-lived perennials that can do well even if they don't reproduce every year.

As you hike, also look for the presence of many insects. Bees, beetles, flies, and other insects are important in the pollination process. Ants loosen the soil, while grasshoppers become meals for animals further up the food chain. It's likely you'll also glimpse larger animals, such as white-tailed deer, while you're here.

This significant parcel was the first project of The Nature Conservancy in Ohio, purchased in 1959 and named a National Natural Landmark in 1967. Lynx Prairie is one of three areas open to the public in the Edge of Appalachia Preserve, which is operated by both TNC and the Cincinnati Museum Center. You might want to combine a hike here with a hike at nearby Buzzardroost Rock. The entire preserve, encompassing 13,000 acres, is home to more than 135 rare plants and animals. Most areas in the preserve are accessible only by permission or through hikes and educational programs offered through the museum or TNC.

Miles and Directions

0.0 Start at the trailhead on the south side of the East Liberty Church cemetery. Walk past the fence and begin on the well-defined trail.

0.2 Come to a fork and the trail register. Begin the Green Loop and take a right.

0.3 Come to a junction. Continue straight to begin the White Loop.

0.5 Arrive at a T intersection. Turn left.

0.6 Hit another T intersection with the Red Loop. Take a right. In about 30 feet the trail forks. Take a right and begin the Red Loop.

0.9 Come to a fork next to the stream. Take a right and cross the stream.

1.0 Return to the junction where you began the Red Trail. Go straight.

1.2 After walking over a boardwalk, come to a junction marked with a post. Continue straight, now back on the Green Loop.

1.3 Hit a fork at the original trail register junction. Take a right.

1.5 Return to the trailhead.

Hike Information

Local information
Adams County Chamber of Commerce; (888) 223-5454; www.adamscountyohchamber. org/main.htm.

Local events and attractions
Serpent Mound State Memorial, Peebles; (800) 752-2757.

Brush Creek Excursions, West Union; (800) 941-5400.

Adams Lake State Park, West Union; (740) 858-6652.

Accommodations
Murphin Ridge Inn, West Union; (877) 687-7446.

Shawnee State Park campground, West Portsmouth; (740) 858-4561; www.ohiodnr.com/parks/parks/shawnee.htm.

32 Day Hike Trail

Shawnee State Forest

Within the 60-mile backpack loop in Shawnee State Forest lies a 7.4-mile loop that's a perfect day hike option. Here in the "Little Smokies" of Ohio, ascend steeply to ridgetops of oak-hickory forest and then walk in cool beech-maple hollows. If you're lucky, you might see the overly harvested ginseng on the forest floor or even the elusive timber rattlesnake. Spring wildflowers and fall foliage draw hikers and photographers from all over the state.

Start: From the East Turkey Lake boat ramp parking lot
Distance: 7.2-mile loop
Difficulty: Moderate to diffcult due to lenght and steep ascents and descents over the ridges
Trail surface: This dirt footpath is narrow but clear; footing can be difficult when walking straight up and down the ridges
Blaze: Blue
Seasons: Best in spring, when the water is flowing and wildflowerss are abundant
Other trail users: Hunters (in season) and equestrains on one portion of the trail
Canine compatibility: Leashed dogs permited

Water: Available at the nature center and at Camp 3
Land status: State forest
Nearest town: Portsmount
Fees and permits: No fees or permits required. For backpacking, self-register at the backpack trail trailhead.
Schedule: Open daily from 6:00 A.M. to 11:00 P.M.
Maps: USGS quad: Pond Run; Maptech Terrain Navigator: Ohio/Southeast
Trail contacts: Shawnee State Forest, West Portsmouth; (740) 858-6685; www.ohionr.com/forestry/Forests/state forests/shawnee.htm

Finding the trailhead: From U.S. Highway 23 in Portsmouth, take State Route 52 west 6.6 miles to State Route 125 (past the state forest headquarters). Turn west (right) onto SR 125 and drive 5.8 miles to the boat ramp and nature center parking lot on the left. *DeLorme: Ohio Atlas and Gazetteer:* Page 84 C3.

The Hike

Shawnee State Forest is often called the Little Smokies of Ohio, in reference to the area's steep hills and narrow hollows. This 63,000-acre forest is by far the state's largest, and when you get an opportunity to peer into the distance, you will see gently undulating ridges unfold as far as the eye can see. Then when you get into the forest to explore it on foot, you'll soon recognize the biodiversity that this geography supports.

Hundreds of millions of years ago, an uplift created the Appalachian or Western Allegheny Plateau. In the time since, water has carved out the resulting landscape. Drainages flow into streams and creeks, and they all make their way to the mighty

Ohio River, which borders Shawnee State Forest to the south. Across the way is Kentucky and more ridges unfolding into the distance.

Just east of the forest is the confluence of the Scioto and Ohio Rivers. Archaic Native Americans inhabited this fertile and accessible spot as far back as 15,000 years ago. By the time Europeans arrived, the Shawnee Indians lived here, hence the name of the state forest. This land was hotly contested in the eighteenth century as the Shawnees defended Lower Town and other settlements and hunting grounds in the Ohio River Valley. But soon enough the Shawnees were driven out.

In 1922 the state of Ohio purchased 5,000 acres of abused land and opened the Theodore Roosevelt State Game Preserve. In the 1930s the Civilian Conservation Corps (CCC) set up six work camps, and young men built roads and lakes in the forest. Over the years, more acreage was acquired. Land oversight changed hands, but it stayed in state ownership—today as Shawnee State Forest and Shawnee State Park. Between state forest and state park lands, more than 60 miles of hiking trails exist for just about any hiking taste. The Shawnee State Forest Day Hike is a good 7.2-mile loop that takes you through much of what this landscape has to show.

Start at Turkey Lake, one of five human-made lakes in the forest (the Turkey Lake earthen dam was built in the 1960s, not by the CCC). From here you'll get your best views along the trail of the surrounding ridges. Enter the forest and begin walking up Williamson Hollow. Almost immediately you'll come upon a large beaver pond. The trail skirts around the beaver pond and then crosses the first of several drainages. Cross this drainage and shortly find yourself ascending a ridge. On this section of trail, look to your right for what looks to be a Native American signal tree. This oak, a couple of hundred years old, was bent horizontally and then allowed to grow straight up from there. Signal trees served as directional markers on long-distance Native American trails, and quite a few remain standing today.

As you'll soon find out, the trail doesn't cross over the ridges too often—but when it does, it goes straight up and then straight down. Be careful, especially when descending the ridges; erosion is a problem, and footing can be sketchy. As you ascend to the drier ridgetops, especially on south-facing slopes, note the forest makeup. Oak and hickory as well as native pitch and shortleaf pines (look for three needles per fascicle) are well adapted here. On the forest floor, look for blueberry bushes. Once you've ascended the ridge and descended back to the stream, especially on north-facing slopes, note how the forest makeup changes. Maple, beech, sycamore, ash, elm, hemlock, and even magnolia trees thrive here. Wildflowers are abundant, and goldenseal is growing everywhere. You'll be lucky to spot ginseng, another medicinal plant, since it has been so heavily poached on the Shawnee State Forest.

◀ *Could this be a Native American signal tree? No one knows for sure, but it's speculated that saplings were bent to serve as directional markers.*

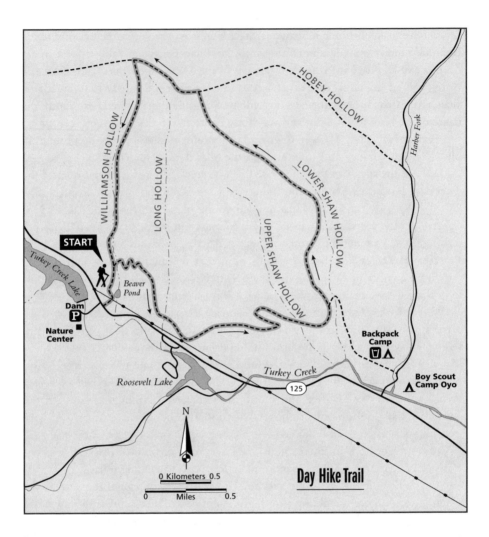

As you cross the rocky streambeds and drainages, turn over a few stones and look for fossils. Reptiles and amphibians are also well represented here, including the endangered timber rattlesnake. (You're probably less likely to see one of these than you are to see ginseng.) Common forest animals such as beaver, fox, white-tailed deer, and turkey are present, and occasional sightings of bobcat and black bear have been reported.

Walk along the sandy ridgetop trail shared with horses before making a final push toward the trailhead on a west-facing slope. Look here for numerous stump sprouts of the American chestnut. These small trees will succumb to the chestnut blight before they hit maturity. After descending to the streambed, walk through a young, dense stand of tulip poplar. This is an example of what the Division of Forestry calls "even-aged management"—otherwise known as a former clearcut. Past that, look for an old sandstone chimney, evidence of a former homestead.

You can make this loop into an overnighter by staying in Camp 3. If you're ready for more miles, even days, hit the 40-mile Shawnee Backpack Trail. Try the south loop first—and come back in fifty years to hike the Wilderness Side Trail when the forest has had a chance to mature undisturbed. Shawnee State Park offers a few shorter day hikes. The best view of Ohio's Little Smokies can be found from the aptly named Lookout Trail.

Miles and Directions:

0.0 Start from the Turkey Lake boat ramp parking lot. Follow the driveway back to SR 125 and cross the road, looking for the wooden trailhead sign. (**FYI:** The trailhead sign says this is a 6.5-mile trail; it's actually longer than that.)

0.2 Come to a junction where the trail turns off to the left. Straight ahead is the beaver pond.

0.5 Hit a fork near the creekbed. Take a right to begin the loop, following the sign for the Day Hike Trail. Soon you will ascend the ridge.

1.5 Descend the ridge to Long Hollow Run. Cross the stream and partially ascend the ridge before coming to a T intersection with the power line right-of-way. Take a left and in about 15 feet reach a junction with an informal side trail. Take a left, pass the power line pole on your right, and ascend the ridge.

2.6 Come to a fork, where the trail splits to go around a fallen beech tree. The right fork is easier. Then cross Upper Shaw Hollow Run and partially ascend the ridge.

3.1 Descend to Lower Shaw Hollow Run and hit a junction. The Day Hike Trail turns left and is marked with a sign. Straight ahead is a side trail to Camp 3 and a potable water source. **Option:** Walk through a hemlock forest to the water and back for about a 1.0-mile round trip.

4.8 Hit a T intersection with a bridle trail. Take a left and follow the ridgetop.

5.6 Come to a junction. Take a left and descend from the ridge to continue on the Day Hike Trail. Straight ahead, the bridle trail continues.

6.8 Arrive back at the first junction where you started the Day Hike Trail loop. Go right.

7.1 Return to the first junction of the trail, near the beaver pond. Take a right.

7.2 Return to SR 125 and the trailhead.

Hike Information

Local information

Portsmouth Area Convention and Visitors Bureau, Portsmouth; (740) 353-1116 or (800) 648-2574; www.portsmouthcvb.org/.

Local events and attractions

Shawnee State Park hosts a Trout Derby the last weekend in April and a Fall Foliage Weekend the third weekend in October. Contact the park for more information at (740) 858-6652.

Check out the **floodwall murals** in Portsmouth, which give a pictoral history of the area.

The Nature Conservancy's Edge of Appalachia Preserve is just west of Shawnee State Forest, in Adams County; (513) 544-2880; nature.org/wherewework/northamerica/states/ohio/.

Accommodations

Shawnee State Park campground; (740) 858-4561.

Shawnee State Park Lodge; (800) 282-7275.

Restaurants

Shawnee State Park Lodge; (740) 858-6621.

Organizations

Buckeye Trail Association, Worthington; (800) 881-3062; www.buckeyetrail.org.

MEDICINAL PLANTS

Even in our technological age, most medicines are still derived from plants before they're copied in the laboratory. Most plants have medicinal characteristics, some more than others. Goldenseal, which grows abundantly in Shawnee State Forest, is used topically as an antibacterial and to treat inflammation. Ginseng, which once grew abundantly in Shawnee State Forest, is used as a general tonic. Wild ginseng is more lucrative than its domesticated relative, selling for as much as $500 a pound. Until recently there was a ginseng season in the Shawnee, but overcollection and poaching have led the forest to ban its collection altogether.

Southwest Ohio Honorable Mentions

○ Brukner Nature Center Trails

If you go for a hike at Brukner Nature Center, you're guaranteed to see a fox, a bald eagle, a great horned owl, or a bobcat. Okay, so maybe it's cheating to view them at the Wildlife Rehabilitation Unit, but these animals are Ohio natives, and some of them live in the forest surrounding the rehab unit as well. Brukner Nature Center is a nonprofit, privately funded preserve with a mission to provide environmental education and wildlife rehabilitation. Combine the outer loop of trails at the preserve to make a 4.3-mile hike that takes you through pine forests, along an oak-hickory ridgetop, and into the Stillwater River Valley. Hang around the interpretive building where you can check out exhibits, the animal rehab unit, a nineteenth-century log home, a totem pole, and an amphitheater around a small pond.

Trail contacts: Brukner Nature Center, Troy; (937) 698–6493; www.tdn-net.com/brukner/.

Finding the trailhead: From I–75 in Troy, turn west onto State Route 55 (exit 73) and drive 2.4 miles to Horseshoe Bend Road. Take a right and drive 2.2 miles to the preserve entrance on the right. Continue all the way to the end of the driveway at the interpretive building parking lot. *DeLorme: Ohio Atlas and Gazetteer:* Page 55 D5.

P Green Trail, Englewood MetroPark

Check out the Green Trail in the East Park section of Englewood MetroPark. Located along the Stillwater River, this park is just a quick trip from downtown Dayton. The 3.0-mile Green Trail features three small waterfalls and a boardwalk through a swamp forest that contains uncommon pumpkin ash trees. Part of the trail follows the Old National Road, constructed for westward expansion after the War of 1812. The South Park section of Englewood is home to the popular Aullwood Audubon Center and Aullwood Garden.

Trail contacts: Five Rivers MetroParks, Dayton; (937) 275–PARK; www.metroparks.org.

Finding the trailhead: From the junction of I–70 and I–75, travel west on I–70 4.5 miles to State Route 48 (exit 29). Drive north on SR 48 for 0.7 mile to U.S. Highway 40 East. Turn right and travel east over the Englewood Dam. Just on the other side of the dam turn left (north) onto ER–1, identified with a MetroPark sign. Across the road is a sign for Aullwood Center. Drive 0.4 mile to a junction. Turn right and drive 0.6 mile to a second junction, where the road curves sharply to the right. Park at the Patty Picnic Shelter. *DeLorme: Ohio Atlas and Gazetteer:* Page 65 A5.

Q Orange Trail, Germantown MetroPark

The 6.8-mile trail that makes a loop around Twin Creek may be Ohio's best-smelling hike. Walk through a mature red cedar forest on the east side of the creek. The cedars are just one example of how Germantown MetroPark is a living example of the process of succession. The property was farmland when the MetroParks purchased it (surrounding land still is in cultivation) and began restoring some of the small native prairies that once existed in western Ohio's landscape. Cedar trees are "pioneer" species that do well on tapped-out soil and are the first trees to grow here. Prairie meets cedar meets deciduous forest, which replaces the cedars as the "climax" plant community. Begin at the nice new visitor center.

Trail contacts: Germantown MetroPark Nature Center; (937) 855–7717; www.metroparks.org.

Finding the trailhead: From I–75 south of Dayton, exit onto State Route 725 West and drive 11.6 miles to Boomershine Road. Turn north (right) and drive 1.0 mile to the park entrance on the right (GM–6). From the park road take the first right to the parking lot at the nature center. *DeLorme: Ohio Atlas and Gazetteer:* Page 65 C4.

R Little Turtle and Blue Jacket Trails, Shawnee Lookout Park

Combine the Little Turtle and Blue Jacket Trails for a 3.3-mile hike to overlooks of the Great Miami and Ohio Rivers. The trails are named after two Native American war chiefs who fought against American federal troops in eighteenth-century battles over the Ohio Valley territories; Little Turtle was a Miami Indian and Blue Jacket was a Shawnee. Human history at this spot dates back a lot further, however, to 15,000 years ago. The hilltop fort and the mounds found here have been thoroughly excavated by archaeologists who have turned up countless artifacts, including arrowheads, tools, tablets with petroglyphs, jewelry, and mortars and pestils.

Trail Contacts: Hamilton County Park District, Cincinnati, OH (513) 941–0120, www.greatparks.org.

Finding the Trailhead: From State Route 50 in Elizabethtown, turn south onto Lawrenceburg Road and drive 0.7 mile to a T intersection. Turn right (west), still on Lawrenceburg Road, and drive 1.5 miles to the park entrance on the left, marked with a sign. Drive 0.7 mile to the trailhead parking on the right for both the Blue Jacket and Little Turtle Trails. *DeLorme: Ohio Atlas and Gazetteer:* Page 74 C1.

S Davis Memorial State Nature Preserve Trails

If you like Fort Hill State Memorial, stop by Davis Memorial, which offers a pleasant 2.5-mile hike, most of which parallels the attractive Cedar Fork Creek. Interpretive signs help you enjoy the hike all the more while you view the rare Sullivantia growing directly out of the Dolomite cliffs, a geologic fault line in the creekbed, and a rich mixed mesophytic forest with excellent spring wildflowers. The statewide Buckeye Trail serves as a connector trail for two small loops on either end.

Trail Contacts: Davis Memorial State Nature Preserve, Peebles; (937) 544–9750; www.ohiodnr.com/location/davis.htm.

Finding the Trailhead: From State Route 32 on the east side of Peebles, turn south onto Steam Furnace Road and travel 0.4 mile to Davis Memorial Road (Township Road 129). Turn east (left) and travel 2.8 miles to the parking lot on the right. *DeLorme: Ohio Atlas and Gazetteer:* Page 84 A2.

OHIO'S LEGENDARY SHAWNEE LEADERS

In the decades leading up to the American Revolution, European-American explorers, trappers, and then settlers made substantial inroads into the territory north of the Ohio River. At the time a handful of Native American nations called this region home or used it for hunting grounds. Clashes soon grew violent between the Native Americans and the homesteaders. The place names we're left with today—Chillicothe, Defiance, Shawnee Lookout—reflect these war-torn times. Many capable leaders emerged on both sides, and two of the most legendary were Shawnees Blue Jacket and Tecumseh.

Blue Jacket was born around 1743 and grew up in a time of treaties ceding the Ohio lands to American and British rule, broken promises, skirmishes, and still more suspect treaties. His origins are a point of contention: Although he is widely known as a white man who grew up a Shawnee, his descendants contradict this claim and maintain that Blue Jacket was born a Shawnee. He was an important player in the defeat of U.S. forces in battles with General Josiah Harmar in 1790 and Arthur St. Clair in 1791 (St. Clair would later become Ohio's first governor). In 1794 Blue Jacket was the leading war chief at the Battle of Fallen Timbers in northwest Ohio, where his forces were defeated by those of General "Mad" Anthony Wayne. This defeat was the beginning of the end for Ohio's Native Americans. Also present at that battle was a young Shawnee warrior named Tecumseh.

Tecumseh means "panther crossing the sky" and refers to the accounts of his birth in 1768: When the Shawnee chief's wife gave birth to this future legend, a shooting star crossed the sky with such brightness and longevity that people were called out of their homes to see it. Tecumseh grew into something of a golden boy, with outstanding skills in hunting, warfare, leadership, and prophecy. His brother, Tenskatawa, was known as "the prophet," but it may have actually been Tecumseh's predictions that Tenskatawa put forth. Tecumseh became best known as an advocate of unity among the many Native American tribes so that they could build a force strong enough to defeat the increasingly invasive federal army. He traveled far and wide to drum up support for this massive effort, while his support back home waned, especially after William Henry Harrison's troops destroyed Prophet's Town while Tecumseh was away.

To close friends, Tecumseh predicted his own death in the Battle of Thames in Ontario, Canada. He reportedly went into battle in disguise in an effort to avoid having his dead body mutilated by American troops. Tecumseh was killed in the battle, but it's unclear whether his body was mutilated, as the American version goes, or if his body was taken away by Shawnees and buried, perhaps in Clark County, as the Shawnee version tells it.

Southeast Ohio

The least populated and least trampled part of Ohio is the southeast. This is also the most rugged section of the state, with narrow hollows and steep ridges supporting a mostly forested landscape. The Ohio River serves as a geographical as well as political boundary on one side. As the region bleeds north and west, the other boundary is also clear to the eye: The edge of the Appalachian Plateau gives way to the glacier-flattened landscape that most of Ohio is known for.

The forests here are very biodiverse. Oak-hickory forests dominate the ridgetops, although maple and beech are well represented in the lowlands. Mixed mesophytic forests are common to southeast Ohio, where a large number of tree species are common, but no single species dominates the canopy. Dysart Woods, Ohio's largest tract of virgin forest, is located here.

Southeast Ohio was home to Native Americans as far back as 15,000 years ago, evidenced by Adena mounds that occasionally dot the landscape. This region was primarily used as hunting grounds for Shawnee Indians when Europeans arrived, and great clashes ensued between Native Americans and European settlers during much of the eighteenth century.

As Native Americans were driven out and settlers proceeded west of the Appalachian Mountains, Ohio River cities served as gateways. Marietta, Ohio's first city, was one of these. Resource-based communities popped up around timber and coal mining operations. Today many of these are ghost towns or shadows of their former selves. The "Hanging Rock" region of southeast Ohio provided much of the growing nation's iron, extracted from sandstone and smelted onsite, using wood-fired blast furnaces. By the turn of the twentieth century, southeast Ohio's landscape was denuded.

In the 1930s the Wayne National Forest began acquiring land, and the Depression-era Civilian Conservation Corps (CCC) began work in earnest. They planted trees and built roads, dams, and many of the shelters and buildings still in use today. The Wayne National Forest has a somewhat unusual configuration in that it is divided into three noncontiguous districts—Athens, Marietta, and Ironton. The Wayne, like all national forests, is a multiple-use public land where timbering and gas development occur, but hiking is accessible in all districts. The Ironton District contains the Vesuvius Recreation Area, where hiking and other outdoor sports do not share space with extraction, hunting, or other activities allowed elsewhere in the Wayne.

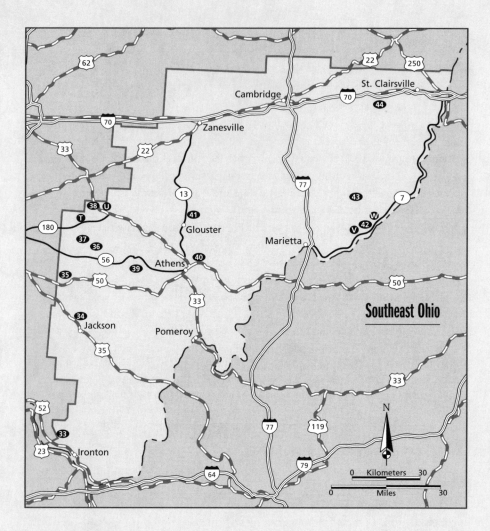

Southeast Ohio

Ohio's state forests are concentrated in the southeast as well. These are also multiple-use lands managed largely for timber, but they also afford ample hiking opportunities. Between national and state forest lands, a number of lengthy day hikes and backpacking options are available.

Some of Ohio's most popular state parks are here in the southeast region. Hocking Hills State Park is home to such well-known attractions as Old Man's Cave, Cedar Falls, and Ash Cave. Burr Oak State Park hosts a lodge and nearly 50 miles of hiking trails in the park and surrounding national forest. Many state parks are anchored by salamander-shaped lakes. No natural lakes exist in this Appalachian Plateau region, so dammed reservoirs take on the shape of the hollows they fill.

33 Lake Vesuvius Lakeshore Trail

Wayne National Forest—Ironton District

Take the 7.4-mile Lake Vesuvius Lakeshore Trail all the way around the reservoir, beginning and ending at the Vesuvius Furnace. This sandstone blast furnace was used to smelt iron ore in the nineteenth and early twentieth centuries. Walk in a deciduous forest along the shore, with water on one side of you and rock outcroppings on the other side. Look for a good lunch spot overlooking the lake, and jump in when it gets hot.

Start: From the parking lot at the dam, across from the iron furnace
Distance: 7.4-mile loop
Approximate hiking time: 3 to 5 hours
Difficulty: Moderate due to length
Trail surface: Dirt
Blaze: White diamond with a blue dot
Seasons: Best April through October
Other trail users: Hikers only
Canine compatibility: Leashed dogs permitted
Water: Available at the boat dock, the beach, and near the dam
Land status: National forest recreation area
Nearest town: Ironton

Fees and permits: No fees or permits required
Schedule: Trails in Wayne National Forest are open 24 hours a day, 365 days a year. The safest time to hike, however, is between dawn and dusk.
Maps: A brochure with topo maps of all hiking and backpacking trails in the Wayne is available for $6.00 at all Wayne National Forest offices. USGS quad: Kitts Hills; Maptech Terrain Navigator: Ohio/Southeast
Trail contacts: Wayne National Forest–Ironton Ranger District, Pedro; (740) 534-6400; www.fs.fed.us/r9/wayne/

Finding the trailhead: From Ironton, travel north on State Route 93 for 6.5 miles and turn east (right) onto County Road 29. Follow the signs 0.9 mile to the parking lot, just past the furnace on the left. *DeLorme: Ohio Atlas and Gazetteer:* Page 85 D7.

The Hike

Lake Vesuvius Recreation Area lies in the heart of the Hanging Rock iron furnace region, named for the outcroppings of ferriferous limestone mined to fuel the iron furnaces that, in turn, fueled the economy of this region between 1818 and 1916. The Vesuvius Furnace (yes, named after the Italian volcano) was built in 1833 to smelt iron ore and was in use until 1906. At its peak the Vesuvius Furnace produced eight to twelve tons of iron each day. Iron munitions from these furnaces were critical to the Union effort during the Civil War.

The Lake Vesuvius Lakeshore Trail begins and ends near the furnace. This rock chimney, built without mortar, is all that remains of a larger blast furnace as well as a storage yard, casting house, scale house, and carpenter and blacksmith shops. Furnace

Where did the lake go? Lake Vesuvius was drained during 2002 so the USDA Forest Service could rebuild the dam.

workers, much like coal miners, lived in company towns and were paid in goods or scrip. The furnaces consumed 300 to 350 acres of timber each year for fuel, so when the industry died, it left behind a denuded landscape.

Enter the Wayne National Forest and Civilian Conservation Corps in the 1930s. The Wayne began purchasing land in 1935, and in 1943 the CCC built an earthen dam near the furnace, creating Lake Vesuvius, a salamander-shaped reservoir. One of the features that makes this hike interesting is how often the trail is pinched between the water and rock outcroppings. There are several choice lunch spots atop the rocks overlooking the lake. When you walk by these outcroppings, look for little bits of iron, noticeably darker and harder than the surrounding sandstone and limestone.

Beginning from the dam, hike the trail clockwise to get the early sun and counterclockwise to try to stay in the shade. The trail generally hugs the lakeside in an oak-hickory forest and through occasional pine plantations. Walking clockwise, look across the lake for views of the dam and a large rock outcropping. Be prepared, however, for the trail often recedes from the lakeshore and moves up and down the ridges. Pass a swimming beach while continuing upstream. As you approach the turnaround point, you will cross over Storms Creek, which feeds the lake. This is a nice area in a creek valley lined by hemlock-dotted rock outcroppings and water-loving sycamore trees. A decent swimming hole awaits the few who venture this far along the trail. This is also the spot where the Lakeshore Trail and the backpack trail diverge.

On the return trip, the views are ever-changing and you get a chance to see how far you've come. Look for signs of beaver activity, and keep an eye open for a good rocky lunch spot if you haven't stopped yet. Toward the end of the loop is the largest rock outcropping, more than 30 feet high. This is a popular spot among hikers, picnickers, and rock climbers. End the walk back at the dam, about 0.5 mile past this point. For a longer hike opt for the Vesuvius Backpack Trail, which shares part of its length with the Lakeshore Trail but continues past the lake and into the forest for a 16.0-mile loop.

Miles and Directions

0.0 Start at the dam, across from the Vesuvius Furnace. Facing the lake from atop the dam, take a left and walk to the road. Turn right and follow the road 0.3 mile to a footbridge that takes you off the road and across the water. Pass a brown building and pick up a trailhead sign for the Lakeshore and Backpack Trails.

0.4 Pass a red-blazed junction for the Rock House Trail to the left. Continue straight, paralleling the lakeside. You will soon find yourself directly across from the dam.

0.7 Pass a stand of cedars and cross a long footbridge. Soon a large rock face will come into view across the lake.

1.1 An old doubletrack joins the trail from behind; in a few hundred feet another doubletrack comes in from the side.

1.2 A wooden post indicates a junction. The backpack trail, blazed with a yellow dot, heads off to the left. Continue straight, along the Lakeshore Trail, blazed with the blue dot.

1.6 The trail comes out at the beach area and rest room/concession building. Water should be available here during summer. Walk past the beach and concession building and pick up the trail again behind the chain-link fence. Look to the trees for blazes.

1.9 The trail rounds a bend and ascends the ridge, now overlooking the lake and heading north. In another 0.5 mile the trail begins to descend again to the lake.

2.6 Cross a footbridge and then enter a more mature forest, including a nice stand of cedars. The trail zigzags back and forth to cross side drainages. (Ascend again to the top of a rock outcropping, which could serve as a nice lunch rock.)

3.2 The trail descends to a fork. Although the right fork is well worn, don't take it. Look for the blazes along the left fork and descend to the bottomlands. (In another 0.5 mile, look for a good swimming hole.)

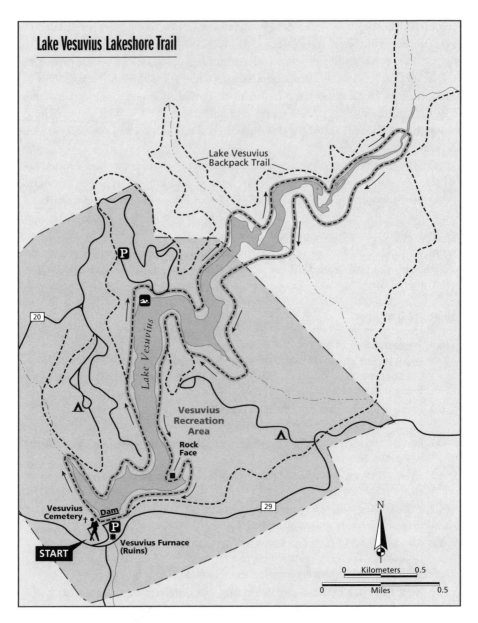

Lake Vesuvius Lakeshore Trail

Lake Vesuvius
Backpack Trail

20

Lake Vesuvius

Vesuvius
Recreation
Area

Rock
Face

Vesuvius
Cemetery

Dam

29

START

Vesuvius Furnace
(Ruins)

N

| 0 | Kilometers | 0.5 |
| 0 | Miles | 0.5 |

3.8 Come to a junction. Straight ahead is the backpack trail. Take a right and cross Storms Creek on the footbridge to remain on the Lakeshore Trail. Begin the return trip now, walking south and west, on the east side of the lake.

4.1 Come to another junction marked with wooden signposts and blazes. Follow the blazes out of the floodplain and up the ridge. Pass hemlocks on the right, and then slowly descend the ridge back down to a couple of stream crossings.

5.5 Reach another rock outcropping that could serve as a nice lunch spot.

6.2 Pass the Whiskey Run Loop Trail on the left (blazed red) and keep walking until the swimming area comes into view across the lake. In a few hundred feet you will see a side trail to the right, which leads to a bench.

6.4 The other end of the Whiskey Run Trail comes in from the left. Cross the footbridge and stay lakeside.

6.9 A series of large rock outcroppings culminate in a large, protruding rock face, a popular spot for recreation area users. Round the corner to begin the last leg of the hike.

7.3 Arrive at the top of the earthen dam. Follow the stairs down.

7.4 Return to the Vesuvius Furnace parking lot.

Hike Information

Local information

Lawrence County Convention and Visitors Bureau, South Point; (800) 408-1334; www.lawrencecountyohio.org/6.htm.

Accommodations

The Vesuvius Recreation Area has two campgrounds, Oak Hill and Iron Ridge; (740) 534-6400. Backcountry camping is allowed in the national forest, but only outside the recreation area boundaries.

UNDERGROUND RAILROAD Iron furnaces weren't the only things burning in this part of the country during the nineteenth century. Antebellum politics were boiling over between the North and South. Several areas in what is now the Wayne National Forest were stops along the Underground Railroad, where people risked their own lives and livelihoods to help escaped slaves on the path to freedom. Underground Railroad routes ran from the slave-holding Southern states to the North (Ohio was part of the Union) and into Canada. For obvious reasons, the routes were unpublished, requiring escaped slaves to rely mostly on the help of sympathetic people from one stop to the next. Human contact was kept to a minimum, but clues were sometimes otherwise available, such as coded quilts hanging on clotheslines. The former loose-knit community of Pokepatch, Ohio, north of where Lake Vesuvius is today, seemed to exist solely as a stop along the Underground Railroad between 1820 and 1870. Pokepatch was home to freed slaves, whites, Native Americans, and people of mixed race. Some of their descendants live in nearby Blackfork today. The Wayne National Forest, through its Historic Black Colleges and University Program, has been working on a database of Underground Railroad sites.

34 Calico Bush and Salt Creek Trails

Lake Katharine State Nature Preserve

The beautiful 5.4-mile trail system in Lake Katharine Preserve is unparalleled in springtime. Home to the northernmost range of umbrella and big leaf magnolia trees, it can look as though the forest itself is one big bloom. That also includes the native mountain laurel, dogwood, redbud, and tulip trees. And as if that's not enough, look underfoot for the hundreds of wildflower species. Walk over the earthen dam that creates Lake Katharine on your way to a cascading waterfall and a hemlock forest. Then find yourself pinched between Little Salt Lick on one side and Sharon conglomerate outcroppings on the other.

Start: From Calico Bush and Salt Creek trailhead next to the parking lot

Distance: 5.4-mile trail system

Approximate hiking time: 2 to 2^1/$_2$ hours

Difficulty: Moderate due to length and several ascents and descents, including stairways.

Seasons: Flowering trees are showy in May and June.

Trail surface: Dirt trail with some boardwalks and stairs

Other trail users: Hikers only

Canine compatibility: Dogs not permitted

Water: No potable water is available along the hike; bring your own.

Land status: State nature preserve

Nearest town: Jackson

Fees and permits: No fees or permits required

Schedule: Open daylight hours year-round

Maps: USGS quad: Jackson; Maptech Terrain Navigator: Ohio/Southeast

Trail contacts: Lake Katharine Nature Preserve, Jackson; (740) 286-2487; www.ohiodnr.com/dnap/location/lake_katharine.html

Finding the trailhead: From State Route 93 in Jackson, turn left on Bridge Street (SR 93 turns to the right). Stay to the right where the road curves at the old-fashioned traffic light and Bridge Street becomes State Street. In about 1.5 miles you will cross two sets of railroad tracks. Just past the second set of tracks, turn right onto Lake Katharine Road, marked by a brown sign. Follow the road 2.0 miles to the parking area. *DeLorme: Ohio Atlas and Gazetteer:* Page 79 D4.

The Hike

The forest in Lake Katharine State Nature Preserve seems like one giant bloom in the spring. Go then and link all three trails in the preserve to take in all the preserve's highlights, including a cascading waterfall, a quiet lake, towering rock walls, wildflowers, and flowering shrubs and trees—including three species of native magnolia trees. Start at the parking area next to the former Camp Arrowhead lodge. Take a nature trail brochure from the trailhead kiosk, then walk past the Calico Bush and Salt Creek trailhead sign and through a young successional forest. When you branch off to the left onto the Calico Bush Trail, stop to take in the self-guided nature trail. Calico bush is a less common name for mountain laurel, a woody shrub that lines a

Magnolia leaf at Lake Katharine State Nature Preserve.

portion of the trail and blooms from May to June. The midsized trees you see blooming in June are umbrella magnolias. This area is at the uppermost portion of the
bigleaf mangolia's range, so these trees are quite rare in Ohio. Their blooms are large
and beautiful, and their leaves grow up to 3 feet in length.

By the time you come to the junction with the Pine Ridge Trail, you will have
already recognized more of the natural features Lake Katharine has to offer: stands
of hemlock and Sharon conglomerate outcroppings. If you look closely at the rock,
you can see that it's made up of rounded quartz pebbles embedded in sandstone. This
rock is evidence of both many years of sedimentation and the fact that moving water
shaped the quartz into its smooth, rounded condition. The trail then takes you across
the earthen dam that creates Lake Katharine, named after the wife of Edwin A.
Jones, who (along with James J. McKitterick) purchased and later donated the land
for a preserve. The preserve purchased more land with federal land and water conservation money in 1976. Canoeing and fishing on Lake Katharine are available by
permit only.

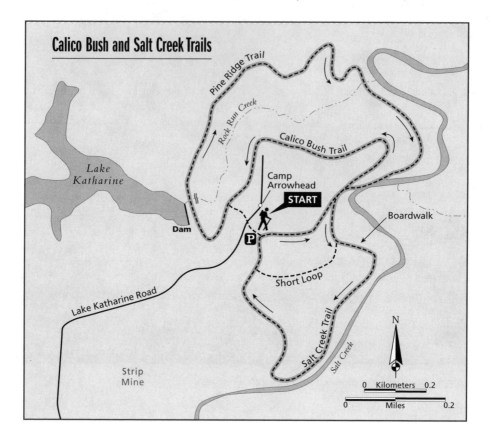

Calico Bush and Salt Creek Trails

Just past the dam is a beautiful spot where water cascades down the rocky bottom of Rock Run Creek. Continue upland among the hemlocks, oaks, and hickories. The trail eventually works its way back down to Little Salt Lick. Spend nearly the rest of the hike walking between rock outcroppings and the creek. Wildflowers are abundant here. In fact, Jackson County is reported to be the most biologically diverse of all Ohio counties. Look for common flowering plants such as spring beauty, solomon's seal, and trillium. You might also get a glimpse of less common species as well, such as the stemless lady's slipper. Tulip trees dominate the canopy here.

The trail is in good shape and is only marked at junctions. Boardwalks and stairs allow you to walk the trails in all types of weather.

Miles and Directions

0.0 Start the hike next to the parking lot at the trailhead sign for the Calico Bush and Salt Creek Trails.

0.3 Come to a staggered junction for all three trails. Turn left, following the sign for the Calico Bush Trail.

0.9 Come to a junction with the Pine Ridge Trail. Continue straight.

1.1 Cross the earthen dam and then cross the stream over a footbridge.

2.0 Take a short spur to the right for an overlook.

2.3 The trail descends to the river by way of switchbacks.

3.3 Arrive again at the staggered junction of all three trails. Keep walking straight ahead, following the signs for the Salt Creek Trail. **Option:** Return directly to the parking lot by taking a right.

4.0 Come to the junction for the short and long loops. Take a left and cross the boardwalk to take the long loop. **Option:** Take the short loop to return to the parking lot. (**FYI:** At the end of the boardwalk, look for a very large old sweetgum tree.)

4.5 Approach a recess cave on the right. The somewhat faint trail turns left here, away from the cave.

5.0 The trail turns right, away from the creek, and ascends to an old road.

5.1 A sign indicates a right turn, off the road and over the drainage.

5.3 Come to a junction with the short loop. Turn left to finish the hike.

5.4 Return to the parking lot.

Hike Information

Local information
www.jacksoncountyohio.org/.

Local events and attractions
Leo Petroglyph is about 5 miles northwest of Jackson. Contact the Ohio Historical Society at (800) 686–1535, or visit www.ohiohistory.org/ places/leopetro/index.html.

Jackson County Apple Festival, third full week of September; www.jacksonapplefestival. com/.

Accommodations
Lake Alma State Park, Wellston; (740) 384–4474.

Maples Bed & Breakfast, Jackson; (740) 286–6067.

Restaurants
The Colonial Restaurant, Jackson; (740) 286–2303.

Hike tours
Ranger-led hikes are offered. Contact the preserve for up-to-date information.

Organizations
Columbus Audubon, Columbus; (614) 451–4591; www.geography.ohio-state. edu/ CAS/.

35 Logan Hollow Trail–North Loop

Tar Hollow State Forest and State Park

The 12.1-mile north loop of the Logan Trail begins and ends at a fire tower that you can climb to get a view of the deciduous forest unfolding in all directions. But the beauty is in the details. Look for wild irises and other spring wildflowers as well as edible plants such as mushrooms, berries, and pawpaws. Hike this well-constructed trail through mature forest, clearcuts, and successional (growing back) woods.

Start: From the fire tower off Forest Road 3
Distance: 12.1 mile loop
Approximate hiking time: 4 to 6 hours
Difficulty: Difficult due to length and hills
Trail surface: Dirt
Blaze: Red
Seasons: Best April through October
Other trail users: Hunters (in season); watch out for the errant mountain biker or horseback rider.
Canine compatibility: Leashed dogs permitted
Water: Available at Sheep Pasture Picnic Area, north of the fire tower on Forest Road 3
Land status: State forest and state park

Nearest town: Adelphi
Fees and permits: No fees or permits required
Schedule: Tar Hollow State Forest is open from 6:30 A.M. to 11:00 P.M. daily.
Maps: USGS quad: Hallsville; Maptech Terrain Navigator: Ohio/Southeast; Buckeye Trail Association Section map: Scioto Trail
Trail contacts: Tar Hollow State Park, Laurelville; (740) 887-4818; www.bright.net/~thollow. Tar Hollow State Forest, c/o Scioto Trail State Forest, Waverly; (740) 663-2523.

Finding the trailhead: From State Route 327 about halfway between State Route 56 and U.S. Highway 50, turn west onto Forest Road 10, marked with a PARK ENTRANCE sign. Travel 3.7 miles to a Y intersection. Turn left (south) onto Forest Road 3 and travel another 1.5 miles to the fire tower. Park on the grass or along the pullout. *DeLorme: Ohio Atlas and Gazetteer:* Page 78, A4.

The Hike

The Tar Hollow region was named after the pine tar that settlers extracted from native pitch pine trees. This tar was used for balms and as a lubricant for machinery. When you start your hike at Tar Hollow from the fire tower, you will immediately see pine trees. But climb up to the top of the tower and get a view of a deciduous forest stretching in all directions. From here you can get an idea of the terrain that lies ahead.

You can spend as much time as you desire hiking Tar Hollow State Forest's 50-plus miles of trails. One of the nicest is the north loop of the Logan Hollow Trail, which is off-limits to equestrians and mountain bikers. The trail is a narrow footpath for its entire length and generally has a backcountry feel. The Logan Hollow Trail was constructed by Boy Scouts in the 1950s and is still maintained by Boy Scouts today. It's named after Chief Logan, who was the leader of the Mingo Nation in the late eighteenth century.

A confluence of two streams in Tar Hollow State Forest.

This particular hike is also a lesson in forest ecology and the politics of multiple use. Since Ohio's state forests are managed for timber, you will begin the hike by walking in a mature forest but will later skirt a fresh clearcut and then walk through a successional forest.

Begin from the fire tower at the top of the ridge and gradually descend to the lowlands. This oak-hickory forest has some mature trees and a brilliant understory. In springtime wild irises are particularly showy, as are other wildflowers such as trillium, wild geranium, and fire pink. A wide variety of ferns help blanket the forest floor as well, including the black-stemmed maidenhair fern. Mushroom hunting is a popular activity in Tar Hollow, where the edible morel and chicken-of-the-woods grow on rotting logs.

The trail is well built, staying along ridgetops and along streambeds for the most part, reducing the number of ascents and descents on this long loop. When exploring along the streams, look for salamanders—several species live here. You may even get a glimpse of the conspicuous five-lined skink, identifiable by its bright blue tail. Don't expect to see the timber rattlesnake, however. Although it is known to inhabit Tar Hollow State Forest, this elusive reptile is on the federal endangered species list.

The trail feels secluded for the first 5 miles. Occasionally you might see some evidence of former land use. For example, look to see old logging roads, recognizable

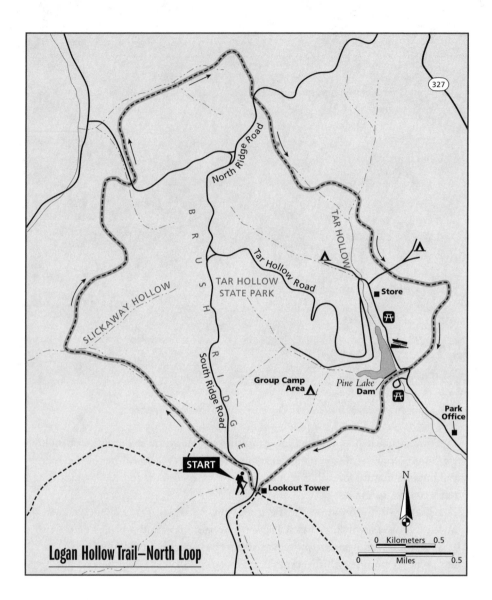

Logan Hollow Trail–North Loop

by flat grades along the slopes. About a mile after crossing Forest Road 16, you will encounter a clearcut just off of the trail; it's shocking if you've never seen one before. These nineteen acres were cut in November 2001. About a mile after that, you will be walking in a successional forest, which was clearcut in sections totaling 126 acres from 1992 to 1994. Note the young trees and a lot of sunlight. There is more than one cache of black raspberries along this section of trail. Also notice the invasive Japanese honeysuckle and poison ivy.

The trail then cuts through Tar Hollow State Park, where you are most likely to run into other hikers along the trail. Walk past a campground and along the earthen dam that creates Pine Lake before reentering the state forest. The last section of the trail, between the park and the fire tower, is joined by the Buckeye Trail, marked with its trademark blue blazes.

A long hike like the Logan Hollow Trail is perhaps most comfortable, weather-wise, in spring or fall. Contact the state forest, however, to learn the dates of hunting season, since hiking during that time would be ill-advised.

Miles and Directions

0.0 Start at the fire tower. Look across FR 3 for the red trailhead sign.

0.2 Come to a fork. Follow the sign to the right to stay on the Logan Trail. To the left, the trail eventually peters out.

0.4 Walk straight through a four-way intersection, keeping an eye on the red blazes.

0.6 Come to the fork where the north and south loops of the Logan Hollow Trail diverge. Take a right.

2.9 A side trail joins from the right. Continue straight.

4.3 Cross Forest Road 16.

6.3 Pass an orange gate and come to Forest Road 4. There are no blazes here. Turn right and walk on the road for about 200 feet. Look for a red blaze and the trail across the road.

7.4 Approach a fork. Take the left fork, following the blazes. To the right is a side trail to the campground.

7.6 Pass another side trail on the right, leading to the campground.

7.7 Come to a four-way intersection. Continue straight, crossing the stream.

8.0 Just before you walk into a campsite, the trail turns sharply left.

10.0 Cross FR 10. Look to your right for the earthen dam that creates Pine Lake. Walk alongside the dam, crossing to the other side. Then cross the footbridge over the spillway and pick up the trail again.

10.1 Hit a fork, marked with a red post. Turn right, ascending the ridge. In about 20 feet cross a doubletrack dirt road.

11.3 The Buckeye Trail joins from the left. Continue straight, following red and blue blazes.

11.6 Walk straight past an old trail and sign for the group campground.

12.0 Pass a trail on the right that leads out to the road.

12.1 Return to the fire tower.

Hike Information

Local information
Ross-Chillicothe Convention and Visitors Bureau; (800) 413-4118; www.visit history.com/home.htm.

Local events and attractions
Horse rentals and mountain bike trails are available in the park.

Tecumseh! outdoor drama, Chillicothe; (866) 775-0700; tecumsehdrama.com/.

Accommodations
Tar Hollow State Park campground; (740) 887-4818.

36 Grandma Gatewood Trail–Old Man's Cave to Ash Cave

Hocking Hills State Park

Begin walking the 5.0 miles from Old Man's Cave to Ash Cave and it won't take long to see why this is one of the state's most popular trails. Descend into Old Man's Creek Gorge and walk by rock features with such names as the Devil's Bathtub and the Sphinx Head. Explore Old Man's Cave, a large recess cave of blackhand sandstone, before continuing downstream in the gorge all the way to Cedar Falls, the area's highest-volume waterfall. Then continue on in an upland forest to Ash Cave, the state's largest recess cave, complete with another waterfall and a forest of old-growth hemlocks.

Start: From Old Man's Cave Visitor Center

Distance: 10.0-mile out-and-back; optional 5.0-mile point to point

Approximate hiking time: 2^1/$_2$ to 3^1/$_2$ hours one way

Difficulty: Difficult due to length and a few portions with steep stairs; optional one-way hike is moderate.

Trail surface: Wide path; mostly dirt with boardwalks and stone stairs

Blaze: Blue

Seasons: Best spring through fall and in winter after a snowfall

Other trail users: Hikers only

Canine compatibility: Leashed dogs permitted

Water: Available at Old Man's Cave Visitor Center, Cedar Falls parking area, and Ash Cave trailhead

Land status: State park

Nearest town: Logan

Fees and permits: No fees or permits required

Schedule: Open daily year-round

Maps: USGS quad: South Bloomingville; Maptech Terrain Navigator: Ohio/Southeast; Buckeye Trail Association Section map: Old Man's Cave

Trail contacts: Hocking Hills State Park, Logan; (740) 385-6841; www.ohiodnr.com/parks/parks/hocking.htm

Finding the trailhead: From U.S. Highway 33 in Logan, turn south on State Route 664 and travel 11.2 miles. Pass the campground on your left and then turn right into the large parking area, across from the Old Man's Cave Visitor Center. Cross the road to the visitor center and pick up the trailhead to the left (east) of the building. The trail is marked with blue blazes, as this is also part of the Buckeye Trail. *DeLorme: Ohio Atlas and Gazetteer:* Page 79 A5.

The Hike

The hike between Old Man's Cave and Ash Cave is rich in both natural and human history, making it a favorite among many hikers. The trail is largely bordered by sandstone walls and features waterfalls, cliffs, hemlock forests, and abundant ferns and wildflowers. If solitude is what you're looking for, try this hike on a weekday or in winter.

Cedar Falls, the highest-volume waterfall in Hocking Hills State Park, was misnamed by European settlers. The falls are surrounded by hemlock trees, not cedars.

Beginning at Old Man's Cave, it's 2.2 miles to Cedar Falls, where you can turn around and take the rim trail back or continue on. It's another 2.8 miles to the Ash Cave trailhead. This trail is named after Emma "Grandma" Gatewood, an Ohio native who was the first woman to through-hike the Appalachian Trail (at age sixty-seven) and a charter member of the Buckeye Trail Association.

You can spend half the day exploring the first half-mile of the trail. As soon as you descend into the gorge, walk upstream, passing the Devil's Bathtub whirlpool on your way to the 30-foot upper falls. Turning back and walking downstream, take notice of all the hard work the Works Progress Administration (WPA) put into the park in the 1930s, creating trails, stone stairs, and tunnels leading to Old Man's Cave.

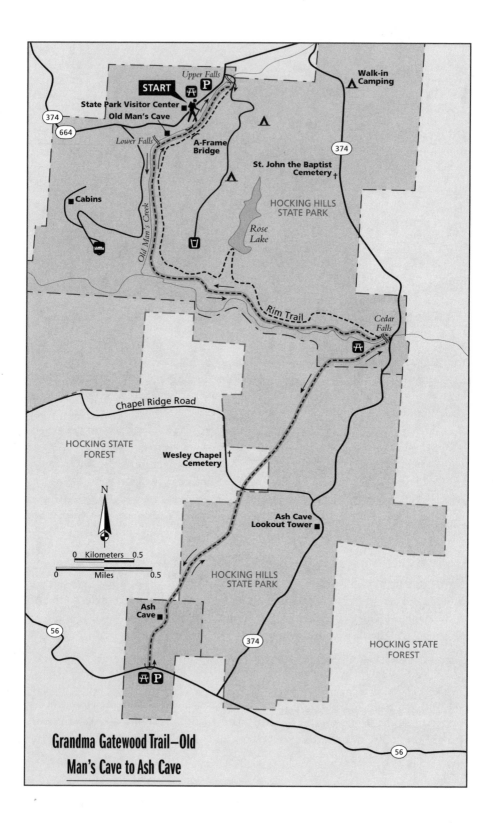

Grandma Gatewood Trail–Old Man's Cave to Ash Cave

Old Man's Cave is named after a hermit, Richard Roe, who made it his home in the eighteenth century. Actually a recess cave eroded through freeze and thaw cycles, Old Man's is 200 feet long, 50 feet high, and 75 feet deep. From Old Man's Cave, look downstream to view the Sphinx Head rock formation.

Continue walking to the 40-foot lower falls, larger in volume than the upper falls and often flanked by rock-skipping youngsters. As you continue downstream enjoy the sandstone walls, ferns, hemlocks, and spring wildflowers, including trillium, wild columbine, jack-in-the-pulpit, Dutchman's breeches, trout lilies, and violets. In July and August look for the endangered round-leafed catchfly growing out of rocky spots. Its brilliant red color will catch your eye.

As you approach the confluence of Old Man's and Queer Creeks, the valley widens and large water-loving white-barked sycamores fill the valley. Look for the smaller, water-loving musclewood trees as well, identifiable by their smooth, sinewy bark.

The trail turns east and takes you along Queer Creek, where the gorge walls are farther apart and still stunning. Approaching Cedar Falls, the gorge again narrows and the path skirts tall, vertical rock faces. Cedar Falls, 55 feet high, are the largest by volume in the Hocking Hills area. They were misnamed by early white settlers, who mistook the hemlocks for cedars.

From Cedar Falls the trail ascends out of the gorge and becomes a mostly upland path in an oak-hickory forest until it arrives at the lip of Ash Cave. It's especially important to keep an eye on children and pets here and to watch your footing. Peer into the state's largest recess cave, measuring 700 feet long, 100 feet deep, and 90 feet high. It is named for the massive amounts of ashes found by early European settlers, believed to be leftovers from fires made by Native Americans over hundreds of years. Follow the rim and then descend into the cave and enjoy views from within of a trickling waterfall and some of the biggest hemlock trees in the state. The remainder of the trail is a handicapped-accessible paved path out to the parking lot, pit toilets, and water. You can return by way of car or bicycle shuttle or by foot the way you came.

Miles and Directions

0.0 Start from the Old Man's Cave Visitor Center. Following the blue blazes, descend into the gorge. Take a left and walk upstream to the upper falls, then turn around and continue downstream.

0.3 Walk through a stone tunnel and emerge in front of Old Man's Cave.

0.5 Descend stairs to the lower falls.

1.0 Approach the confluence of Old Man's and Queer Creeks. Take a left, following Queer Creek and the signs to Cedar Falls.

1.5 Pass benches and a trail sign.

2.0 Come to a T intersection. Take a left, following the sign for Cedar Falls.

2.2 Take the wooden stairs out of the gorge, following both blue and yellow blazes. At the top look across the road for a post with a blue blaze. Walk toward the post and then to the orange gate. Walk along the road past the orange gate.

2.8 The trail leaves the road at a U-turn. It's clearly blazed.

3.5 Cross Chapel Ridge Road.

4.5 Approach the rim of Ash Cave. Take the wooden stairs down into the cave.

5.0 Finish at the Ash Cave trailhead. Return the way you came, or pick up your shuttle here.

10.0 Return to the visitor center.

Hike Information

Local information
Hocking Hills Region homepage: www.hockinghills.com.

Accommodations
Hocking Hills State Park Campground; (740) 385–6165.
Hocking Hills State Park Cottages; (740) 385–6841.

Restaurants
Hocking Hills State Park dining lodge; (740) 385–6841.

Hike tours
Ranger-led hikes are offered in-season, including the annual Hocking Hills Winter Hike. Contact the park for up-to-date information.

"GRANDMA" GATEWOOD
The trail from Old Man's Cave to Ash Cave is known as the Grandma Gatewood Trail. It's named after Emma "Grandma" Gatewood, an Ohio native who is best known as the first woman to through-hike the Appalachian Trail (AT). But that's where the story just starts to get interesting. Grandma Gatewood completed her through-hike in 1955 at age sixty-seven—and in tennis shoes, to boot! She was clearly unfazed by the demands of keeping up with the latest advancements in gear technology. Her provisions included a blanket, a shower curtain, a tin cup, beef jerky, and cheese. She didn't even carry a backpack; she just slung a sack over one shoulder. Some refer to Grandma Gatewood as "the patron saint of ultralightweight backpackers."

Her advice to other long-distance hikers? "Head is more important than heel." And as if once wasn't enough, this mother of eleven through-hiked the AT again in 1957 and in 1964. Reportedly Old Man's Cave to Ash Cave remained her favorite hike. She began the annual Hocking Hills Winter Hike, now the largest event of the year, and she was a founding member of the Buckeye Trail Association (BTA). She died in 1973 at age eighty-five.

37 Rim and Gorge Trails

Conkles Hollow State Nature Preserve

One of the state's best trails, Conkles Hollow provides a rare experience in Ohio: vistas. From sandstone overlooks, view the hollow, rock outcroppings, and forested ridges unfolding into the distance. Walk around the rim of this beautiful hollow, and be sure to hike the Gorge Trail as well, where wildflowers bloom in springtime profusion. A hemlock forest, diverse wildlife, and a waterfall are other attractions along this 3.1-mile trail system.

Start: From the parking lot

Distance: 3.1-mile trail system

Approximate hiking time: 1 to 2 hours

Difficulty: Rim Trail is moderate due to a steep ascent out of the gorge and some difficult footing. Gorge Trail is an easy short and flat trail.

Trail surface: Dirt

Blaze: None; trails are well traveled and marked at junctions.

Seasons: Best in April and May for wildflowers and September and October for fall foliage

Other trail users: Hikers only

Canine compatibility: Dogs not permitted

Water: Available at the parking lot

Land status: State nature preserve

Nearest town: Logan

Fees and permits: No fees or permits required

Schedule: Open dawn to dusk year-round

Maps: USGS quad: South Bloomingville; Maptech Terrain Navigator: Ohio/Southeast

Trail contacts: Conkles Hollow State Nature Preserve, Logan; (740) 420-3445; www.ohiodnr.com/dnap/location/conkles_hollow.html

Finding the trailhead: From U.S. Highway 33 in Logan, turn south on State Route 664 and drive 11.8 miles to the Hocking Hills State Park Visitor Center. From the visitor center it's another 1.6 miles to a T intersection with State Route 374. Turn right (north) and travel 1.0 mile to Big Pine Road. Turn right again and continue 0.2 mile to the parking lot on the left. *DeLorme: Ohio Atlas and Gazetteer:* Page 79 A5.

The Hike

One of Ohio's most scenic hikes, Conkles Hollow offers the Rim Loop Trail, which loops 200 feet above the gorge, affording views of nearby and faraway ridges, waterfalls, forests, and sandstone outcroppings. This is not a trail for those with a fear of heights. The out-and-back Gorge Trail, which lies between walls only 100 to 300 feet apart, will take you through some of the most biodiverse areas in the state. You can expect to see as many as fifty wildflower species blooming at once in spring while hiking to a beautiful waterfall tumbling into a box canyon.

Conkles Hollow lies several miles beyond the reach of the last glacier to come through Ohio. But like so many other places in the state, the glacier affected this area

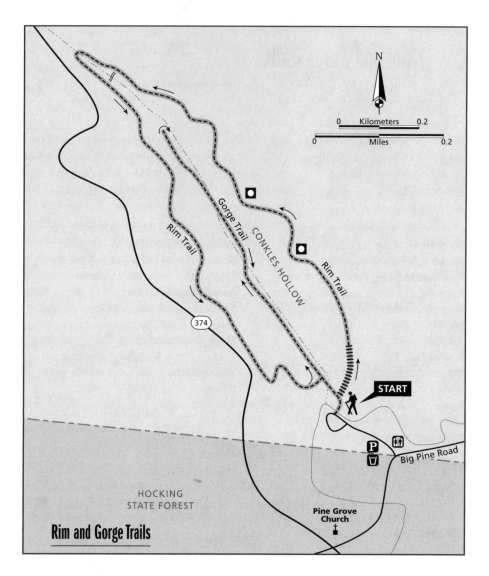

Rim and Gorge Trails

drastically. Formerly part of the north-flowing Teas River Valley, the waterways in this region were pushed—and sometimes reversed—to their current configuration, flowing south to the Ohio River. This highly biodiverse region offers myriad variations in topography, soils, and microclimes. More than 1,200 plant species grow in the Hocking Hills region.

The hike begins with an ascent to the top of the gorge's rim, where you'll be pleased with a rare treat in Ohio: views from rock outcroppings that allow you to see into the distance. Take in the hardwood forests on the ridgetops, peer into the hollow below, and view the sandstone outcroppings themselves. Just before the turn-around point on the trail, an observation deck allows you to view a 90-foot seasonal waterfall dropping into the gorge.

But don't just hike the Rim Trail and neglect all the life there is to see in the gorge itself. The cool microclime in Conkles Hollow supports towering evergreen hemlock, Canada yew, and yellow birch. Spring wildflowers include Dutchman's breeches, trillium, solomon's seal, violets, and a number of native orchid species, to name just a few. An unnamed tributary to Big Pine Creek has carved a narrow gorge through layers of sandstone, providing 200 feet worth of living geology lesson in how weathering affects different types of rock. The soft layers of blackhand sandstone have eroded away faster than surrounding rock, leaving recess caves and creating slump blocks, which now lie in the valley. These slump blocks are covered in ferns, wildflowers, and hemlocks. You can hike all the way to the bottom of the waterfall where it pours into a narrow, moist greenspace. Stop and listen for a minute to the falling water, breezes, and the many nesting and migrating birds found here, including the flutelike song of the hermit thrush and the intensifying call of the ovenbird.

Humans have inhabited the hollow and its surroundings for generations. Conkles is named after a German immigrant, W. J. Conkle, who carved his initials into the rock in 1797. Reportedly, old timers remember another carving in the hollow: an arrow marking the spot across the gorge where a treasure of sorts was buried. As the story goes, a small group of Native Americans robbed some European settlers on the Ohio River, then returned to this hollow and stashed the money in a high-up recess cave. They reached the hiding place by felling one of two hemlocks growing near the cave. They used the hemlock as a ladder and then dropped it to the ground, planning to return later and use the second hemlock to access the goods. But when they returned a storm had felled the other hemlock, so the money remains in the cave to this day.

Miles and Directions

0.0 Start at the bridge along the cul-de-sac portion of the drive. Cross the creek and follow the trail to the left as it passes an informational kiosk and then approaches the stairs to begin the Rim Trail. Turn right and ascend the stairs out of the gorge. At the top of the stairs, the trail curves left and makes its way to the gorge's rim.

0.4 Come to the first sandstone outcropping overlook.

0.5 Reach the second overlook.

0.9 Arrive at the wooden overlook above the waterfall.

1.0 Walk over the creek on a footbridge. Return on the west side of the gorge, walking downstream.

1.7 Descend the stairs back into the gorge.

1.9 Reach the trailhead for the Gorge Trail. Turn left and walk upstream.

2.4 Come to the end of the Gorge Trail, at the bottom of the falls.

3.0 Return to the Gorge Trail trailhead the way you came. Continue straight.

3.1 Arrive back at the starting point.

Hike Information

Local information

Hocking Hills Region homepage: www. hockinghills.com.

Logan-Hocking Chamber of Commerce; (740) 385-6836; www.logan-hockingchamber.com/.

Accommodations

Hocking Hills State Park Campground; (740) 385-6165.

Hocking Hills State Park Cottages; (740) 385-6841.

About seventy-five cabins, bed-and-breakfasts, and lodges are located in the Hocking Hills region. Visit www.hockinghills.com for a listing.

Restaurants

Hocking Hills State Park dining lodge; (740) 385-6841.

Local events and attractions

Hocking Hills State Park (740-385-4402; www.ohiodnr.com/parks/parks/hocking.htm) surrounds Conkles Hollow, which is a state nature preserve. The park is home to excellent hikes, including Old Man's Cave to Ash Cave, Cantwell Cliffs, and Rockhouse.

Rockbridge State Nature Preserve, Rockbridge; (614) 265-6543; www.ohiodnr.com/odnr/dnap/dnap.html.

International Washboard Festival, held in Logan, usually on Father's Day weekend. Contact the Logan-Hocking Chamber of Commerce or the Columbus Washboard Company in Logan at (800) 343-7967.

Hike tours

Naturalist-led hikes are offered throughout the year. Contact the Department of Natural Areas and Preserves for a schedule at (614) 265-6453; www.ohiodnr.com/dnap.

38 Hemlock to Creekside Meadows Loop

Clear Creek Metro Park

Clear Creek Valley is where the last glacier's advance ended. The result is a beautiful creek surrounded by a biodiverse forest. Begin and end next to Clear Creek and make a 3.0-mile loop on the appropriately named Hemlock and Fern Trails (there are more than forty fern species in the park). Enjoy the sandstone outcroppings and the many bird species that call this place home.

Start: From the pullout/trailhead on Clear Creek Road

Distance: 3.0-mile loop

Approximate hiking time: 1 to 1$\frac{1}{2}$ hours

Difficulty: Easy; short and well maintained

Trail surface: Dirt

Blaze: Hemlock Trail, blue hemlock tree; Fern Trail, green fern; Creekside Meadows Trail, yellow flower

Seasons: Best April through October

Other trail users: Hikers only

Canine compatibility: Leashed dogs permitted

Water: Available at the Barnebey Hambleton picnic area

Land status: Columbus Metro Park

Nearest towns: Lancaster, Logan

Fees and permits: No fees or permits required

Schedule: Open daily year-round until dark

Maps: USGS quad: Rockbridge; Maptech Terrain Navigator: Ohio/Southeast

Trail contacts: Columbus Metro Parks, Westerville; (614) 508-8000; www.metroparks.net

Finding the trailhead: From U.S. Highway 33 between Lancaster and Logan, turn west onto County Road 116 (Clear Creek Road), marked with a small brown sign. Drive 2.1 miles to the fishing access pullout on the left, across from the Hemlock Trailhead. If you hit the Fern Picnic Area, you've gone too far. **DeLorme: Ohio Atlas and Gazetteer: Page 69 D5.**

The Hike

Although it's part of the Columbus Metro Park system, Clear Creek is located in the Hocking Hills region, 30 miles southeast of the I–270 outerbelt. The Metro Parks made a good choice by going a little farther afield to purchase this special land in 1996. Unlike the more urban parks, Clear Creek is arguably underutilized and has a well-maintained system of 10-plus miles of hiking trails. More trails are planned.

Geologists believe that the Wisconsinan Glacier terminated its advance in today's Clear Creek Valley some 20,000 years ago. Clear Creek is now the central feature of the valley and the park. Its riffling waters sparkle in the sun as anglers fish for brown trout, smallmouth bass, and rock bass. Tributaries to Clear Creek make their way through narrow, verdant drainages, often lined by sandstone cliffs.

By hiking the Hemlock Trail and returning by way of the Fern and Creekside Meadows Trails, you can get a nice sampling of all the park has to offer. Begin near Clear Creek and walk along a ravine. This cool, moist environment is home to its namesake hemlocks and ferns. Naturalists have identified forty fern species in the

Clear Creek is where geologists believe the last glacier terminated its advance.

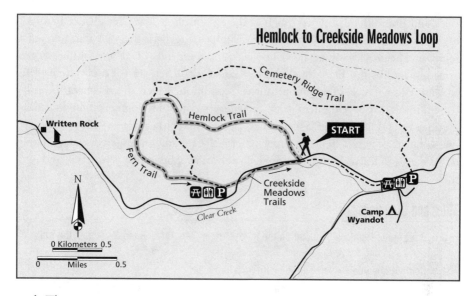

park. The more common ones you'll see include Christmas, wood, maidenhair, and sensitive fern, as well as ebony spleenwort and polypody fern. As you ascend the 300-foot ridge, conditions get drier and the forest becomes dominated by red and white oak. If you are observant, you may notice some young stump sprouts of American chestnut. These trees will succumb to the chestnut blight before reaching fruit-bearing age. Near the intersection of the Fern and Cemetery Ridge Trails, look for mountain laurel and reindeer moss, species usually associated with Southern Appalachian balds. After descending again to the creek valley on the Fern Trail, join the Creekside Meadows Trail and follow it back to the trailhead. Notice a thick understory of scouring rush (horsetail) growing alongside the creek, underneath the sycamores that lean over the water in search of sunlight. In the field near the Fern Picnic Area, look for late summer wildflowers such as wingstem, oxeye, sweet William, joe-pye weed, ironweed, and goldenrod.

In addition to the 1,200 plants that grow in the Clear Creek watershed, more than 150 bird species call this place home (on average, 300 species of birds are found in Ohio each year). The nearby Prairie Warbler Trail allows the hiker a chance to see some of the eighteen species of warbler that nest in the park. Moving up the food chain, deer and beavers are very active in the park. And if you're lucky, you might see a resident bobcat or signs of its presence.

Humans have called the Clear Creek Valley home for thousands of years. In the Written Rock recess cave, located along Clear Creek Road, there are V-shaped grooves cut into a sandstone boulder. Archaeologists believe these were ax polishers, used by the Late Woodland prehistoric peoples. Other evidence of human activity in the cave has been vandalized by more recent humans.

Like so many other preserves today, the fate of the land in the Clear Creek Valley could have easily been very different. Oscar Barneby and the families of Allen F.

Beck and Emily Benua owned much of the land in the Clear Creek Valley before it became a park. In the 1960s there was a proposal to dam the valley and create a reservoir. The project was defeated, however, and these individuals and families began donating land to the Franklin County Metro Parks. The Metro Parks system plans to keep Clear Creek in a "semiprimitive" condition, which means it will be protected from most development, even recreation-related development such as campgrounds and miniature golf. Several trails allow visitors to explore much of the park, but some areas are off-limits in order to protect rare and endangered species. Contact the park to learn about naturalist-led backcountry hikes that go off-trail and into these areas.

Miles and Directions

0.0 Start at the Hemlock Trailhead on the north side of Clear Creek Road. Walk past the trailhead sign and follow the stream.

1.5 Come to the intersection with the Fern Trail. Turn right.

1.7 Continue straight past the junction with the Cemetery Ridge Trail on the right.

2.3 Come to the junction of the Fern Trail loop. Continue straight (downslope).

2.5 Arrive at Clear Creek Road. Cross the road and walk through the Fern Picnic Area. Pick up the Creekside Meadows Trail in the picnic area, marked with a trailhead sign, and continue straight, heading downstream.

3.0 Return to the trailhead.

Hike Information

Local information

Hocking Hills Region homepage: www.hockinghills.com.
Logan-Hocking Chamber of Commerce; (740) 385-6836; www.logan-hockingchamber.com/.

Accommodations

Hocking Hills State Park Campground; (740) 385-6165.
Hocking Hills State Park Cottages; (740) 385-6841.
About seventy-five cabins, bed-and-breakfasts, and lodges are located in the Hocking Hills region. Visit www.hockinghills.com for a listing.

Restaurants

Hocking Hills State Park dining lodge; (740) 385-6841.

Local events and attractions

Nearby parks with excellent hikes include **Rockbridge** and **Conkles Hollow Nature Preserves** (614-265-6543; www.ohiodnr.com/dnap).
Hocking Hills State Park (740-385-4402; www.ohiodnr.com/parks/parks/hocking.htm) is home to a number of excellent hikes, including short forays into Rock House and Cantwell Cliffs.
International Washboard Festival, held in Logan, usually on Father's Day weekend; contact the Logan-Hocking Chamber of Commerce or the Columbus Washboard Company in Logan at (800) 343-7967.

Hike tours

Park naturalist programs are held evenings and on weekends. Contact the park for information; (614) 508-8000.

39 Peninsula to Olds Hollow Trail

Lake Hope State Park and Zaleski State Forest

Lake Hope is a dammed, salamander-shaped body of water that's the central feature of this state park, which is adjacent to the Zaleski State Forest. Begin a 4.2-mile day hike from the Hope Furnace, a leftover from the region's bygone iron smelting days. Walk along the lakeshore in a nice second-growth oak-hickory forest. Then head into the forest and walk by a recess cave and a pioneer cemetery and into a minigorge before returning in a wetland area.

Start: From Lake Hope Furnace parking lot
Distance: 4.2-mile figure eight
Approximate hiking time: $1^1/_2$ to $2^1/_2$ hours
Difficulty: Moderate due to length and hills, including a descent into a narrow and sometimes slick gorge
Trail surface: Dirt
Blaze: None, but part of Olds Hollow Trail follows Zaleski Backpack Trail, blazed orange.
Seasons: Best from mid-April through mid-October
Other trail users: Hikers only
Canine compatibility: Leashed dogs permitted

Water: Available at parking lot
Land status: State park
Nearest towns: Zaleski, McArthur
Fees and Permits: No fees or permits required
Schedule: Open year-round from dawn to dusk
Maps: USGS quad: Mineral; Maptech Terrain Navigator: Ohio/Southeast
Trail contacts: Lake Hope State Park, McArthur; (740) 596-5253; www.ohiodnr.com/parks/parks/lakehope.htm

Finding the trailhead: From State Route 56 south of Nelsonville, turn south onto State Route 278 and travel 4.9 miles to the Hope Furnace parking lot on the right. *DeLorme: Ohio Atlas and Gazetteer:* Page 79 B7.

The Hike

Begin and end your hike at Lake Hope State Park at the namesake Hope Furnace, built in the nineteenth century as an iron ore smelter. Ohio was once one of the nation's leading iron producers, and some of the items made from the ore in this area included munitions for the Union Army during the Civil War. The forests here were cleared in order to fuel these furnaces, most of which had shut down by 1900. Since then, a second-growth oak-hickory forest has come back nicely.

After exploring the furnace you will begin the Peninsula Trail by walking along the edge of Lake Hope, a salamander-shaped body of water created by an earthen dam stopping up Big Sandy Creek (also called Sandy Run), just upstream from its confluence with Raccoon Creek. All lakes in southeast Ohio are human-made, since the topography does not support natural lakes. They all take on the familiar look of dammed hollows. Although you are hiking along the water's edge, you will find

Sycamore trees tower over Hope Furnace in Lake Hope State Park.

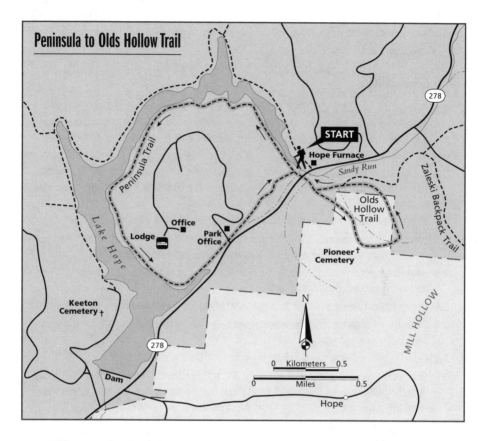

Peninsula to Olds Hollow Trail

yourself in an upland oak-hickory forest because this is actually an upland trail. Look along the lakeshore for signs of a very active beaver population. You should see their dens as well as dams and stumps. This path forms a circle around the dining lodge and cabins, making it very accessible to guests.

You can pick up the Olds Hollow Trail at the end of the Peninsula Trail. Cross the road and begin hiking both Olds Hollow and the Zaleski Backpack Trails. The Olds Hollow Trail diverges from the backpack trail and takes you to some interesting sights, including recess caves and an old pioneer cemetery, where the sandstone grave inscriptions are slowly eroding. This secluded hike also takes you through a small yet striking gorge. In springtime look on the forest floor for wildflowers, including such common species as wild geranium, bloodroot, and blue-eyed Mary. The rare yellow lady's slipper also blooms here. As you complete this loop you will walk parallel to a wetland area. Look here for water-loving birds, including ducks, kingfishers, and great blue herons. And as always, keep an eye out for wild turkeys and white-tailed deer.

> ▶ Raccoon Creek, 99 miles long, is said to be the world's longest creek. One hundred miles would make it a river.

Many other hiking options are available in Lake Hope State Park and Zaleski State Forest, including a 23.5-mile backpack loop with a nice 10-mile day hike option along the backpack trail.

Miles and Directions

0.0 Start at the Hope Furnace. After exploring the furnace walk to the road and turn right (south). Walk over the bridge, then look for wooden stairs to your right. Ascend the stairs and follow the path to a wooden footbridge. The trailhead is here, marked with a wooden sign. Take a right.

0.8 Cross a footbridge and see a sign for a spur trail to the left, taking you to the lodge and cabins at the top of the ridge. Continue straight on the Peninsula Trail, passing some other informal trails on the left that lead to the top of the ridge.

2.0 Cross a footbridge and continue straight; the trail here moves away from the lake.

2.1 Cross the lodge road and follow the grass about 100 feet past the WELCOME TO LAKE HOPE STATE PARK sign. You will see a wooden trailhead where you reenter the woods.

2.6 Hit a T intersection and a wooden sign directing you right to stay on the Peninsula Trail (left to the cabins and lodge).

2.9 Return to the original trailhead. Turn right across the footbridge and come out at the road.

3.0 Cross the road and pick up the trailhead for both Olds Hollow Trail and the Zaleski Backpack Trail. Cross the footbridge and turn left.

3.1 Come to a fork. Follow the sign right onto the Olds Hollow Trail.

3.5 Pass an old pioneer cemetery on the right. The trail continues slightly to the left and down from the cemetery. In a few hundred feet you will come to a sandstone-lined gorge. Walk down the steps into the gorge and turn left, passing two small waterfalls. Cross a footbridge to the other side of the stream and continue walking along it.

3.6 Come to the junction with Kings Hollow Trail (the Zaleski Backpack Trail). Continue straight, picking up the orange blazes that signify the backpack trail.

4.1 Return to the junction that began the Olds Hollow loop. Continue straight.

4.2 Return to the trailhead.

Hike Information

Local information

Vinton County Chamber of Commerce; (740) 596-5033; www.vintoncounty.com.

Local events and attractions

Lake Hope State Park has a number of facilities, including a beach, boat rental, dining lodge, cabins, campground, and the nearby Zaleski backpack trail.

The Vinton County Wild Turkey Festival is an annual May event; (740) 596-5033

Accommodations

Lake Hope State Park cabins and campground; (740) 596-5253.

Restaurants

Lake Hope State Park dining lodge; (740) 596-5253.

MOONVILLE GHOST
Stories about the ghost of Moonville Tunnel, located in the Zaleski State Forest, are a mixture of fact and fiction. (But, as they say, never let the facts get in the way of a good story.) Moonville was once a stop on the Marietta and Cincinnati Railroad and was home to up to one hundred persons, mostly employed by the furnaces and the coal mines. In 1859 a man was, in fact, killed when he was run over by a train. Who he was and exactly what happened, however, are less clear. Perhaps the most popular story claims that Moonville was in the throes of a plaguelike epidemic. Fearing exposure, the train's crew refused to stop in town. But supplies in Moonville were dwindling, so the town appointed one man to stop the train in order to save them all—but the train ran him down. Over the years there have been a number of reported sightings of the Moonville Ghost. If you're brave, you might follow the bed of the tracks to the sandstone-and-brick tunnel at night. If not, well, there's a reason they're called day hikes.

40 Lakeview Trail

Strouds Run State Park

Walk around Dow Lake in an attractive, healthy second-growth oak-hickory forest on the ridgetops and beech-maple in the valleys. Walk through white pine plantations, near a Native American mound, and by a pioneer cemetery. Look for the active beaver population. Spring wildflowers and fall foliage are highlights of this 6.8-mile horseshoe trail in a state park just 5 miles from Ohio's funkiest small town.

Start: From the trailhead past the beach parking lot
Distance: 8.3-mile loop; optional 6.8-mile horseshoe
Approximate hiking time: 2^1/$_2$ to 3^1/$_2$ hours
Difficulty: Moderate due to length
Trail surface: A mostly flat, dirt (often muddy) trail
Blaze: Orange
Seasons: Best April through October
Other trail users: Hunters (seasonal)

Canine compatibility: Leashed dogs permitted
Water: Available near the concession stand
Land status: State park
Nearest town: Athens
Fees and permits: No fees or permits required
Schedule: The park closes at 11:00 P.M. daily
Maps: USGS quad: Athens; Maptech Terrain Navigator: Ohio/Southeast
Trail contacts: Strouds Run State Park, Athens; (740) 592-2302; www.ohiodnr.com/parks/parks/strouds.htm

Finding the trailhead: From U.S. Highway 33 in Athens, exit south onto Columbus Road (exit 13) and drive 2.1 miles to Columbia Avenue (at the top of the hill with a traffic light). Turn left (east) and drive 1.1 miles to a fork at the third stop sign. Take the right fork and continue 0.3 mile to a T intersection with County Road 20 (Strouds Run Road). Turn right (east) and drive 3.2 miles to the beach entrance on the right. From the beach parking lot, continue to the small gravel lot beyond it. The trailhead is on the far side of the gravel lot, marked with a sign. **Option:** Just past the park entrance sign on the right is a small parking lot at the terminal trailhead. You can drop off a bicycle or car here if you want to set up a shuttle. *DeLorme: Ohio Atlas and Gazetteer:* Page 80 B2.

The Hike

When the Strouds family arrived in Athens County in the early 1800s, they probably came on the Ohio River and then traveled upstream on the Hocking River to the confluence of what is now known as Strouds Run. Today an earthen dam has turned the lower portion of Strouds Run into Dow Lake, and Strouds Run State Park offers more than 10 miles of secluded hiking trails just a few minutes away from funky, progressive Athens.

The Stroudses and other early settlers followed in the footsteps of the prehistoric Adena people, who built the mounds in the park and throughout the area, and later the Shawnee Nation. At the time of the Strouds family's arrival, this land was known

The Lakeview Trail overlooks Dow Lake at Strouds Run State Park.

as the Northwest Territory. The Ohio Company, a private group formed to purchase land, bought the land now encompassing Athens, Meigs, and Washington Counties from Congress; and Ohio University was established—on paper. Settlement was encouraged as part of an overall plan to develop a town and a university.

The university encouraged growth in the area, but so, too, did the discovery of coal. Much of the land surrounding what is now Strouds Run State Park was mined for both clay and coal. Athens County produced several varieties of brick from this clay, some of which still paves area streets. Although the forests were largely cleared, the park now contains some of the nicest second- and third-growth forests in the region. A small tract of old-growth forest also stands on private property near the park in Athens County.

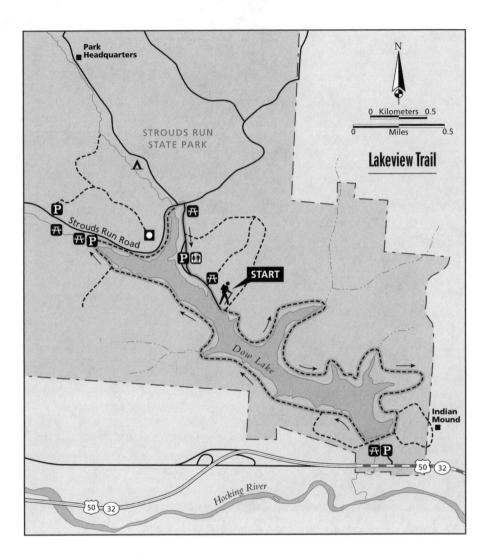

Many visitors to southeast Ohio bypass Strouds Run in favor of the more popular Hocking Hills region. Although this park does not contain the striking gorges and waterfalls of the Hocking Hills, the trade-off is more-secluded trails, away from the masses. The longest of these is the Lakeview Trail, which as the name implies, follows the edge of Dow Lake. Although the park widened this trail to practically a road a few years ago, nature has bounced back and the trail mostly resembles a footpath again.

Begin from the beach area and walk in a mature forest of sycamore, tulip, and maple trees close to the lake, with an upland oak-hickory forest on the ridges above. You'll occasionally walk through white pine plantations. Spring wildflowers are abundant and include spring beauty, blue-eyed Mary, phlox, violet, trillium, hepatica, and Dutchman's breeches. Morel mushrooms grow in several hollows. Flowering trees line the lakeside; especially noticeable are the dogwoods (although their numbers are diminishing due to a fungal blight) and redbud. A little later in the spring, tulip poplars display their eponymous flowers. Hike along a trail covered with flower-petal confetti. In summer, wetland plant species flourish, including cattails, rose mallows, and arrowhead. Fall brings consistent views of colorful foliage. Winter is most often cold and brown, but the park takes on a new luster after a snowfall.

About halfway into the trail on each side of the lake, it's unlikely you'll see or hear other human activity, save for fishing boats on the water. Beavers are quite active on Dow Lake, especially in the first big inlet from the trailhead. Several side trails shoot off the Lakeview Trail. These include the Indian Mound Trail, which takes you past an old Adena mound that is difficult to recognize. Near the terminal trailhead is a side trail leading up a beautiful hollow to a pioneer cemetery.

If time permits, hike the separate Beaver Pond Trail around dusk. You are sure to see a lot of beaver activity and perhaps other wildlife activity as well. Bird-watching can be quite good in the park; commonly-seen species include Canada goose, turkey vulture, red-winged blackbird, cardinal, and kestrel. There have been reported sightings in the park of bobcat, black bear, and bald eagle.

Miles and Directions

0.0 Start at the trailhead located past the beach area parking lot. Walk to the end of the smaller gravel parking area and look for the trailhead sign. In a few hundred feet, the trail forks. To the left is the Broken Rock Trail. Stay right, near the lake.

1.1 At the edge of the inlet, the trail forks. Take a right here, crossing the stream. There's a faint blaze on a sycamore tree. Stay lakeside.

3.4 You will see a smattering of boulders to the left of the trail and a blaze for the Lake Trail opposite the boulders on the right. Continue straight. **Option:** Take a left here to go on the Indian Mound Trail, which follows the ridgetop. In about 100 feet, come to a fork. You can take either one; they both lead to the dam. The left fork is flat; the right fork is steep, but shorter.

3.6 The forks rejoin at the trailhead for the Indian Mound Trail, next to the dam. (**FYI:** Atop the dam or on the grass near the water, you can find a lunch spot. There's a picnic area at the bottom of the dam, but no water is available here.)

3.8 After crossing the dam, come to a sign for the Sycamore Trail. Take a right to stay lakeside. **Option:** Following the Sycamore Trail covers about the same distance as staying on the Lakeview Trail but Sycamore climbs the ridge before rejoining Lakeview.

4.1 The Sycamore Trail rejoins the Lakeview Trail. Continue straight ahead along the lake. The Pioneer Cemetery Trail starts on the left.

6.8 Just past the trailhead for the cemetery, finish at the picnic area. Pick up your shuttle, or walk between the road and the lake back to the beginning trailhead.

8.3 If you continued on foot, return to the trailhead.

Hike Information

Local information

Athens County Convention and Visitors Bureau; (800) 878-9767; www.eurekanet.com/~athenscvb/outdoors.html.

Local events and attractions

The Hockhocking-Adena bike path extends 17 miles from Athens to Nelsonville; www.seorf.ohiou.edu/~xx088.

Check out the **Athens International Street Fair,** usually held the third weekend in May.

Athens is well known for its annual **Halloween street party,** held the Saturday night closest to Halloween.

Accommodations

Strouds Run State Park campground; (740) 592-2302.

Restaurants

Casa Nueva in Athens is a worker-owned Mexican-American restaurant with plenty of vegetarian and vegan options; (740) 592-2016; www.casanueva.com.

Big Chimney Bakery, just east of the park, specializes in European hearth breads; (740) 592-4147; www.bigchimney.com.

Purple Chopstix Restaurant, Athens; (740) 592-4798.

Organizations

Athens Trails is a hiking and trails group based in Athens; (740) 593-6572; www.gasp.athens.oh.us/trails.shtml.

Buckeye Forest Council, The Plains; (740) 797-7200; www.buckeyeforestcouncil.org.

41 Lakeview Trail

Burr Oak State Park

There are plenty of options for hiking around Burr Oak Lake, since some 50 miles of trail exist here where state park meets national forest. Hikes vary from short to long day hikes as well as an 18.0-mile backpack trail. Adjacent to the state park is Wayne National Forest and the 15.0-mile Wildcat Hollow Backpack Trail. Try the highlight: a 5.8-mile out-and-back hike between Tom Jenkins Dam and Dock 4. Views are consistently good on this truly lakeside trail.

Start: From Tom Jenkins Dam

Distance: 5.8-mile out-and-back; optional 2.9-mile point-to-point

Approximate hiking time: 2 to 3 hours

Difficulty: Easy; short and flat

Trail surface: Mostly flat dirt trail

Blaze: Yellow

Seasons: Best April through October

Other trail users: Hunters (seasonal)

Canine compatibility: Leashed dogs permitted

Water: Available at Tom Jenkins Dam

Land status: State park

Nearest town: Glouster

Fees and permits: No fees or permits required

Schedule: Open year-round from dawn to dusk

Maps: USGS quad: Corning; Maptech Terrain Navigator: Ohio/Southeast

Trail contacts: Burr Oak State Park, Glouster; (740) 767-3570; www.ohiodnr.com/parks/parks/burroak.htm

Finding the trailhead: From the junction of State Routes 13 and 78 in Glouster, continue north on Route SR 13 for 2.7 miles to the railroad tracks. Past the tracks, look for a right turn to the Tom Jenkins Dam at Mile 2.9. Park in the lot atop the dam. **Option:** If you choose to shuttle, continue north on SR 13 a half mile from the dam and turn right (east) onto County Road 107. Drive 1.0 mile and turn right onto Beach Road, marked by a huge state park sign. Drive to the bottom of the hill and turn right into the parking lot at Dock 4. *DeLorme: Ohio Atlas and Gazetteer:* Page 70 D2.

The Hike

Burr Oak State Park is named after this particular winged-branch, large-acorn oak tree. The forests here are dominated by a variety of oaks as well as hickories. The focal point of the park is Burr Oak Lake, a dammed salamander-shaped body of water that is surrounded by 28 miles of trails. A campground, cabins, and a lodge make this a popular multiday destination for hikers and other fun-seekers.

The Lakeview Trail begins at Tom Jenkins Dam picnic area. In 1950 the Army Corps of Engineers dammed the East Branch of Sunday Creek to create Burr Oak Lake. A rock outcropping over the water here is a favorite spot for jumping in. The trail parallels the lakeshore among oak, hickory, and beech trees. Watch for the yellow blazes to help you stay on track when you see informal side trails. Spring wild-

The view from the trail at Burr Oak State Park.

flowers and fall foliage make this an especially nice walk. In spring look for spring beauty, Dutchman's breeches, trillium, hepatica, and bloodroot.

As you hike, you're likely to see anglers and boaters enjoying Burr Oak Lake. Looking inland, you might see the abundant white-tailed deer and wild turkey. The trail often follows the very edge of the lake, so views are consistently good. You will watch the dam disappear slowly behind as you take in some new vistas. Toward the end of this section near Dock 4, Burr Oak Lodge comes into spectacular view across the lake to the east. This is best seen in the evening light.

Miles and Directions

0.0 Start at the Tom Jenkins Dam. From the parking lot, look to the sign for the backpacking trail. *Do not follow the sign.* Instead, walk past it and straight through the picnic area. Just past the picnic shelter, you will see the wooden trailhead sign for the Lakeview Trail.

0.2 The trail veers away from the lake, edging the stream. At this point you will pick up white diamond blazes in addition to the yellow blazes. When you see the double white blaze, cross the stream and head back to the main body of the lake.

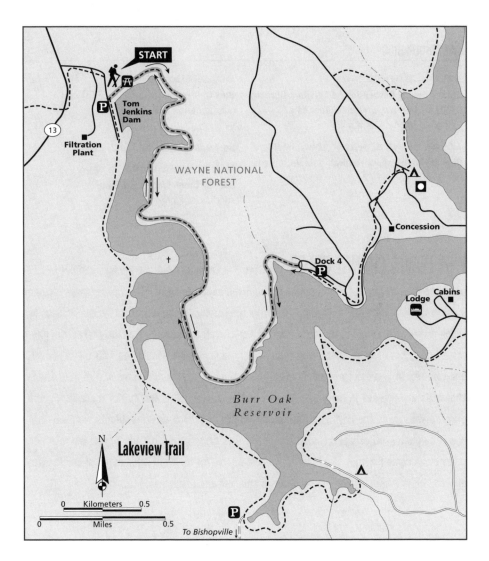

0.7 You will cross a large stream. Beware: The stream crossing occurs before the blazes. In a few hundred feet you will cross another stream, but the cherry tree that holds the blaze has fallen. Cross and walk slightly to the left, ascending the ridge. Continue ascending about halfway up the ridge. The trail stays there for a while, crossing some more drainages.

1.2 The trail cuts to the left, crossing a ridge, and then immediately descends; the blazes are not apparent here.

1.5 The trail finishes its descent to the lakeside.

2.0 Cross a couple of footbridges, then walk through some brambles.

2.6 The lodge will come into view across the lake, and Dock 4 will be visible straight ahead.

2.9 The trail curves eastward and finishes at Dock 4. **Option:** Finish the hike here if you shuttled.

5.8 Return to the dam trailhead.

Hike Information

Local information

Athens County Convention and Visitors Bureau; (800) 878-9767; www.eurekanet.com/ ~athenscvb/outdoors.html.

Local events and attractions

Glouster Chili Pepper Festival, held in September; (740) 767-4772.

Accommodations

Burr Oak Lodge (800-282-7275) and campground (740-767-3570).

Restaurants

Burr Oak Lodge; (800) 282-7275.

Other resources

Sunday Creek Watershed Group; sundaycreek.org/.

WHY LEAVES CHANGE COLOR

The Burr Oak Lakeside Trail is especially popular in fall, when the bright colors of turning leaves accent the landscape. But what makes leaves change color in the fall? As most of us remember from grade school, photosynthesis is the process by which plants turn sunlight into sugar for food. The chemical chlorophyll, an integral part of photosynthesis, gives leaves their green color. Other chemicals are associated with the other colors you see in leaves: carotenoids with yellow and orange; anthocyanins with red. These chemicals are present in leaves all along, but the chlorophyll green masks them during the growing season. As the days shorten and the nights approach freezing, plants begin to shut down the photosynthesis process. As the chlorophyll disappears from the leaves, the reds and yellows can come through. Maple trees are best known for their fall color, with red maple turning red; sugar maple turning yellow, orange, and red; and black maple turning yellow.

42 Archers Fork Trail

Wayne National Forest—Marietta District

This 9.5-mile loop trail offers a sampling of the natural, resource, and human history that defines Ohio's Appalachian region. Start from an old cemetery and walk along ridgetops and in hollows. Pass two attractive runs, a natural bridge, recess caves, and rock outcroppings surrounded by mountain laurel. Spring wildflowers in this mixed mesophytic forest are outstanding. Hike it in a day or make it into an overnighter, since backcountry camping is allowed in the national forest.

Start: From the cemetery off Shay Ridge Road
Distance: 9.3-mile loop
Approximate hiking time: 4 to 5 hours
Difficulty: Difficult due to length and hills
Trail surface: A dirt path that crosses a number ridges and several streams
Blaze: White diamond with a blue dot in the middle
Seasons: Best mid-April through mid-October
Other trail users: Mountain bikers, hunters (seasonal)
Canine compatibility: Leashed dogs permitted
Water: No potable water is available along this long and difficult trail; bring enough water or a purifier.

Land status: National forest
Nearest town: New Matamoras
Fees and permits: No fees or permits required
Schedule: Wayne National Forest trails are open 24 hours a day, 365 days a year. Day hikes are best done from dawn to dusk.
Maps: A brochure with topo maps of all hiking and backpacking trails in the Wayne is available for $6.00 at all Wayne National Forest offices. USGS quad: Rinard Mills; Maptech Terrain Navigator: Ohio/Southeast
Trail contacts: Wayne National Forest–Marietta District, Marietta; (740) 373-9055; www.fs.fed.us/r9/wayne/

Finding the trailhead: From State Route 260 between Bloomfield and New Matamoras, turn south onto Shay Ridge Road (Township Road 34). Drive 1.4 miles to the brown NORTH COUNTRY SCENIC TRAIL sign. Turn left and park by the cemetery on the left. Do not try to continue along the road past the cemetery, it's deeply rutted and there's no parking farther down. *DeLorme: Ohio Atlas and Gazetteer:* Page 72 D2.

The Hike

Think Appalachia—hollows, coal mines, bluegrass music, rural life. Now think Appalachian Ohio. Yep, there is such a thing, and Archers Fork lies in the heart of Ohio's hill country. Hike the Archers Fork Loop Trail and walk through a microcosm of the natural, human, and resource history that defines this region.

The USDA Forest Service started purchasing land in the 1930s, when much of it had already been depleted of its timber and other natural resources. Today the Wayne National Forest comprises 233,000 acres within a purchase boundary of 834,000 acres. Wayne National Forest's purchase boundaries are the lines Congress

Irish Run Natural Bridge on Archers Fork Trail in Wayne National Forest.

has drawn within which the Wayne can buy land. It looks vast, but in reality the Wayne's actual holdings look more like the shotgun blasts you see on target-practice road signs here. Private inholdings make up most of the area within purchase boundaries. Some locals resent the Wayne because of the lack of a tax base. But other locals, as well as the Wayne's many visitors, take advantage of the many recreational opportunities it provides. (In 2001 a state representative introduced a bill that would place a moratorium on land acquisition for the Wayne. Forest users, environmental groups, property owners, and the Wayne National Forest combined forces and defeated the bill.)

The Wayne's management plan is a schizophrenic attempt to satisfy all industry and public desires. Timbering, oil and gas development, and coal mining proposals exist side by side with legal and illegal ATV, equestrian, mountain bike, and hiking trails. Be sure to stay on the designated trail lest you stray onto private land.

This landscape retains a rugged side as well. If you make the 9.3-mile loop into an overnighter, listen for the incessant call of the whippoorwill until you hear the hooves of white-tailed deer just outside the tent. But this is a doable, if difficult, day hike. Walk quietly and keep an eye out for fox. Look on the trail for signs of raccoons and wild turkey scratch—they often kick up large areas of leaf litter while looking for grub.

Begin the hike at an old cemetery just up the hill from a recess cave. At the top of the cave, you may notice a hole. The erosion process will someday enlarge this hole to the point where the cave technically becomes a rock bridge, but that's prob-ably a long ways off. Continue along the ridgetop, looking down on the first of many attractive stream valleys. Sycamore, beech, and maple grow in the moist bottomlands, while the up-lands are usually dominated by oak and hickory. Some of these slopes are more mixed, though, so look also for cherry, tulip poplar, ash, walnut, and basswood. Understory trees and shrubs include dogwood, redbud, pawpaw, and spicebush.

Soon the trail arrives at its most conspicuous geologic point, Irish Run natural bridge, a sandstone outcrop-ping that measures 51 feet long and 39 feet high. There are other small but at-tractive rock faces and recess caves along the trail. Look in spring for hepatica, ramps, trillium, jack-in-the-pulpit, and other flowers in bloom. Although uncommon in these parts, flowering mountain laurel also grows around these rock faces.

▶ When hiking, stop by cemeteries along the trail, especially old cemeteries. There are two interesting things to look for: First, note the names on the headstones. This will give you a good idea of the settlement patterns of the region. Are these names Irish, Italian, English, Amish? Is it a mix? If so, jobs (for example, coal mining) probably attracted people from near and far to the area. A second thing to look for are the trees in the cemetery. You're likely to find some stately old trees that have thrived for many years in favorable conditions—that is, few other trees competing for sunlight.

Before you finish the loop you will walk along Archers Fork and Jackson Run and cross Irish Run. These streams may be impassable during high water in spring. Expect also to walk along some access roads to contemporary and "historic" (read abandoned) oil wells. If you want to extend your hike, a connecting path leads to the Covered Bridge Trail. Or try the North Country Trail, which joins Archers Fork for a while and then continues both north and south.

Miles and Directions

0.0 Start from the cemetery. Follow the white blaze down the gravel road, then pick up blue blazes with directional arrows. Turn left and descend to a fork and a sign that says HIKER TRAIL, marked also with blue and white blazes. Take a right, just before the top of the recess cave.

0.5 Come to a sign for a short side trail to the left leading to the natural bridge. Explore the bridge and then return to this point and continue on.

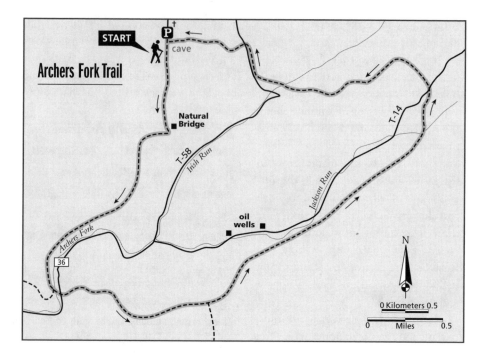

Archers Fork Trail

0.7 Hit an unimproved dirt road. Take a right and follow the road up the ridge. In a few hundred feet the trail turns off the road to the left. Pass a gate and continue walking on another unimproved road.

1.0 Pass some old oil wells and turn left.

1.2 The trail turns right and becomes a footpath again.

1.8 In the lowlands paralleling the stream, reach a fork. Take the right fork onto a grassy mowed path.

2.3 Come to a junction with the connector to the Covered Bridge Trail. Turn left, staying with both the blue and the white blazes.

2.5 Cross Township Road 36.

3.7 After walking on a doubletrack for a while, pass a gate and reach a junction with an access road. Continue straight and follow the road.

4.0 Come to a junction. The North Country National Scenic Trail (blazed blue) takes off to the right. Take a left, following the white blazes and a signpost for the Archers Fork Trail. Almost immediately, hit a fork. Turn right, looking for the white blaze. Again almost immediately, there's a side trail to the right. *Don't take it.* Instead continue straight. In less than 100 yards, the doubletrack veers right. Go straight, staying with the blazes.

6.0 Descend across a drainage and then to a streambed. You will see signs for the Ohio View Trail, unfortunately also blazed with white diamonds/blue dots. Continue straight ahead, crossing the streambed. Ascend the ridge by way of switchbacks.

6.5 Cross Township Road 14. Continue straight on the trail until you hit a T intersection. Turn left and continue along the ridgetop.

7.7 Descend to Township Road 58 and turn right. Walk a few hundred feet to a poorly marked trail to the left. If you see a blue blaze on the roadside, you've gone too far. You can turn around and see the trail more clearly from this point.

8.5 Descend back down to Township Road 411 and cross it. The trail soon forks. Take the left—the blazes here may be obscured by foliage. Walk under power lines in the bottomland. The mowed trail turns right and ascends the ridge steeply.

9.3 Return to the cave near the start. Cross over the top of the cave and continue straight. Return the way you came to the cemetery.

Hike Information

Local information

Marietta/Washington County Convention and Visitors Bureau, Marietta; (800) 288-2577; www.mariettaohio.org/.

Local events and attractions

Lamping Homestead, Covered Bridge, and Ohio View Trails are also located in the Marietta District of the Wayne National Forest.

Accommodations

Backcountry camping is permitted in Wayne National Forest. Two national forest campsites are close to the trail, located at either end of the Covered Bridge Trail. However, the WNF reports that vandalism has occured here.

Organizations

North Country National Scenic Trail; www.northcountrytrail.org/gts/index.htm.

43 Lamping Homestead Trail

Wayne National Forest—Marietta District

This 4.0-mile loop trail is one of the most secluded in the state. Begin at the nine-teenth-century Lamping family homestead. Walk around a small fishable pond and into a deciduous forest dotted here and there with white pine plantations. Ascend ridges 600 to 800 feet above the river valleys, and walk in biodiverse hollows. Over-look Clear Fork and return to where you started, circling a Native American mound and the old Lamping family cemetery.

Start: From the picnic area next to the parking lot.

Distance: 4.0-mile loop

Approximate hiking time: 1^1/$_2$ to 2 hours

Difficulty: Moderate due to some steep sections and some difficult footing

Trail surface: Dirt

Blaze: White diamond

Seasons: Best April through October

Other trail users: Hunters (seasonal)

Canine compatibility: Leashed dogs permitted

Water: None available; bring your own.

Land status: National forest

Nearest town: Graysville

Fees and permits: No fees or permits required

Schedule: Wayne National Forest trails are open 24 hours a day, 365 days a year. Day hikes are best done from dawn to dusk.

Maps: A brochure with topo maps of all hiking and backpacking trails in the Wayne is available for $6.00 at Wayne National Forest offices. USGS quad: Rinard Mills; Maptech Terrain Navigator: Ohio/Southeast

Trail contacts: Wayne National Forest–Marietta District, Marietta; (740) 373-9055; www.fs.fed.us/r9/wayne/

Finding the trailhead: From Marietta, take State Route 26 North 35.3 miles to State Route 537. Turn left (west) and drive 1.6 miles to Township Road 307. Take a left and drive 0.2 mile to the sign for the Lamping Homestead picnic area. Turn left into the parking lot. *DeLorme: Ohio Atlas and Gazetteer:* Page 72 C2.

The Hike

The Lamping Homestead Trail is one of the most secluded hiking trails in Wayne National Forest, if not the state. Not only is it far from just about anywhere, but the trail never crosses a road or suffers from a lot of human intrusion. Wayne National Forest literature suggests that this old homestead still looks much as it did in the early 1800s, when the Lamping family lived here.

Situated well into the Western Allegheny–Appalachian Plateau, the Lamping Homestead and much of Morgan County are home to some of the steepest ridges in Ohio, with an average 600- to 800-foot elevation gain from creek to ridgetop. This is the land where the last glacier pushed the flow of the former Teas and Steubenville Rivers backward into the newly created (geologically speaking) Ohio River, which cuts a valley through the Appalachian Plateau. Monroe County has

Lamping cemetery at Lamping Homestead.

historically been known as Little Switzerland—but not because of the steep slopes. Rather it's because this area was heavily settled by Swiss immigrants.

The hike begins at a picnic area situated where the homestead once was. Walk through a small white pine plantation and begin circling around a fishable pond created by a small earthen dam. The trail soon turns away from the pond and follows an attractive stream that feeds the pond. Look for beech and maple trees lower down and oak trees on the ridgetops. Understory species include pawpaw and spicebush. Springtime brings common wildflowers such as spring beauty, trillium, and wild geranium.

Ascend to a small opening and walk by the only gas well you'll see on the hike and then through another white pine plantation. Soon you will have the option to take a shorter loop back to the picnic area. Continuing on, the trail works its way along other small tributaries to the Clear Fork, an attractive creek that flows into the Little Muskingum River. There are some views of the Clear Fork Valley. The forest is lush and ferns grow in the cool, damp drainages. Walk quietly and keep an eye out for white-tailed deer, wild turkey, ruffed grouse, and fox.

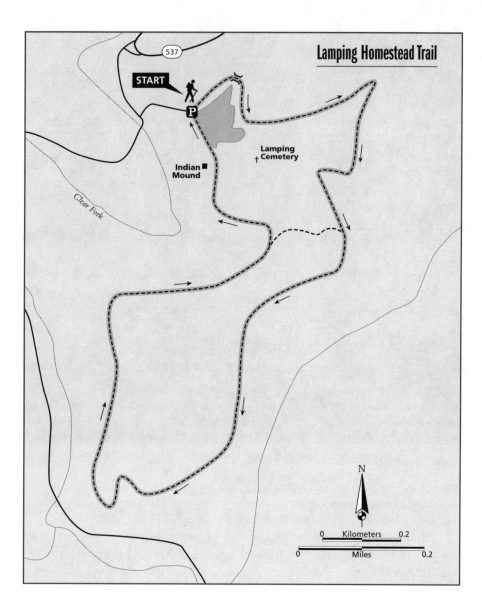

START

P

Lamping
† Cemetery

Indian
Mound

Clear Fork

537

N

| 0 | Kilometers | 0.2 |
| 0 | Miles | 0.2 |

As you approach the end of this loop, you will see evidence of the people who lived here long before the Lampings. The trail skirts the base of a large conical Adena mound. Look for a side trail to the old Lamping cemetery atop the mound. Finish the hike by walking over the dam and back to the picnic area.

Miles and Directions

0.0 Start from the picnic area next to the parking lot. Walk past the gate and toward the lake. Take a left and walk through the pines, following white blazes.

0.2 The trail curves to the right and crosses a footbridge. In a few hundred feet, the trail turns away from the pond and slowly ascends the ridge, paralleling the stream.

0.6 Turn right and cross over the stream.

1.0 Reach the top of the ridge and then approach a wooden sign for the short loop. To continue on the long loop, walk straight ahead. **Option:** Take a right to return on the short loop for a 1.8-mile round-trip hike. You will soon cross an old road and walk through another pine plantation.

1.4 The trail turns sharply left and crosses a drainage. Then it begins a gradual descent.

2.0 The trail curves to the right and ascends slightly. You can see Clear Fork Creek from here.

2.1 Cross an old doubletrack road.

3.7 Come to the junction with the short loop trail, entering from the right. Continue straight ahead, descending to the bottomlands.

4.0 Approach a large Native American mound and circle halfway around it. Then cross the dam and return to the picnic area where you started.

Hike Information

Local information

Monroe County Office of Economic Development and Tourism; (740) 472-0169; www.monroecountyohio.net/.

Local events and attractions

Archers Fork, Covered Bridge, and Ohio View Trails are also located in the Marietta District of the Wayne National Forest.

Accommodations

There is a nice primitive campground at **Lamping Homestead.**

Neighboring **Clearwater Creek Campground** in Graysville has electric sites; (740) 934-2331.

44 Red and Blue Trails

Dysart Woods

What this 1.5-mile trail lacks in length, it makes up for in significance. If you want to get a sense of what the first Europeans settlers saw when they encountered North America's eastern hardwood forests, come to Dysart Woods, Ohio's largest tract of virgin forest. This rich mixed mesophytic forest is home to ancient oaks and tulip poplars that measure more than 5 feet in diameter. Expect to climb up and down ridges and over fallen logs on this trail in an undisturbed forest.

Start: From the parking area
Distance: 1.5-mile figure eight
Approximate hiking time: 1 hour
Difficulty: Moderate due to a lot of ups and downs and several large fallen tree trunks over the trail
Trail surface: A hilly dirt trail occasionally blocked by fallen logs
Seasons: Best April through October
Other trail users: Hikers only
Canine compatibility: Dogs not permitted
Water: None available; bring your own.

Land status: Owned by Ohio University; open to the public
Nearest town: St. Clairsville
Fees and permits: No fees or permits required
Schedule: Open daily year-round from dawn to dusk
Maps: USGS quads: Armstrong Mills, Hunter; Maptech Terrain Navigator: Ohio/Southeast
Trail contacts: Ohio University, Athens; www.plantbio.ohiou.edu/epb/facility/dysart/dysart.htm

Finding the trailhead: From I-77 in St. Clairsville, turn south onto State Route 9 (exit 216) and travel 7.8 miles to State Route 14. Turn west (right) and drive 1.0 mile to Dysart Road, marked by a large wooden sign. Turn left (south) and travel 0.2 mile to a fork. Take the right fork, following the large sign for Dysart Woods. Drive 0.8 mile to a small gravel parking lot on the left. Look downhill for two blue markers indicating the trailhead. ***DeLorme: Ohio Atlas and Gazetteer:*** Page 72 A4.

The Hike

For all the times your eyes scanned a landscape and you thought, *I wonder what it was like to discover this place,* go to Dysart Woods and indulge this daydream. Home to Ohio's largest remaining tract of virgin forest, Dysart Woods allows you to get a glimpse of what the eastern hardwood forests looked like to Native Americans and, later, European settlers. Trees 300 to 400 years old continue to thrive in this fifty-acre National Natural Landmark.

Beginning on the Blue Trail, walk down into a ravine. You will see a rich mixed mesophytic forest, common in this part of the state. Pay close attention and you will begin to notice the characteristics that make this forest special. Most obvious are the smattering of trees as large as 5 feet in diameter. A number of these giants are con-

A massive tulip tree snag stands at Dysart Woods.

centrated on the small loop of the Blue Trail, so be sure to take it. Some of the most noticeable here are tulip poplars, so called in reference to their yellow-and-orange tuliplike flowers. Look on the trail for petals in springtime, because you probably won't see the flowers growing in the trees. Tulips are tall, straight, self-pruning trees whose first branches in dense woods are 40 to 50 feet from the ground. Scientists refer to tulip poplars as tulip trees because they are not actually in the poplar family. Giant snags make good homes for a number of animal species. Look for the squared-off holes of the pileated woodpecker.

The Blue Trail ends at Ault Dysart Road. Both the road and the woods are named after the Dysart family, who for several generations preserved the woods they owned before handing ownership over to The Nature Conservancy and then Ohio University. When you cross the road and begin the Red Trail, you will descend into the valley. On the other (upland) side of the stream, approach some of the biggest trees at Dysart. The largest is a tulip tree whose bottom half stands as a snag while its top half lies on the ground nearby. This tree, with a diameter of 64 inches, was struck by lightning in 1995. Because the core was rotten when it fell, no one knows the tree's exact age, but it's estimated to be about 400 years old.

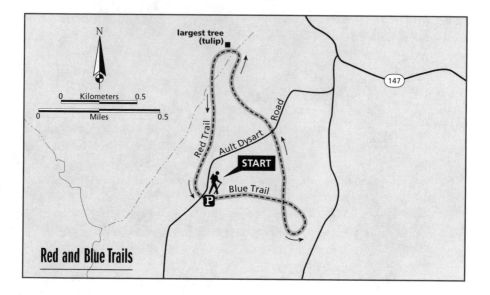

Red and Blue Trails

Standing snags and fallen trees left to rot are notably common here. The forest is left untouched in an effort to preserve its natural state. What makes this a "virgin" forest is that it has encountered little or no human disturbance. The forest has never been logged or thinned; it hasn't been occupied by a homestead, fenced, used for grazing animals, farmed, or otherwise disturbed by humans (except, of course, for this hiking trail).

Due to the shade cast by a dense canopy, the understory of this forest is clearer than in a younger forest. Common understory plants include witch hazel, pawpaw, and spicebush. In spring look for such flowers as trout lily, trillium, and spring beauty. In summer look for sweet cicely. Mosses, ferns, and fungi tend to be more widespread here than in a disturbed forest.

Researchers use Dysart Woods as a laboratory for studying forest ecosystems. These remnant old-growth forests are the best measure we have today for how a healthy, functioning forest ecosystem works and how natural disturbances affect them. These forests tend to be reserves of biological diversity and also serve as living museums that provide a climatic history of the area. Tree rings indicate periods of drought, fire,

▶ A mixed mesophytic forest is one in which about twenty to twenty-five tree species are common, but none dominate the canopy. Trees found in a mixed mesophytic forest include beech, tulip tree, basswood, sugar maple, red oak, white oak, and hemlock. Depending on where you are, some species drop out while others come in, including birch, cherry, ash, magnolia, sour gum, black walnut, and hickory. Mixed mesophytic forests are known to be very biologically rich, often containing more than 1,000 plant species.

and human impact. Finally, as you stroll through these magnificent woods, ponder the philosophical questions that surround the place. How do we measure the worth of a forest? In board feet? In biological diversity? Intrinsic value? What are the roles humans have played in the demise of the eastern hardwood forests, and what is our role in preserving what's left and being stewards of the forests that are still growing?

Miles and Directions

0.0 Start at the parking area. Look downhill to two blue markers that indicate the Blue Trail trailhead.

0.2 Come to a T intersection. Turn right here to walk a small loop on the Blue Trail. This loop contains some of the preserve's larger trees.

0.4 Pass an old wooden sign on the right (there's nothing on it). The trail curves to the left.

0.5 Return to the junction of the Blue Trail loop. Walk straight, following signs for the Red Trail.

0.7 The Blue Trail ends at Ault Dysart Road. Cross the road; angle off to the left a bit and pick up the Red Trail, marked with a sign.

0.9 Cross the stream over two footbridges and then begin to ascend the ridge.

1.0 Come to the largest tulip tree. Its bottom half stands as a snag, while its top half lies on the ground. In about 75 feet approach a giant white oak. The trail continues to the left (downslope) of the oak, *not* to the right.

1.1 Cross the stream again over a footbridge. The rest of the trail is uphill. Look for the red blazes. You will have to climb over some large fallen logs.

1.5 Return to Ault Dysart Road and the parking area.

Hike Information

Local information
Belmont County Tourism Council; (740) 695-4359; www.bctc.itgo.com/events.htm.

Local events and attractions
Annual **Drover's Trail Festival** celebrates the bovine equivalent of the National Road; www.droverstrail.com.

Accommodations
Barkcamp State Park campground, Belmont; (740) 484-4064; www.ohiodnr.com/parks/parks/barkcamp.htm.

Restaurants
Gasber's Fine Day Restaurant, St. Clairsville; (740) 695-0125.

A NEW THREAT Dysart Woods is still intact because several generations of the Dysart family protected it from logging. Its greatest threat may lie ahead, however. The Ohio Division of Mines and Reclamation has given a permit to the Ohio Valley Coal Company to conduct long-wall mining near the woods. Ohio University, The Buckeye Forest Council, and Dysart Defenders are all engaged in a legal battle to prevent the mining. Some predict that mining might draw groundwater away from the woods and damage, if not kill, the trees. If you're considering a trip to Dysart Woods, go soon. To express your concerns, contact your state elected representatives. Call the Legislative Public Information Office at (800) 282–0253, or log on to the State of Ohio home page legislature link: www.legislature .state.oh.us.

Honorable Mentions Southeast Ohio

T Buckeye Trail through Hocking Hills State Forest

Love the Hocking Hills but hate the crowds? The statewide Buckeye Trail (BT) traces a path through the Hocking Hills State Forest, and while some sections are mobbed (think Old Man's Cave to Cedar Falls), others are hardly even known. A case in point is the 2.5-mile section between Rocky Fork and Kreashbaum Roads. Starting from a small pullout along Rocky Fork Road, walk into a dense hemlock forest. Downslope is Rocky Fork, and upslope to your left are some nice sandstone outcroppings. The understory is relatively bare, so don't think about flowering plants; rather, look for the easy-to-see mushrooms that grow on the many rotting logs and stumps here. The trail dips down and crosses Rocky Fork at an attractive spot of sandstone outcroppings, small caves, and a fern-covered floor. You can continue to Kreashbaum Road, but the trail quality goes downhill between the creek and Kreashbaum as it travels through younger successional forests and then skirts a fresh clearcut. But definitely take the BT as far as the creekbed and return for a nearly 5.0-mile round-trip. You probably won't see another soul.

Trail contacts: Hocking State Forest, Rockbridge; (740) 385–4402; www.ohio dnr.com/forestry/Forests/stateforests/hocking.htm.

Finding the trailhead: From U.S. Highway 33 west of Logan, turn onto State Route 180 west and drive 4.0 miles to the junction with State Route 678 South. Turn left and drive 1.3 miles to Kreashbaum Road, on the left. Turn onto Kreashbaum and drive 0.7 mile to Rocky Fork Road (Township Road 232) on the left. Make a sharp left turn onto this gravel road and drive 1.0 mile to a pullout on the right, marked with a double blue blaze that indicates a turn onto the Buckeye Trail. *DeLorme: Ohio Atlas and Gazetteer:* Page 69 D6 and Page 79 A5.

U Rockbridge State Nature Preserve

The main attraction at this preserve is Ohio's longest natural bridge, measuring nearly 100 feet long and featuring a 50-foot waterfall. Both of the preserve's trails can be combined to make a 2.6-mile hike. Begin by walking a long, narrow right-of-way between two farm fields and then enter the woods, where you will see spring wildflowers such as crested dwarf iris, trillium, bloodroot, and trailing arbutus. Other attractions include migrating warblers, views of the Hocking River, and more rock features, including a small rock shelter. There is also canoe access from the Hocking River. This spot was popular with Wyandot In-

▶ There are sixty-five to seventy known rock bridges in Ohio. It's possible that more have yet to be documented.

dians and, later, Hocking Canal travelers. Be sure to stay on designated trails; you will be near private property at all times. Hunters may be on adjacent private property, so be aware of hunting season dates.

Trail contacts: Rockbridge State Nature Preserve, Rockbridge; (740) 420–3445; www.ohiodnr.com/dnap/location/rockbridge.html.

Finding the trailhead: From U.S. Highway 33 in Hocking County (near the state rest area), turn north onto Township Road 124/503 (Dalton Road). Take an immediate right and follow the signs 0.7 mile to a parking area on the left. The trail is located just past the information kiosk. *DeLorme: Ohio Atlas and Gazetteer:* Page 69 D6.

V Covered Bridge Trail, Wayne National Forest

The highlight of this 5.0-mile point-to-point trail is what lies at each end: a century-old covered bridge. Once numbering in the thousands, only about 140 covered bridges exist in Ohio today. Each bridge/trailhead crosses the scenic Little Muskingum River where steep wooded slopes meet farmland in the river valley. The trail itself moves away from the river to upland oak-hickory forests and crosses some attractive tributaries. From the Covered Bridge Trail, you can take a connector trail to Archers Fork and the North Country Trail. Stay on the designated trail, since private land abuts the Wayne throughout this portion of the national forest. Primitive campgrounds are located at either trailhead, but vandalism is a threat in this remote area.

Trail contacts: Wayne National Forest—Marietta District; (740) 373–9055; www.fs.fed.us/r9/wayne/.

Finding the trailhead: From State Routes 7 and 60 in Marietta, take State Route 26 north 17.7 miles to a brown forest service trailhead sign on the right that reads CANOE ACCESS HUNE BRIDGE. Take a right onto Duff Road and leave your car in the camping area. To shuttle, return to SR 26 and continue north another 3.0 miles to the Haught Bridge, visible right next to the road. Turn right onto Tice Run Road (County Road 406) and park by the covered bridge. *DeLorme: Ohio Atlas and Gazetteer:* Page 72 D2.

W Ohio View Trail, Wayne National Forest

The 7.0-mile point-to-point Ohio View Trail could be better described as the Ohio Glimpse Trail. And the glimpse you do get is overlooking an industrial complex! But don't be discouraged, this well-designed trail weaves through mature oak-hickory forests on the slopes and beech-maple forests in the bottomlands. Wind your way around a number of attractive streams and drainages. Go in springtime to see a riot of wildflowers and in autumn for the striking colors of fall foliage. Get a permit to collect some nontimber forest products like morel and chicken-of-the-woods mushrooms, pawpaw fruits, and medicinal plants like yellowroot, bloodroot, blue cohosh, and black cohosh. Watch closely for blazes toward the northern end of this trail; the route sometimes deviates from the forest service map due to changes in oil and gas access roads.

Trail contacts: Wayne National Forest—Marietta District; (740) 373–9055; www.fs.fed.us/r9/wayne/.

Finding the trailhead: The trailhead is marked with a sign on State Route 7 in Beavertown. To shuttle, continue north to New Matamoras, where you turn onto State Route 260 and travel west 2.0 miles to the trailhead on the left. The trailhead sign is easy to miss; if you hit County Road 9, you've gone too far. *DeLorme: Ohio Atlas and Gazetteer:* 73 C7.

In Addition: Ohio's Backpack Trails

If you're looking for a few more miles, a backcountry experience, or a secluded camping spot, try one of Ohio's backpack trails. Most backpack trailheads do not have maps stocked, so contact the appropriate agency before heading out. Also bring a water purifier, since reliable water sources can be few and far between. Most of these trails require a free backcountry permit or self-registration at the trailhead.

Burr Oak Backpack Trail

Walk around the perimeter of Burr Oak Lake on an 18.0-mile trail that provides some excellent views of the lake from the comfortable shade of a maturing forest. There are some nice rock features and even a Native American signal tree—an old

Backpacking in the Shawnee State Forest.

tree that Native Americans bent down as a sapling to mark a direction on long-distance routes. Begin from Boat Dock 1 and take the Buckeye Trail along the east side of the lake or the Backpack Trail along the west side of the lake to one of several primitive campsites or the main campground. Alternately, begin along the north side of the lake, at the campground or at the Wildcat Hollow Trailhead, and spend the night at the lodge.

Trail contacts: Burr Oak State Park, Glouster; (740) 767–3570; www.ohiodnr.com/parks/parks/burroak.htm.

Finding the trailhead: From State Route 13 in Glouster, turn east onto State Route 78 and drive 4.1 miles to the park entrance on the left, marked with a sign. Take a left onto the park drive and drive straight to the park office. *DeLorme: Ohio Atlas and Gazetteer:* Page 70 D2.

East Fork State Park Trails

There are three lengthy trails on the south side of East Fork Lake. Combine them any way you want to make an overnighter or a several-day trip. Closest to the lakeshore is the 14.0-mile Backpack Trail. Paralleling that and circling the entire lake is the 32.0-mile Steve Newman Worldwalker Perimeter Trail, named after a native son who became the first person to circle the globe entirely on foot. He spent the last night of his travels in East Fork State Park before returning home. Largely sharing the same route with the Perimeter Trail is the Buckeye–North Country–American Discovery Trail. This multinamed trail continues beyond park boundaries to the east and west. There are four backcountry campsites available; get a permit from the park office. Horses are permitted on the Perimeter Trail, and illegal equestrian use has extended to the Backpack Trail as well.

Trail contacts: East Fork State Park, Bethel; (513) 734–4323; www.ohiodnr.com/parks/park/eastfork.htm.

Finding the trailhead: From I–275 in Cincinnati, travel east on State Route 32 for 10.0 miles to Half Acre Road. Turn south (right) and drive 0.8 mile to Old State Route 32. Take a left and drive 0.1 mile to the park entrance on the right. Drive straight ahead to the park office. *DeLorme: Ohio Atlas and Gazetteer:* Page 75 D7.

Logan Trail

If the north loop of the Logan Trail in Tar Hollow State Forest leaves you wanting more, you can access the backpack camp on the south loop and keep on going. The entire figure-eight trail makes a good 21.0-mile overnight trip, but the campsite is located near the intersection of the loops, so two day hikes from a base camp might be more appropriate. Begin and end at the fire tower, where you can look out on a sea of deciduous forest. In springtime look for showy wildflowers and hunt for edible mushrooms. Complete the figure eight in its entirety, or, better yet, do the north loop then hop on the well-constructed Buckeye Trail, which bisects the south loop. On the south side expect to share old logging roads with equestrians. The Logan Trail is named after the eighteenth-century chief of the Mingo Nation, a Native American tribe that lived in Pennsylvania and Ohio.

Trail contacts: Tar Hollow State Forest, Waverly; (740) 663–2523; www.ohiodnr.com/forestry/Forests/stateforests/tarhollow.htm.

Finding the trailhead: From State Route 327 about halfway between State Route 56 and U.S. Highway 50, turn west onto Forest Road 10, marked with a park entrance sign. Travel 3.7 miles to a Y intersection. Turn left (south) onto Forest Road 3 and travel another 1.5 miles to the fire tower. Park on the grass or along the pull-out. *DeLorme: Ohio Atlas and Gazetteer:* Page 78, A4.

Mohican Memorial State Forest Bridle Trails

The day hikes in Mohican State Park are home to the area's main attractions: the Clear Fork of the Mohican River, Big and Little Lyons Falls, and a covered bridge. Two campgrounds also serve the park. But if you want to get a backcountry experience, head out on the adjacent Mohican Memorial State Forest's 24 miles of hiking and bridle trails (some portions are open to mountain biking as well). This is a way to get away from the crowds that can overwhelm the park's most popular trails. Of course, this time you'll be sharing the also-popular bridle trails with both people and horses. Check in with the state forest office for a free permit (required) and information about backcountry campsites. Dogs are not allowed in backcountry campsites.

Trail contacts: Mohican Memorial State Forest, New Philadelphia; (330) 339–2205; www.ohiodnr.com/forestry/Forests/stateforests/mohicanow.htm.

Finding the trailhead: From I–71 south of Mansfield, exit on State Route 96 and drive about 18 miles to the state forest offices on the left. *DeLorme: Ohio Atlas and Gazetteer:* Page 49 D7.

Morgan Sisters and Symmes Creek Trails

Good luck finding the trailhead, better luck staying on the overgrown trail, and forget about finding the virgin forest said to grow here. Nevertheless, the Morgan Sisters and Symmes Creek Trails in the Ironton District of the Wayne National Forest offer day-hike and backpacking options of 2, 4, 6, 8, or 14 miles. Try one or both trails (two loops with a connector) in fall through spring, when keeping on the well-blazed path shouldn't be difficult. Camp along Symmes Creek, but don't pitch your tent where an all-terrain vehicle might run you over. There's a lot of ATV use here. Some parts of the trail are in nice second-growth forest, and wildflowers are good spring through fall. Look for the old one-room schoolhouse, but don't fall into the well!

Trail contacts: Wayne National Forest, Ironton Ranger District, Pedro; (740) 532–3223; www.fs.fed.us/r9/wayne/.

Finding the trailhead: From State Route 93 in Oak Hill, turn east onto State Route 233 and drive 9.0 miles to Pumpkintown Road (an unmarked gravel road on the left at a bend, near the top of a hill on Route 233). Take a left and drive 0.9 mile to the first (gravel) road on the right, also unmarked. Take a right and drive 0.2 mile to a pullout at the end of the road, just past the small lake on the left. *DeLorme: Ohio Atlas and Gazetteer:* Page 86 B2.

Shawnee Backpack Trail

Shawnee State Forest is often called the Little Smokies, in reference to the area's steep hills and narrow hollows. The name Shawnee, of course, comes from the Native Americans who were living here when European settlers arrived. There are 40 miles worth of backpacking trails in this very bio-diverse mixed mesophytic forest, divided into north and south loops. The south loop takes you through the 8,000-acre backcountry management area, which is managed in part for rare and endangered species. Indeed, this is one trail where you have a chance to see wild ginseng growing on the forest floor. The endangered timber rattlesnake also makes the Shawnee its home. Unfortunately, the folks who constructed the trails here never heard of switchbacks, so hit the Stairmaster before strapping on your pack and hiking straight up and down the ridges. Plan your route according to water conditions: Creeks can run dry in summer, the trail is often on the ridgetop, and potable-water tanks provided by the state forest are sometimes empty. The Shawnee State Forest is also home to Ohio's only wilderness area. Designated in 1972, the wilderness area is off-limits to timbering, roads, and any other development. But it's by no means an old-growth forest yet, so plan to come back in fifty years.

▶ If you arrive at park or forest headquarters during office hours and they're not too busy, you may be able to get somebody to drop you off at a trailhead in order to set up a shuttle. This is especially true in more-remote areas, where vandalism is more of a threat to unattended vehicles.

Trail contacts: Shawnee State Forest, West Portsmouth; (740) 858–6685; www.ohiodnr.com/forestry/Forests/stateforests/shawnee.htm.

Finding the trailhead: From U.S. Highway 23 in Portsmouth, take U.S. Highway 52 west 6.6 miles to State Route 125 (past the state forest headquarters). Turn west (right) onto Route 125 and drive 6.6 miles to the backpacking trailhead parking lot on the left. *DeLorme: Ohio Atlas and Gazetteer:* Page 84 C3.

Vesuvius Backpack Trail

If you enjoyed the Lakeshore Trail at Lake Vesuvius in the Ironton District of Wayne National Forest, take it up a notch and head out on the Vesuvius Backpack Trail, a 16.0-mile loop that shares the Lakeshore Trail but then extends out into the forest along ridges and creek valleys. The redbuds and dogwoods blooming in springtime make a great show (although the dogwoods are succumbing to a fungal blight). Wildflowers and rock outcroppings in the Hanging Rock region are impressive as well.

Trail contacts: Wayne National Forest, Ironton Ranger District, Pedro; (740) 532–3223; www.fs.fed.us/r9/wayne/.

Finding the trailhead: From Ironton, travel north on State Route 93 for 6.5 miles and turn east (right) onto County Road 29. Follow the signs 0.9 mile to the furnace parking lot. *DeLorme: Ohio Atlas and Gazetteer:* Page 85 D7.

Wildcat Hollow Backpack Trail

This popular trail in the Athens District of Wayne National Forest largely follows ridgetops and features excellent spring wildflowers and fall foliage. Attractions include an old one-room schoolhouse and an old farmhouse. Expect also to see oil wells and access roads. In dry weather it may be difficult to find a good water source. The trail is a 15.0-mile loop with an optional 5.0-mile day hike.

Trail contacts: Wayne National Forest, Athens Ranger District; (740) 753–0101; www.fs.fed.us/r9/wayne/.

Finding the trailhead: From State Route 13 between Corning and Glouster, turn east onto Irish Ridge Road (County Road 16). Drive 0.1 mile to a junction, where Irish Run turns left. Take a left here and drive 1.9 miles to a second junction. Turn right onto Dew Road (the road is not marked, but there is a sign here for the Wildcat Hollow trailhead). Drive 1.6 miles to the trailhead parking lot on the left. *DeLorme: Ohio Atlas and Gazetteer:* Page 75 D7.

Zaleski Backpack Trail

Only about ninety minutes from Columbus, the 26.0-mile Zaleski State Forest Backpack Trail is perhaps the most popular backpack trail in the state. From the official trailhead at the Hope Furnace, you can start on a Friday night and make it to the first campsite just 1.5 miles into the trail. Several access points allow you to trim the mileage when necessary, including a 10.0-mile day hike that also starts from the Hope Furnace. Hike in some mature second-growth forest, near a brand-new clearcut, and through a former strip mine site. Walk through a young successional forest and a pine plantation. A side loop takes you past a pioneer cemetery and through a minigorge. There's even an overlook where you might glimpse the Moonville Ghost's swinging lantern at night.

Trail contacts: Zaleski State Forest, Zaleski; (740) 596–5781; www.ohiodnr.com/forestry/Forests/stateforests/zaleski.htm.

Finding the trailhead: From State Route 56 south of Nelsonville, turn south onto State Route 278 and travel 4.9 miles to the Hope Furnace parking lot on the right. *DeLorme: Ohio Atlas and Gazetteer:* Page 79 B7.

In Addition: Ohio's Long Trails

Buckeye Trail

When Emma "Grandma" Gatewood finished becoming the first woman to through-hike the Appalachian Trail, she returned to her home state of Ohio and hatched a new plan. With a few other dedicated folks, the Buckeye Trail Association (BTA) formed in 1959 with a mission to connect the Ohio River to Lake Erie with a footpath.

At nearly 1,300 miles in the length, the Buckeye Trail (BT) is now the longest hiking trail within one state in the country. The BT's southern terminus is along the Ohio River at Cincinnati's Eden Park. From there the trail circles around the state to the northern terminus at Headlands Beach in Mentor, on Lake Erie. The trail then completes the circle back down to the Ohio. In the meantime it crosses forty counties in just about every fashion possible: through state parks and forests, along abandoned railroad rights-of-way, through private lands, on bike paths, and along the road. The scenery is equally diverse: deep forests to farmland, rocky outcrops to lakeshore, boardwalks to waterfalls.

Only about 40 percent of the trail is off-road, but don't let that discourage you: Sections up to 70 miles in length are off-limits to motorized traffic. The BTA, an all-volunteer effort, is working to get the entire trail off-road. You can simply "follow the blue blazes" for the BT's entire length, or you can purchase section maps that detail the route in increments of about 50 miles each. Organized "circuit hikes" allow you to hike with a group one weekend a month along sections of the BT until you complete the entire length; on this schedule, it takes about five years to do the whole route. To help with trail building or maintenance, to make a donation, or to get information on group hikes, contact the BTA at (800) 881–3062 or visit www.buckeyetrail.org.

North Country Trail

Following the successful completion of the Appalachian Trail and the Pacific Crest Trail, Congress designated these two mountainous footpaths as National Scenic Trails in 1968. At about the same time, the USDA Forest Service came up with a plan to build the North Country National Scenic Trail (NCT). Today the NCT has a proposed route of 4,175 miles that weave through seven northern states: North Dakota, Minnesota, Wisconsin, Michigan, Ohio, Pennsylvania, and New York.

A full 1,050 of these miles will be through Ohio, and much of the NCT follows the same path as the Buckeye Trail (BT). The NCT's characteristics are varied, combining natural, recreational, historic, and cultural features.

The NCT enters northwest Ohio from Michigan, west of Toledo. It joins the BT and follows the Miami and Erie Canal towpath down toward Cincinnati, where it turns east through southern Ohio. The NCT and BT diverge in southeast Ohio,

The Buckeye Trail and the North Country Trail often follow the same route, as they do here along Piedmont Lake.

where the NCT continues through the Marietta District of Wayne National Forest. It then veers northward to Beaver Creek State Park, where it takes an eastward turn and continues to Pennsylvania. Volunteer groups in several states further the aims of the NCT. Log on to their Web site for more information: www.northcountry-trail.org/gts/index.htm.

American Discovery Trail

Once complete, the American Discovery Trail (ADT) will be the nation's only coast-to-coast nonmotorized trail. Spanning from Cape Henlopen State Park in Delaware to Point Reyes National Seashore near San Francisco, the trail has a total proposed length of 6,300 miles. The ADT connects five National Scenic Trails and ten National Historic Trails along the way. Like the Buckeye and the North Country Trails, it combines wilderness with urban experiences and links everything in between.

Coming from the west, optional north and south routes of the ADT converge in Elizabethtown, Ohio, west of Cincinnati. The ADT then follows the path of the Buckeye Trail for most of southern Ohio before diverging in the southeast part of the state, where it continues to Belpre before crossing the Ohio River into West Virginia. For route, volunteer, and other information, visit www.discoverytrail.org.

The Art of Hiking

When standing nose to snout with a bear, you're probably not too concerned with the issue of ethical behavior in the wild. But let's be honest. How often are you nose to snout with a bear? For most of us, a hike into the "wild" means loading up the 4-Runner with everything North Face and driving to a toileted trailhead. Sure, you can mourn how civilized we've become—how GPS units have replaced natural instinct and Gore-Tex, true-grit—but the silly gadgets of civilization aside, we have plenty of reason to take pride in how we've matured. With survival now on the back-burner, we've begun to reason—and it's about time—that we have a responsibility to protect, no longer just conquer, our wild places; that they, not we, are at risk. So please, do what you can. Now, in keeping with our chronic tendency to reduce everything to a list, here are some rules to remember.

Zero impact. Always leave an area just like you found it—if not better than you found it. Avoid camping in fragile meadows and along the banks of streams and lakes. Use a lightweight camp stove versus building a wood fire. Pack up all of your trash and extra food and carry it out with you. Bury or pack out human waste at least 200 feet from water sources and under six to eight inches of topsoil. Don't bathe with soap (even biodegradable soap) in a lake or stream. Even your body oils (especially if you're wearing sunscreen) can contaminate water sources, so try to take water in a container at least 200 feet from water sources and wash and rinse there. Remember to dump the wastewater away from water sources. Another option is to use prepackaged moistened towels to wipe off sweat and dirt.

Leave no weeds. Noxious weeds tend to out-compete (overtake) our native flora, which in turn affects animals and birds that depend on them for food. Noxious weeds can be harmful to wildlife. Yes, just like birds and furry critters, we humans can carry weed seeds from one place to another. Here are a couple of things hikers can do to minimize the spread of noxious weeds. First, learn to identify noxious weeds and exotic species. You can obtain information pamphlets from the USDA Forest Service or Ohio State University Cooperative Extension (www.ag.ohio-state.edu/). Second, regularly clean your boots, tents, packs, and hiking poles of mud and seeds. Brush your dog to remove any weed seed. Avoid camping and traveling in weed infested areas.

Stay on the trail. It's true, a path anywhere leads nowhere new, but purists will just have to get over it. Paths serve an important purpose; they limit our impact on natural areas. Straying from a designated trail may seem innocent, but it can cause damage to sensitive areas—damage that may take years to recover, if it can recover at all. Even simple shortcuts can be destructive. So, please, stay on the trail.

Keep your dog under control. You can buy a flexi-lead that allows your dog to go exploring along the trail, while allowing you the ability to reel him in should another hiker approach or should he decide to chase a deer. Always obey leash laws and be sure to bury your dog's waste or pack it out in resealable plastic bags. Don't let your dog harass wildlife, and a dog on leash may also alert you to nearby wildlife you might otherwise miss.

Respect other trail users. Often you're not the only one on the trail. With the rise in popularity of multi-use trails, you'll have to learn a new kind of respect, beyond the nod and "hello" approach you're used to. You should first investigate whether you're on a multi-use trail, and assume the appropriate precautions. When you encounter motorized vehicles (ATVs, motorcycles, and four-wheel drives), be acutely aware. Though they should always yield to the hiker, often they're going too fast or are lost in the buzz of their engine to react to your presence. If you hear activity ahead, step off the trail just to be safe. Now, you're not likely to hear a mountain biker coming, so the best bet is to know whether you share the trail with them. Cyclists should *always* yield to hikers, but that's of little comfort to the hiker. Be aware. When you approach horses or pack animals on the trail, always step quietly off the trail, preferably on the downhill side, and let them pass. If you're wearing a large backpack, it's often a good idea to sit down.

Preparedness

It's been said that failing to plan means planning to fail. So do take the necessary time to plan your trip. Whether going on a short day hike or an extended backpack trip, always prepare for the worst. Simply remembering to pack a copy of the *U.S. Army Survival Manual* is not preparedness. Although it's not a bad idea if you plan on entering truly wild places, it's merely the tourniquet answer to a problem. You need to do your best to prevent the problem from arising in the first place. These days the word *survival* is often replaced with the pathetically feeble term *comfort*. In order to remain comfortable (and to survive if you really want to push it), you need to concern yourself with the basics: water, food, and shelter. Don't go on a hike without having these bases covered. And don't go on a hike expecting to find these items in the woods.

Water. Even in frigid conditions, you need at least two quarts of water a day to function efficiently. Add heat and/or taxing terrain and you can bump that figure up to one gallon. That's simply a base to work from—your metabolism and your level of conditioning can raise or lower that amount. Unless you know your level, assume that you need one gallon of water a day. Now, where do you plan on getting the water?

Natural water sources can be loaded with intestinal disturbers, such as bacteria and viruses. *Giardia lamblia,* the most common of these disturbers, is a protozoan parasite that lives part of its lifecycle as a cyst in water sources. The parasite spreads when mammals (humans included) defecate in water sources. Once ingested, Giardia can induce cramping, diarrhea, vomiting, and fatigue within two days to two weeks after ingestion. Giardia is treatable with the prescription drug Flagyl. Fluid loss due to diarrhea can be helped by drinking an electrolyte solution, such as Gatorade. If you believe you've contracted Giardia, see a doctor immediately.

Treating water. The best and easiest solution to avoid polluted water is to carry your water with you. Yet, depending on the nature of your hike and the duration, this may not be an option—seeing as one gallon of water weighs 8.5 pounds. In that case, you'll need to look into treating water. Regardless of which method you choose, you should always carry some water with you, in case of an emergency. Save this reserve until you absolutely need it.

There are three methods of treating water: boiling, chemical treatment, and filtering. Boiling is the safest, if not simplest method because it's not dependent on variables (i.e. brand name or proper dosage). If you boil water, it's recommended that you do so for 10 to 15 minutes, though some will say just bringing the water to a boil is enough. Many may find this method impractical, since you're forced to exhaust a good deal of your fuel supply. You can opt for chemical treatment (e.g. Potable Aqua), which will kill Giardia but will not take care of other chemical pollutants. Other drawbacks to chemical treatments are the unpleasant taste of the water after it's treated and the length of time it takes for them to be effective. You can remedy the former by adding powdered drink mix to the water. Filters are the preferred method for treating water. Filters (check the instructions to make sure) remove Giardia, organic and inorganic contaminants, and don't leave an aftertaste. Some filters also remove viruses. Water filters are far from perfect as they can easily become clogged or leak if a gasket wears out. It's always a good idea to carry a backup supply of chemical treatment tablets in case your filter decides to quit on you.

Food. If we're talking about "survival," you can go days without food, as long as you have water. But we're talking about "comfort" here. Try to avoid foods that are high in sugar and fat like candy bars and potato chips. These food types are harder to digest and are low in nutritional value. Instead, bring along foods that are easy to pack, nutritious, and high in energy (e.g. bagels, nutrition bars, dehydrated fruit, gorp, and jerky). Complex carbohydrates and protein are your best food friends. If you are on an overnight trip, easy-to-fix dinners include rice or pasta dinners and soup mixes. A few spices are lightweight and can really perk up a meal. Freeze-dried meals are nice for long trips, but are expensive and bulky. If you do a lot of long backpacks, invest in a dehydrator. For a tasty breakfast, you can fix hot oatmeal with brown sugar and reconstituted milk powder topped off with banana chips. If you like a hot drink in the morning, bring along herbal tea bags or hot chocolate. If you are a coffee junkie, you can purchase coffee that is packaged like tea bags. Pre-package all of your meals in heavy-duty resealable plastic bags to keep food from spilling in your pack. These bags can be reused to pack out trash. Pre-packaging also minimizes extra trash in the form of boxes and cans. Avoid bringing glass containers into the backcountry as broken glass can pose some serious problems. A good book on back-country cooking is *Wilderness Ranger Cookbook* by Brunell and Swain from The Globe Pequot Press.

Shelter. The type of shelter you choose depends less on the conditions than on your tolerance for discomfort. Shelter comes in many forms—tent, tarp, lean to, bivy sack, cabin, cave, etc. If you're camping in the desert, a bivy sack may suffice, but if you're near treeline and a storm is approaching, a better choice is a three or four season tent. Tents are the logical and most popular choice for most backpackers as they're lightweight and packable—and you can rest assured that you always have shelter from the elements. Before you leave on your trip, anticipate what the weather and terrain will be like and bring the type of shelter that will work best for your comfort level.

Finding a campsite. If there are established campsites, stick to those. If not, start looking for a campsite early—like around 3:30 or 4:00 P.M. Stop at the first appropriate site you see, remembering that good campsites are found and not made. Depending on the area, it could be a long time before you find another suitable location. Pitch your camp in an area that's reasonably level and clear of underbrush (which can harbor insects and conceal approaching animals). Make sure the area is at least 200 feet from fragile areas like lakeshores, meadows, and stream banks. Tree saplings and flowering plants are easily damaged, so avoid plopping your tent on top of them. In addition, watch out for poison ivy and thorny plants like greenbrier and multiflora rose.

If you are camping in stormy, rainy weather, look for a rock outcrop or a shelter in the trees to keep the wind from blowing your tent all night. Be sure that you don't camp under trees with dead limbs that might break off on top of you. Also, try to find an area that has an absorbent surface, such as sandy soil or forest duff. This, in addition to camping on a surface with a slight angle, will provide better drainage. By all means, don't dig trenches to provide drainage around your tent—remember you're practicing minimum-impact camping.

If you're in bear country, steer clear of creek beds or animal paths. If you see any signs of a bear's presence (i.e. scat, footprints), relocate. You'll need to find a campsite near a tall tree where you can hang your food and other items that may attract bears such as deodorant, toothpaste, or soap. Carry a lightweight nylon rope with which to hang your food. As a rule, you should hang your food at least 15 feet from the ground and four feet away from the tree trunk. You can put food and other items in a waterproof stuff sack and tie one end of the rope to the stuff sack. To get the other end of the rope over the tree branch, tie a good size rock to it and gently toss the rock over the tree branch. Pull the stuff sack up until it reaches the top of the branch and tie it off securely. Don't hang your food near your tent! If possible, hang your food at least 100 feet away from your campsite. Alternatives to hanging your food are bear-proof plastic tubes and metal bear boxes. Chipmunks, ground squirrels, and raccoons will also steal your food if you don't hang it.

Lastly, think of comfort. Lie down on the ground where you intend to sleep and see if it's a good fit. Bring along an insulating pad for warmth and extra comfort. The days of using pine boughs or digging a hip depression in the ground are long gone. And for the final touch, have your tent face east. You'll appreciate the warmth of the morning sun and have a nice view to wake up to.

First Aid

If you plan to spend a lot of time outdoors hiking, spend a few hours and bucks to take a good wilderness first-aid class. You'll not only learn first-aid basics, but how to be creative miles from nowhere. The Red Cross offers basic first-aid and CPR classes. Some outdoor organizations and universities offer Wilderness First Response courses. Find the nearest Red Cross office by going to www.redcross.org/oh/ohiostate/.

Now, we know you're tough, but get 10 miles into the woods and develop a blister, and you'll wish you had carried a first-aid kit. Face it; it's just plain good sense. Many companies produce lightweight, compact first-aid kits, just make sure yours contains at least the following:

- band aids
- moleskin, duct tape or athletic tape, and/or Band-Aid's Blister Relief Compeed
- various sterile gauze and dressings
- white surgical tape
- an ace bandage
- an antihistamine
- aspirin, ibuprofen, or acetaminophen
- Betadine solution
- First-aid book
- Tums
- tweezers
- scissors
- anti-bacterial wipes
- triple-antibiotic ointment
- plastic gloves
- sterile cotton tip applicators
- a thermometer

Here are a few tips for dealing with and hopefully preventing certain ailments.

Sunburn. To avoid sunburn, wear sunscreen (SPF 15 or higher), protective clothing, and a wide-brimmed hat when you are hiking in sunny weather. If you do get sunburned, treat the area with aloe vera gel and protect the area from further sun exposure. Protect your eyes by wearing sunglasses with UV protection, too!

Blisters. First try to prevent blisters. Break in your boots, wear appropriate socks, and then, if you're prone to blisters, apply moleskin, Compeed, Bodyglide

(888–263–9454), duct tape, or athletic tape *before* you start hiking to help decrease friction to that area. In case a blister develops despite your careful precautions, an effective way to treat it is to cut out a circle of moleskin and remove the center—like a donut—and place it over the blistered area. Cutting the center out will reduce the pressure applied to the sensitive skin. Then put Second Skin in the hole and tape over the whole mess. Second Skin (made by Spenco) is applied to the blister after it has popped and acts as a "second skin" to help prevent further irritation.

Insect bites and stings. The most troublesome of Ohio's insects are mosquitoes and yellow jackets. A simple treatment for most insect bites and stings is to apply hydrocortisone 1 percent cream topically and to take a pain medication such as ibuprofen or acetaminophen to reduce swelling. If you forgot to pack these items, a cold compress or a paste of mud and ashes can sometimes assuage the itching and discomfort. Remove any stingers by using tweezers or scraping the area with your fingernail or a knife blade. Don't pinch the area as you'll only spread the venom.

Some hikers are highly sensitive to bites and stings and may have a serious allergic reaction that can be life threatening. Symptoms of a serious allergic reaction can include wheezing, an asthmatic attack, and shock. The treatment for this severe type of reaction is epinephrine (adrenaline). If you know that you are sensitive to bites and stings, carry a pre-packaged kit of epinephrine (e.g. Anakit), which can be obtained only by prescription from your doctor. Also carry an antihistamine such as Benadryl.

Ticks. As you well know, ticks can carry disease, such as Lyme disease. The best defense is, of course, prevention. If you know you're going to be hiking through an area littered with ticks, wear long pants and a long sleeved shirt. At the end of your hike, do a spot check for ticks (and insects in general). If you do find a tick, coat the insect with Vaseline or tree sap to cut off its air supply. The tick should release its hold, but if it doesn't, grab the head of the tick firmly—with a pair of tweezers if you have them—and gently pull it away from the skin with a twisting motion. Sometimes the mouthparts linger, embedded in your skin. If this happens, try to remove them with a disinfected needle. Clean the affected area with an anti-bacterial cleanser and then apply triple antibiotic ointment. Monitor the area for a few days. If irritation persists or a white spot develops, see a doctor for possible infection.

Poison ivy. These skin irritants can be found most anywhere in North America and come in the form of a bush, having leaflets in groups of three. Learn how to spot the plants. The oil they secrete can cause an allergic reaction in the form of blisters, usually about 12 hours after exposure. The itchy rash can last from ten days to several weeks. The best defense against these irritants is to wear protective clothing and to apply a non-prescription product called IvyBlock to exposed skin. This lotion is meant to guard against the effects of poison ivy and can be washed off with soap and water. If you know you've been exposed, look for some jewelweed (spotted touch-me-not) and crush the juicy stem and leaves and apply to your skin. Only do this if you're in an area where it's legal to pick plants and where there is an abundant supply. Thin the stand carefully by taking a small plant that will likely be out-competed anyway. Jewelweed is an effective antidote to poison ivy for many people. After you return home, wash the area as soon as possible with soap and cool water. Taking a cool shower after you return home from your hike will also help to remove any lingering oil from your skin (hot water opens your pores). Should you contract a rash from this plant, use Benadryl or a similar product to reduce the itching. If the rash is localized, hydrocortisone cream or calamine lotion can help reduce itching and dry up the area. If the rash has spread, either tough it out or see your doctor about getting a dose of Cortisone (available both orally and by injection).

Snakebites. First off, snakebites are rare in North America. Unless startled or provoked, the majority of snakes will not bite. If you are wise to their habitats and keep a careful eye on the trail, you should be just fine. Though your chances of being struck are slim, it's wise to know what to do in the event you are.

If a *non-poisonous* snake bites you, allow the wound to bleed a small amount and then cleanse the wounded area with a Betadine solution (10 percent povidone io-dine). Rinse the wound with clean water (preferably) or fresh urine (it might sound ugly, but it's sterile). Once the area is clean, cover it with triple antibiotic ointment and a clean bandage. Remember, most residual damage from snakebites, poisonous or otherwise, comes from infection, not the snake's venom. Keep the area as clean as possible and get medical attention immediately.

If you are bitten by a *poisonous* snake, remove the toxin with a suctioning device, found in a snakebite kit (like the Sawyer Extractor). If you do not have such a de-vice, squeeze the wound—don't cut it and do *not* use your mouth for suction as the venom will enter your bloodstream through the vessels under the tongue and head straight for your heart. Then, clean the wound just as you would a non-poisonous bite. Tie a clean band of cloth snuggly around the afflicted appendage, about an inch or so above the bite (or the rim of the swelling). This is *not* a tourniquet—you want to simply slow the blood flow, not cut it off. Loosen the band if numbness ensues. Remove the band for a minute and re-apply a little higher every ten minutes. (Do *not* try to apply ice to the bite wound achieve slower blood flow.)

If it is your friend who's been bitten, treat him or her for shock—make him comfortable, have him lie down, elevate the legs, and keep him warm. Immobilize the affected area and remove any constricting items such as rings, watches, or re-strictive clothing—swelling may occur. Splint the extremity that was bitten and keep it lower than the heart. Monitor for shock. Keep your friend hydrated but avoid painkillers and alcohol. Once your friend is stable and relatively calm, hike out to get help. The victim should get treatment within 12 hours, ideally, which usually consists of a tetanus shot, antivenin, and antibiotics.

Now, if you are alone and struck by a poisonous snake, stay calm. Hysteria will only quicken the venom's spread. Follow the procedure above and do your best to reach help. When hiking out, don't run—you'll only increase the flow of blood throughout your system. Instead, walk calmly.

Ohio is home to only three poisonous snakes: the copperhead, the eastern massasauga, and the timber rattlesnake. The timber rattlesnake is an endangered species and you are far more likely to get struck by lightning than bitten by one of these. The massasauga and the timber are both rattlers, and all three of these species have two defining characteristics: triangular heads and elliptical pupils. Cooperheads tend to bite more than any other species, but their bites are rarely fatal.

Dehydration. Have you ever hiked in hot weather and had a roaring headache and felt fatigued after only a few miles? More than likely you were dehydrated. Symptoms of dehydration include fatigue, headache, and decreased coordination and judgment. Dehydration can also make you more susceptible to hypothermia and frostbite. When you are hiking, your body's rate of fluid loss depends on the outside temperature, humidity, altitude, and your activity level. On average, a hiker walking in warm weather will lose four liters of fluid a day. That fluid loss is easily replaced by normal consumption of liquids and food. However, if a hiker is walking briskly in hot, dry weather and hauling a heavy pack, he can lose one to three liters of water an hour. It's important to always carry plenty of water and to stop often and drink fluids regularly, even if you aren't thirsty. One way to tell if you're adequately hydrated is to check the color of your urine. It should be clear. The darker yellow it is, the more dehydrated you are. With a little creativity, you can check the color in the backcountry. You can also pinch the skin on the back of your hand. If it quickly lowers itself, you're OK. If it remains in a peak, you're dehydrated.

Heat exhaustion is the result of a loss of large amounts of electrolytes and often occurs if a hiker is dehydrated and has been under heavy exertion. Common symptoms of heat exhaustion include cramping, exhaustion, fatigue, lightheadedness, and nausea. You can treat heat exhaustion by getting out of the sun, eating high energy foods, and drinking an electrolyte solution made up of one teaspoon of salt and one tablespoon of sugar dissolved in a liter of water. Drink this solution slowly over a period of one hour. Drinking plenty of fluids (preferably an electrolyte solution like Gatorade) can also prevent heat exhaustion. When drinking a lot of water, remember to snack while you drink. If you don't, you'll disrupt the electrolyte balance as you lose body salt through sweating, and possibly develop hyponatremia (water intoxication). Symptoms include nausea, vomiting, frequent urination, and altered mental states. Avoid hiking during the hottest parts of the day and wear breathable clothing, a wide brimmed hat, and sunglasses.

Hypothermia is one of the biggest dangers in the backcountry—especially for day hikers in the mild weather. That may sound strange, but imagine starting out on a hike in spring when it's sunny and 60°F out. You're clad in nylon pants and a cotton T-shirt. About halfway through your hike, the sky begins to cloud up and in the next hour a light drizzle begins to fall, and the wind starts to pick up. Before you know it, you are soaking wet and shivering—the perfect recipe for hypothermia. More advanced signs include decreased coordination, slurred speech, and blurred vision. When a victim's temperature falls below 91°F, the blood pressure, breathing, and pulse plummet, possibly leading to coma and death.

To avoid hypothermia, always bring a windproof/rainproof shell, a fleece jacket, Capilene tights or rainpants, gloves, and hat when you are hiking in the mountains. Avoid wearing 100 percent cotton clothing as it does not dry easily and provides no warmth when wet. Learn to adjust your clothing layers based on the temperature. If you are climbing uphill at a moderate pace you will stay warm, but when you stop for a break you'll become cold quickly, unless you add more layers of clothing. Keeping hydrated and well nourished are also important in avoiding hypothermia.

If a hiker is showing advanced signs of hypothermia, dress her in dry clothes and make sure she is wearing a hat and gloves. Place her in a sleeping bag in a tent or shelter that will protect her from the wind and other elements. Give her warm fluids to drink and keep her awake. Put water bottles filled with warm water in the crotch and armpits to help warm her.

Frostbite. When the mercury dips below 32°F, your extremities begin to chill. If a persistent chill attacks a localized area, say your hands or your toes, the circulatory system reacts by cutting off blood flow to the affected area—the idea being to protect and preserve the body's overall temperature. And so it's death by attrition for the affected area. Ice crystals start to form from the water in the cells of the neglected tissue. Deprived of heat, nourishment, and now water, the tissue literally starves. This is frostbite.

Prevention is your best defense against this situation. Most prone to frostbite are your face, hands, and feet—so protect these areas well. Wool is the material of choice because it provides ample air space for insulation and draws moisture away from the skin. However, synthetic fabrics have recently made great strides in the cold weather clothing market. Do your research. A pair of light silk or polypro liners under your regular gloves or mittens is a good trick to keeping warm. They afford some additional warmth, but more importantly they'll allow you to remove your mitts for tedious work without exposing the skin.

Now, if your feet or hands start to feel cold or numb due to the elements, warm them as quickly as possible. Place cold hands under your armpits or bury them in your crotch. Carry hand and foot warmers if you can. If your feet are cold, change your socks. If there's room in your boots, add another pair of socks. Do remember though that constricting your feet in tight boots can restrict blood flow and actually make your feet colder more quickly. Your socks need to have breathing room if they're going to be effective. Dead air provides insulation. If your face is cold, place your warm hands over your face or simply wear a head stocking (called a balaclava).

Should your skin go numb and start to appear white and waxy but is still cold and soft, chances are you've got superficial frostbite. Rewarm as quickly as possible with skin-to-skin contact. No damage should occur. Do *not* let the area get frostbitten again!

If your skin is white and waxy but dents when you press on it, you have partial thickness frostbite. Rewarm as you would for superficial frostbite, but expect swelling and blisters to form. Don't massage the affected area, but do take ibuprofen for pain and reduction of tissue damage. If blisters form, you need to leave the back-country.

If your skin is frozen hard like an ice cube, you have full thickness frostbite. Don't try to thaw the area unless you can maintain the warmth. In other words, don't stop to warm up your frostbitten feet only to head back on the trail. You'll do more damage than good. Tests have shown that hikers who walked on thawed feet did more harm, and endured more pain, than hikers who left the affected areas alone. Do your best to get out of the cold entirely and seek medical attention—which usually consists of performing a rapid rewarming in warm water (104°F to 108°F) for 20 to 30 minutes. Get to a doctor as soon as possible.

The overall objective in preventing both hypothermia and frostbite is to keep the body's core warm. Protect key areas where heat escapes, like the top of the head, and maintain the proper nutrition and hydration levels. Foods that are high in calories aid the body in producing heat. Never smoke or drink alcohol when you're in situations where the cold is threatening. By affecting blood flow, these activities ultimately cool the body's core temperature.

Natural Hazards

Besides tripping over a rock or tree root on the trail, there are some real hazards to be aware of while hiking.

Lightning. Thunderstorms are common to Ohio in the spring and summer and also occur in the fall. Lightning is generated by thunderheads and can strike without warning, even several miles away from the nearest overhead cloud. Keep an eye on cloud formation and don't underestimate how fast a storm can build. The bigger they get, the more likely a thunderstorm will happen. Lightning takes the path of least resistance, so if you're the high point, it might chose you. Ducking under a rock overhang is likewise dangerous as you form the shortest path between the rock and ground. Avoid standing under the only or the tallest tree. If you have an insulating pad, squat on it. Avoid having both your hands and feet touching the ground at once and never lay flat. Minimize yourself as a target. If you hear a buzzing sound or feel your hair standing on end, move quickly as an electrical charge is building up. For additional information check out the National Lightning Safety Institute's Web site at www.lightningsafety.com.

Flash floods. The spooky thing about flash floods is that they can appear out of nowhere from a storm many miles away. Always climb to safety if danger threatens. Flash floods usually subside quickly, so be patient and don't cross a swollen stream.

Bears. The black bear is making a comeback in the eastern part of Ohio. Here are some tips in case you and a bear scare each other. Most of all, avoid scaring a bear. Watch for bear tracks (five toes) and droppings (sizable with leaves, partly digested berries, seeds, and/or animal fur). Talk or sing where visibility or hearing are limited. Keep a clean camp, hang food, and don't sleep in the clothes you wore while cooking. Be especially careful in spring to avoid getting between a mother and her cubs. In late summer and fall bears are busy eating berries and acorns to fatten up for winter, so be extra careful around berry bushes and oak brush. If you do encounter a bear, move away slowly while facing the bear, talk softly, and avoid direct eye contact. Give the bear room to escape. Since bears are very curious, it might stand upright to get a better whiff of you, and it may even charge you to try to intimidate you. Try to stay calm. If a bear does attack you, fight back with anything you have handy. Unleashed dogs have been known to come running back to their owners with a bear close behind. Keep your dog on a leash or leave it at home.

Hunting. Hunting is a popular sport in Ohio, and it seems as if it's always one sort of hunting season or another. Contact the Ohio Department of Natural Resources Division of Wildlife for information on hunting seasons at www.ohiodnr.com/wildlife or (800) WILDLIFE. When it comes to the one-week gun season for deer (usually in November or December), just avoid the public lands where hunting is allowed (you will be considerably outnumbered by people with guns in their hands) and opt for parks and preserves where hunting is not allowed. It's always a good idea to wear at least one article of clothing that's hunter orange.

Trip Planning

Planning your hiking adventure begins with letting a friend or relative know your trip itinerary so they can call for help if you don't return at your scheduled time. Your next task is to make sure you are outfitted to experience the risks and rewards of the trail. This section highlights gear and clothing you may want to take with you to get the most out of your hike.

Day Hikes
- daypack
- water and water bottles/water hydration system
- food and high energy snacks
- first-aid kit
- headlamp/flashlight with extra batteries and bulbs
- maps and compass/GPS unit
- knife/multi-purpose tool
- sunscreen and sunglasses
- matches in waterproof container and fire starter
- insulating top and bottom layers (fleece, wool, etc.)
- raingear
- winter hat and gloves
- wide-brimmed sun hat

- insect repellant
- backpacker's trowel, toilet paper, and resealable plastic bags
- whistle and/or mirror
- space blanket/bag
- camera/film
- guidebook
- watch
- water treatment tablets
- wet ones or other wet wipes
- hand and foot warmers if hiking high
- duct tape for repairs
- extra socks
- gaiters depending on season

Overnight Trip (plus what's listed for Day Hikes)
- backpack and waterproof rain cover
- bandanna
- biodegradable soap
- collapsible water container (2–3 gallon capacity)
- clothing (extra wool socks, shirt and shorts, long pants)
- cook set/utensils and pot scrubber
- stuff sacks to store gear
- extra plastic resealable bags
- garbage bags
- journal/pen
- nylon rope to hang food
- long underwear
- permit (if required)
- repair kit (tent, stove, pack, etc.)
- sandals or running shoes to wear around camp and to ford streams
- sleeping bag
- waterproof stuff sacks (one for hanging food)
- insulating ground pad
- hand towel
- stove and fuel
- tent and ground cloth
- toiletry items
- water filter

Appendix A: Hike Index

Best Hikes for Birding
3. Boardwalk Trail, Maumee Bay State Park (NW)
38. Hemlock to Creekside Meadows Loop, Clear Creek Metro Park (SE)
5. Northshore Loop, North Pond, and East Quarry Trails, Kelleys Island State Park (NW)
U. Rockbridge State Nature Preserve (SE)
10. Seven Ponds, South Point, and Lonesome Pond Loop Trails, Tinkers Creek State Nature Preserve (NE)
C. Sheldon Marsh State Nature Preserve (NW)
4. South Beach Trail, East Harbor State Park (NW)
12. Vondergreen Trail, Beaver Creek State Park (NE)

Best Hikes to See Native American Earthworks
25. Earthworks Trail to Sun Serpent Effigy, Fort Ancient State Memorial (SW)
29. Gorge to Fort Trail Loop, Fort Hill State Memorial (SW)
43. Lamping Homestead Trail, Wayne National Forest (SE)
R. Little Turtle and Blue Jacket Trails, Shawnee Lookout Park (SW)
14. Overlook and Dripping Rock Trails, Highbanks Metro Park (C)

Best Kid-friendly Hikes
N. Battelle–Darby Creek Metro Park (C)
23. Big Woods and Sugar Bush Trails, Hueston Woods State Nature Preserve (SW)
3. Boardwalk Trail, Maumee Bay State Park (NW)
O. Brukner Nature Center (SW)
K. Butternut Nature Trail, Malabar Farm State Park (NE)
25. Earthworks Trail to Sun Serpent Effigy, Fort Ancient State Memorial (SW)
24. Flat Fork Ridge Trail to Pioneer Village, Caesar Creek State Park (SW)
17. Flint Ridge to Creek Trail Loop, Flint Ridge State Memorial (C)
21. Glen Helen Loop Trail, Glen Helen Preserve (SW)
36. Grandma Gatewood Trail, Hocking Hills State Park (SE)
15. Oak Trail, The Dawes Arboretum (C)
Q. Orange Trail, Germantown Metropark (SW)
14. Overlook and Dripping Rock Trails, Highbanks Metro Park (C)
F. Rocky River Reservation (NE)
27. Rowe Woods Trails, Cincinnati Nature Center (SW)

Best Hikes along Scenic Rivers and Streams

28. Barrett's Rim Trail, Highlands Nature Sanctuary (SW)
S. Davis Memorial State Nature Preserve (SW)
21. Glen Helen Loop Trail, Glen Helen Preserve (SW)
I. Glens Trail, Gorge Metro Park (NE)
29. Gorge to Fort Trail Loop, Fort Hill State Memorial (SW)
13. Hemlock Gorge to Lyons Falls Trail, Mohican State Park (NE)
38. Hemlock to Creekside Meadows Loop, Clear Creek Metro Park (SE)
20. Little Miami River Loop, Clifton Gorge State Nature Preserve and John Bryan State Park (SW)
8. Stanford House to Brandywine Falls Loop, Cuyahoga Valley National Park (NE)
12. Vondergreen Trail, Beaver Creek State Park (NE)

Best Hikes to View Rock Features

42. Archers Fork Trail, Wayne National Forest (SE)
28. Barrett's Rim Trail, Highlands Nature Sanctuary (SW)
23. Big Woods and Sugar Bush Trails, Hueston Woods State Nature Preserve (SW)
K. Butternut Nature Trail, Malabar Farm State Park (NE)
11. Cascade Falls to Devil's Icebox Loop, Nelson-Kennedy Ledges State Park (NE)
S. Davis Memorial State Nature Preserve (SW)
24. Flat Fork Ridge Trail to Pioneer Village, Caesar Creek State Park (SW)
17. Flint Ridge to Creek Trail Loop, Flint Ridge State Memorial (C)
21. Glen Helen Loop Trail, Glen Helen Preserve (SW)
I. Glens Trail, Gorge Metro Park (NE)
29. Gorge to Fort Trail Loop, Fort Hill State Memorial (SW)
36. Grandma Gatewood Trail, Hocking Hills State Park (SE)
9. Haskell Run to Ledges Trail, Cuyahoga Valley National Park (NE)
38. Hemlock to Creekside Meadows Loop, Clear Creek Metro Park (SE)
6. Hinckley Lake to Whipps Ledges Trail Loop, Hinckley Reservation (NE)
33. Lake Vesuvius Lakeshore Trail, Wayne National Forest (SE)
20. Little Miami River Loop and Spur Trail, Clifton Gorge State Nature Preserve and John Bryan State Park (SW)
5. North Shore Loop, North Pond, and East Quarry Trails, Kelleys Island (NW)
14. Overlook and Dripping Rock Trails, Highbanks Metro Park (C)
U. Rockbridge State Nature Preserve (SE)
30. Trail to Buzzardroost Rock, Edge of Appalachia Preserve (SW)

Best Hikes for Solitude

42. Archers Fork Trail, Wayne National Forest (SE)
28. Barrett's Rim Trail, Highlands Nature Sanctuary (SW)

V. Covered Bridge Trail, Wayne National Forest (SE)

S. Davis Memorial State Nature Preserve (SW)

H. Eagle Creek State Nature Preserve (NE)

43. Lamping Homestead Trail, Wayne National Forest (SE)

15. Oak Trail, The Dawes Arboretum (C)

W. Ohio View Trail, Wayne National Forest (SE)

Best Hikes to See Old-growth Forests or Trees

28. Barrett's Rim Trail, Highlands Nature Sanctuary (SW)

23. Big Woods and Sugar Bush Trails, Hueston Woods State Nature Preserve (SW)

1. Cottonwood to Toadshade Loop, Goll Woods State Nature Preserve (NW)

29. Gorge to Fort Trail Loop, Fort Hill State Memorial (SW)

13. Hemlock Gorge Trail, Mohican State Park (NE)

44. Red and Blue Trails, Dysart Woods (SE)

22. Three Sisters to Sycamore Ridge Loop, Sugarcreek Metropark (SW)

Best Trails with Vistas

3. Boardwalk Trail, Maumee Bay State Park (NW)

18. Five Oaks to Kokomo Wetland Trail, Slate Run Metro Park (C)

G. Frazee House to Bridal Veil Falls, Cuyahoga Valley National Park (NE)

9. Haskell Run to Ledges Trail, Cuyahoga Valley National Park (NE)

33. Lake Vesuvius Lakeshore Trail, Wayne National Forest (SE)

41. Lakeview Trail, Burr Oak State Park (SE)

5. North Shore Loop, North Pond, and East Quarry Trails, Kelleys Island (NW)

15. Oak Trail, The Dawes Arboretum (C)

37. Rim and Gorge Trails, Conkles Hollow State Nature Preserve (SE)

C. Sheldon Marsh State Nature Preserve (NW)

30. Trail to Buzzardroost Rock, Edge of Appalachia Preserve (SW)

Best Trails to See Waterfalls

28. Barrett's Rim Trail, Highlands Nature Sanctuary (SW)

34. Calico Bush and Salt Creek Trails, Lake Katharine Nature Preserve (SE)

21. Glen Helen Loop Trail, Glen Helen Preserve (SW)

29. Gorge to Fort Trail Loop, Fort Hill State Memorial (SW)

36. Grandma Gatewood Trail—Old Man's Cave to Ash Cave, Hocking Hills State Park (SE)

P. Green Trail, Englewood MetroPark (SW)

20. Little Miami River Loop, Clifton Gorge State Nature Preserve and John Bryan State Park (SW)

13. Hemlock Gorge to Lyons Falls Trail, Mohican State Park (NE)
11. Cascade Falls to Devil's Icebox Loop, Nelson–Kennedy Ledges State Park (NE)
 7. Buckeye Trail: Red Lock to Boston Store, Cuyahoga Valley National Park (NE)
U. Rockbridge State Nature Preserve (SE)
 8. Stanford House to Brandywine Falls, Cuyahoga Valley National Park (NE)

Best Wheelchair-accessible Hikes

36. Ash Cave Trail, Hocking Hills State Park (SE)
 3. Boardwalk Trail, Maumee Bay State Park (NW)
20. Little Miami River Loop, Clifton Gorge State Nature Preserve (SW)
 5. North Pond Trail, Kelleys Island (NW)
C. Sheldon Marsh State Nature Preserve (NW)
22. Portions of Sugarcreek MetroPark (SW)

Appendix B: Resources (Government, State, and Local Groups)

Public Land Management Agencies

Ohio Department of Natural Resources
Division of Forestry
Columbus, OH
(614) 265–6694
www.ohiodnr.com/forestry/default.htm

Ohio Department of Natural Resources
Division of Natural Areas and Preserves
Columbus, OH
(614) 265–6453
www.ohiodnr.com/dnap/

Ohio Department of Natural Resources
Division of Parks and Recreation
Columbus, OH
www.ohiodnr.com/parks

Wayne National Forest
Athens Ranger District (Headquarters)
(740) 753–0101
www.fs.fed.us/r9/wayne/

Hiking and Trail Groups

American Discovery Trail
www.discoverytrail.org

Athens Trails
Athens, OH
(740) 593–6572
www.gasp.athens.oh.us/trails.shtml

Boy Scouts
There are several local Boy Scout chapters; look in the white pages of your phone book for more information.

Buckeye Trail Association
Worthington, OH
(800) 881–3062
www.buckeyetrail.org

Cleveland Hiking Club
www.clevelandhikingclub.com

Columbus Outdoor Pursuits
Columbus, OH
(614) 447–1006
www.outdoor-pursuits.org

Cuyahoga Valley Trails Council
www.nps.gov/cuva/friends/cvtc.htm

Maumee Valley Volkssporters
Maumee, OH
(734) 847–0641
www.geocities.com/Yosemite/Gorge/4120

North Country Scenic Trail
www.northcountrytrail.org/gts/index.htm

Ohio Parks and Recreation Association
Westerville, OH
(614) 895–2222
www.opraonline.org

Environmental and Conservation Groups

Audubon Ohio
Columbus, OH
(614) 224–3303
www.audubon.org/states/oh/

Buckeye Forest Council
The Plains, OH
(740) 797–7200
www.buckeyeforestcouncil.org

Chagrin Land Conservancy
Novelty, OH
(440) 729–9621
www.crlc.cc/

Earth Day Coalition
Cleveland, OH
(216) 281–6468
www.earthdaycoalition.org/

EarthSave
Cincinnati, OH
(513) 929–2500
cincinnati.earthsave.org/

EcoCity Cleveland
Cleveland Heights OH
(216) 932–3007
www.ecocitycleveland.org

Environmental Education Council of Ohio
Akron, OH
(330) 761–0855
www.eeco-online.org

IMAGO
Cincinnati, OH
(513) 921–5124
www.sustainable.doe.gov/success/imago.shtml

Ohio Citizen Action
Cleveland, OH
(216) 861–5200
www.ohiocitizen.org

Ohio Division of Soil and Water Conservation
Columbus, OH
(614) 265–6610
www.ohiodnr.com/soilandwater/

Ohio Ecological Food and Farm Association
Columbus, OH
(614) 421–2022
www.oeffa.org/

Ohio Environmental Council
Columbus, OH
(614) 487–7506
www.theoec.org/

Ohio Greenways
Peninsula, OH
(330) 657–2055
www.ohiogreenways.org/

The Ohio to Erie Trail
Columbus, OH
(614) 451–8776
www.ohiotoerietrail.org

Rivers Unlimited
Cincinnati, OH
(513) 761–4003
www.riversunlimited.org/

Sierra Club—Ohio Chapter
Columbus, OH
(614) 461–0734
ohio.sierraclub.org

The Nature Conservancy
Ohio Chapter Main Office
Dublin, OH
(614) 717–2770
nature.org/wherewework/northamerica/
states/ohio/

Western Wildlife Corridor
Cincinnati, OH
(513) 921–9453
www.westernwildlifecorridor.org/

The Wilds
Cumberland, OH 43732
(740) 638–5030
www.thewilds.org

Appendix C: Further Reading

Braun, Emma Lucy. *The Woody Plants of Ohio: Trees, Shrubs, and Wood Climbers Native, Naturalized, and Escaped* (Ohio State University Press).

Collective authors. *Ohio Birds* (The Globe Pequot Press).

Dean, Tanya West & W. David Speas, George W. Knepper (ed.). *Along the Ohio Trail* (Ohio Auditor of State).

Eckert, Allan W. *That Dark and Bloody River: Chronicles of the Ohio River* (Bantam Doubleday Dell).

Genheimer, Robert A. (ed.). *Cultures Before Contact: The Late Prehistory of Ohio and Surrounding Regions* (Ohio Archaeological Council Inc.).

Gross, W. H. "Chip". *Ohio Wildlife Viewing Guide* (The Globe Pequot Press).

Lafferty, Michael B. (ed.). *Ohio's Natural Heritage* (The Ohio Academy of Science).

Minardi, Kay Wert. *Short Bike Rides in Ohio* (The Globe Pequot Press).

Newcomb, Lawrence & Gordon Morrison. *Newcomb's Wildflower Guide* (Little, Brown & Co).

Ostrander, Stephen (ed.). *The Ohio Nature Almanac: An Encyclopedia of Indispensable Information About the Natural Buckeye Universe* (Orange Frazer Press).

Pacheco, Paul J. (ed.). *A View From The Core: A Synthesis of Ohio Hopewell Archaeology* (The Ohio Archaeological Council Inc.).

Quinley, Mary. *52 Ohio Weekends* (McGraw-Hill/Contemporary Books).

Ramey, Ralph. *50 Hikes in Ohio* (Countryman Press).

Romain, William F. *Mysteries of the Hopewell: Astronomers, Geometers, and Magicians of the Eastern Woodlands* (University of Akron Press).

Sibley, David Allen. *The Sibley Guide to Birds* (National Audubon Society).

Vincent, Adam. *Mountain Bike America Ohio* (The Globe Pequot Press).

Vonada, Damaine (ed.). *The Ohio Almanac* (Orange Frazer Press).

Wharton, Mary E. & Roger W. Barbour. *A Guide to the Wildflowers and Ferns of Kentucky* (University Press of Kentucky).

———*Trees and Shrubs of Kentucky* (University Press of Kentucky).

Woodward, Susan and Jerry N. McDonald. *Indian Mounds of the Middle Ohio Valley* (Blacksburg, Virginia: McDonald and Woodward Publishing Co.).

Woodyard, Chris. *Haunted Ohio* (I–IV) (Kestrel Publishing).

Zimmermann, George and Carol. *Ohio: Off the Beaten Path* (The Globe Pequot Press).

About the Author

When she's not writing, Mary Reed is usually hiking, climbing, cycling, paddling, or hatching plans for her next outdoor adventure. Although she has trekked as far afield as Guatemala's highlands to Nepal's Annapurna region, some of her favorite places in the world are within a day's drive from her home in Athens, Ohio.